The Social Gospel

The Social Gospel

Religion and Reform in Changing America

RONALD C. WHITE, Jr. and
C. HOWARD HOPKINS

With an essay by
John C. Bennett

Temple University Press
Philadelphia

Temple University Press, Philadelphia 19122
© 1976 by Temple University. All rights reserved
Published 1976
Printed in the United States of America

International Standard Book Number: 0-87722-083-2 cloth; 0-87722-084-0 paper
Library of Congress Catalog Card Number: 75-34745

Contents

Illustrations

Page 1: "Washington Gladden as a Present-Day Crusader." From *Ohio State Journal,* April 9, 1905, p. 1. Courtesy of the Ohio Historical Society.

Page 49: "Government Troops Battle Strikers in First Nationwide Strike by Railroad Workers in 1877." Courtesy of Hyperion Press, Inc.

Page 99: Willis D. Weatherford (1875–1970). Courtesy of Willis D. Weatherford, Jr.

Page 127: "Where Cross the Crowded Ways of Life," by Frank Mason North, 1903. From *The Hymnal of the Protestant Episcopal Church in the United States of America* (1940).

Page 197: "The New Ally of the Knights of Labor—Does the Catholic Church Sanction Mob Law?" From *Puck,* March 23, 1887, pp. 60–61. Courtesy of the Firestone Library of Princeton University.

Page 241: Walter Rauschenbusch (1861–1918). Collection of C. Howard Hopkins.

Page 283: Excerpt from the report of the section "Confessing Christ Today," Fifth Assembly of the World Council of Churches, Nairobi, 1975.

What Is the Social Gospel?

The story of the social gospel is one of the most distinctive chapters in the American experience. Historian Carl Degler has summed it up in this way: "The acceptance of the social gospel spelled the transformation of American Protestantism."[1] Always more than a traditional religious movement, the social gospel stepped outside the churches to intersect the political, social, and economic forces of changing America. The social gospel was born in post–Civil War America, and grew to maturity in the era of Progressivism. Its impact continued long after its demise was forecast following World War I with the coming of the politics of normalcy and the theology of neo-orthodoxy. Emerging with renewed vigor in the turbulent 1960's as one of the not always recognized roots of the variegated social justice movement, extensions of the social gospel can be seen today among groups hitherto associated with different histories and orientations.

The purpose of this volume is to restate and re-vision the social gospel. Thirty-five years after its publication, C. Howard Hopkins' *The Rise of the Social Gospel in American Protestantism, 1865–1915*, is still the authoritative chronicle of the movement. However, recent years have seen a surge of both social activism and historical reflection that make the story of the social gospel worth retelling and redefining. There is need now to enlarge the definition of the social gospel even as its geographical, religious, and social boundaries are redrawn and expanded. In one sense "social gospel" refers to an historical movement that supposedly came to an end a half-century ago. But in another sense it speaks of a social consciousness and mission that is being renewed in every succeeding generation.

Toward the end of the progressive era, the social gospel was defined by one of its adherents as "the application of the teaching of Jesus and the total message of the Christian salvation to society, the economic life, and social institutions . . . as well as to individuals."[2] Christianity, to be sure, has exhibited social dimensions throughout its history, but what is here identified as the social gospel was basically an indigenous movement growing within the matrix of American Protestantism. Interacting with the changing realities and problems of an increasingly industrialized and urbanized nation, the social gospel viewed itself as a crusade for justice and righteousness in all areas of the common life. The crusade recruited articulate ministers and lay persons who publicized their new points of view as pastors, educators, editors, and directors of reform organizations.

The social gospel is a phenomenon that is difficult to define or contain. At the popular level, the words "social gospel" have become part of everyday language and thus have become so overused or misused as to obscure their generic and historic meaning. Along with such words as "puritan" or "fundamentalist," the words "social gospel" bear a meaning and evoke an interest that carry beyond the student's or scholar's precise historical, sociological, or theological concerns. Just as the word "fundamentalist" has been applied and misapplied to diverse and sometimes contradictory religious phenomena, just so "social gospel" often is used to cover a multitude of saints and sinners. It has been used as a label or a libel depending on the bias of the speaker. It can imply meaningful social involvement or meddling sociological interference.

Among scholars, there has come a renewed interest in the social gospel from many quarters. In his foreword to the 1967 paperback edition of *The Rise of the Social Gospel,* Howard Hopkins delineated "issues and relationships" involving the social gospel that were "still unexplored." Much work has gone on since that invitation, and this volume contains some of the fruits of both new research and reinterpretation. Now in his nineties, Dores R. Sharpe, secretary to Walter Rauschenbusch in 1912 and author of the official Rauschenbusch biography in 1942, reports that interest in and inquiries about Rauschenbusch have increased dramatically in the past half-dozen years (one reason for the inclusion of a good amount of Rauschenbusch material in this volume). Josiah Strong, a "forgotten" leader of the social gospel, is being rediscovered. Many so-called secondary figures are receiving biographical treatments to fill out the larger story. The geographical boundaries of the movement are being redrawn to include the South. Long-forgotten reform efforts—race, women, and anti-imperialism, for example—can now be seen alongside better-known and admittedly more vigorous efforts in the industrial arena. The social gospel's contribution to the ecumenical movement is attracting more attention. Finally, social gospel parallels and connections with Catholicism and Judaism are suggested here but still await more investigation.

This volume combines source documents and critical essays woven

together by an historical narrative. The primary sources take a variety
of forms—addresses, articles, sermons, platforms of reform organizations. We have attempted to balance the ideological and institutional
aspects of the story with its appeal to popular culture—thus the inclusion of hymns, prayers, and tracts. Some of the primary sources are
now out of print; others were never published. The critical essays encompass the work of established scholars and younger interpreters.
Essays were prepared especially for this volume by William B. Gravely,
Philip D. Jordan, and Paul Toews. We are especially pleased to have a
final reappraisal of the social gospel contributed by John C. Bennett.
For readers to whom the subject matter is new, the narrative and the restatement of classic social gospel materials are presented as a fascinating
and sometimes complex story. For more knowledgeable students, the
heretofore unpublished source materials and the new essays can provide
the opportunity for re-visioning the social gospel.

As a guide for understanding and interpreting the materials, there
are some issues the reader might want to consider. Posed in the form of
questions, these issues are presented to sensitize the reader to related
questions he or she may want to ask. Taken together, they can help
bring into perspective the major contributions of the social gospel.

1. *Is the social gospel chiefly a response to external events, or is it
rather the expression of the internal continuity of aggressive American
religion?*

As a result of Arthur M. Schlesinger's seminal essay of 1931, "A
Critical Period in American Religion, 1875–1900," American religion
came to be examined in terms of a challenge-response framework.
Schlesinger had suggested that American religion in the last quarter of
the nineteenth century was reshaped by the way it met the challenge of
urbanization and industrialization on the social-political front, and
Darwinian thought and German biblical criticism on the intellectual
front. Schlesinger's emphasis was on reaction rather than initiative.
Aaron I. Abell, *The Urban Impact on American Protestantism* (1943),
and Henry F. May, *Protestant Churches and Industrial America* (1949),
reflect the stimulus-response attitude in their explanations of the social
gospel; social causation rather than ideological or theological causation
is the dominant rationale.

Another interpretive framework has tended to stress the internal
continuity and dynamic of American religion. H. Richard Niebuhr set
the tone for this position in his classic work *The Kingdom of God in
America,* written in 1937. In the preface Niebuhr confessed his dis-

satisfaction with the "sociological" approach that had dominated his own earlier work, *The Social Sources of Denominationalism:*

> Though the sociological approach helped to explain why the religious stream flowed in these particular channels it did not account for the force of the stream itself; while it seemed relevant enough to the institutionalized churches it did not explain the Christian movement which produced these churches; while it accounted for the diversity in American religion it did not explain the unity which our faith possesses despite its variety; while it could deal with the religion which was dependent on culture it left unexplained the faith which is independent, which is aggressive rather than passive, and which molds culture instead of being molded by it.[3]

In our own day Sidney Mead and Robert T. Handy have emphasized the dynamism and integrity of American religious traditions. Handy has forged the thesis that the period 1830–1930 can best be understood as a more or less continuous attempt by American Protestantism to "Christianize America" first through revivalism and then through the social gospel. One of the most able historians of the social gospel, Handy states, in the introduction to *The Social Gospel in America:* "The response to the problems of an urbanized and industrialized society was shaped by the patterns of thought and action that had long been characteristic of American Protestantism."[4] Accentuating continuity over discontinuity, aggressive as opposed to defensive religion, Handy's viewpoint has implications for such issues as the theological precursors of the social gospel and the movement's decline and revival.

It must not be assumed that these two interpretive schemes are at every point contradictory or that they are held exclusively by any one person. Historiography is changing and growing even as the social gospel needs to be re-visioned. Thus, Henry F. May, in the 1967 introduction to the paperback edition of *Protestant Churches in Industrial America,* observes:

> Much more than I realized as I wrote it, this book was dominated by the assumptions about American religious history of the late Arthur M. Schlesinger. . . . As the book's most acute critics have pointed out, it usually takes for granted Professor Schlesinger's organization of late nineteenth-century American religious history in terms of challenge and response.

May believes that in our reflections on external challenge we should also be cognizant of "the inner vitality and continuity of the religious tradition that shaped the response."[5]

In detecting the often subtle differences between these two viewpoints, one needs to be aware of starting points and perspectives. Thus, Donald B. Meyer, in *The Protestant Search for Political Realism, 1919– 1941* (1960), comments: "The social gospel could be regarded as, in a sense, reform with a Protestant gloss, the gloss interesting but inessential. Reform first, religion second." Meyer goes on to add, however, that from another perspective "it would be possible to regard reform as the social gospel unconscious of its religious debts. Religion first, reform second."[6] It will be important, then, to keep in mind these two starting points, and perspectives in between, in approaching the documents and essays that follow.

2. *How did the social gospelers understand the new urban world?*

Again and again social gospelers were shaped by interaction with the new world of the American city. Washington Gladden commented upon his first contact with Brooklyn, New York:

> The city, from the first day, was a thing stupendous and overpowering, a mighty monster, with portentous energies. To one who had nursed his fancies for the greater part of his life in the solitude of a back country farm, and who had breasted no currents of life stronger than those which meander through the streets of a quiet village, the contact with the strenuous life of the great city was a revelation.[7]

On June 1, 1886, Walter Rauschenbusch began his duties as pastor of the Second German Baptist Church, ministering to the tenement dwellers of what was called the Hell's Kitchen neighborhood of New York City. In the beginning Rauschenbusch's strategy of ministry was quite orthodox, preaching and pastoring with the idea of saving souls and building them up in the faith. Very quickly he discovered that Hell's Kitchen was not a safe place for saved souls. Working in the midst of the city, he then began to formulate a program of social action.

Josiah Strong summed it up for many when he wrote, "The city is the nerve center of our civilization. It is also the storm center."[8] If the social gospel was in large part a response to urbanization and industrialization, the question that emerges is, How did these reformers envision the making and remaking of the city? Would the shape of the city be formed out of nostalgia for rural America or from a tough-minded acceptance of the urban experience? Put another way, Was the city to be the peril or the promise of the new America?

In approaching this issue, it is well to be aware of the ambivalence present in both the perceptions of the city and the prescriptions for change. It is possible to argue that the social gospel, as the bridge from an agrarian to an urban religion, brought its best exponents and tools to the city. Open to the new social sciences, the best of the new breed of sociologists, such as Graham Taylor of Chicago, operated from a social gospel basis. The social gospelers did not speak about the city only from the pulpit. From the social survey to institutional churches to social settlement houses, new techniques and strategies were brought to bear. Washington Gladden was elected to the city council in Columbus, Ohio, in 1900 as an Independent. Gladden did not campaign actively; his election was a tribute to his many years of work for the reorganization of the municipal government. Samuel M. "Golden Rule" Jones, friend of Gladden and reform mayor of Toledo, was one of the most celebrated of the municipal leaders of the progressive era. Jones' Society of Applied Christianity was the ideological schoolhouse for the spreading of his social gospel brand of city politics.

It is possible, however, to paint municipal reform in different colors. It has been suggested that the order sought by advocates of the social gospel, and indeed many other progressives, was that of rural and small-town America. Critics have pointed to the heavy emphasis on saloons and related social vices plus efforts at immigration restriction as indications that rural values dictated city politics. For all their talk against an isolated individualism, to what degree did these leaders move beyond the personalism of the small town to deal with the impersonal structures of the emerging cities?

3. *To what extent is the social gospel a theological movement, and what is its theology?*

To be sure, theology was a part of the social gospel, but its critics, both contemporaries and later commentators, have pointed out that it was fundamentally a social movement. Did not Walter Rauschenbusch, certainly the foremost theologian of the social gospel—so the argument runs—admit in the opening sentences of his *A Theology for the Social Gospel:* "We have a social gospel. We need a systematic theology large enough to match it and vital enough to back it"?[9] But this was in 1917, Rauschenbusch was dead within a year, and no serious theological formulation was then forthcoming.

Observers of the growth of the social gospel have pointed out that the movement coalesced more around action than belief. Persons and organizations were drawn together because of pressing social needs. This tendency to emphasize action culminated in the founding of the

Federal Council of Churches in 1908. If there was any agreement by the various churches, it was on the famous Federal Council's "Social Creed of the Churches" rather than on a more traditional theological creed.

In the decade after World War I the social gospel and theological liberalism came under heavy attack from what became known as neoothodoxy. European theologian W. A. Visser 't Hooft, in *The Background of the Social Gospel in America* (1928), and Americans such as the Niebuhr brothers, Reinhold and Richard, criticized the optimistic formulations of a theology that did not deal seriously enough with either the transcendence of God or the reality of sin and evil.

In the light of these criticisms it is well to be alert to the basic issue of the theological foundations of the social gospel. What are they? Are they tacked on to what is basically social reform, or does reform emerge from theology? Part of the answer may be found in the way the questions are framed.

Washington Gladden was not a theologian by reason of academic training—he did not complete a seminary course—but it is possible to argue that his lifelong study of theology always informed his social consciousness. A contemporary observed:

> The Christianity to be applied was very clearly conceived by Dr. Gladden. Behind his social mission there has been from the first not only Christian motive, but a definite, tangible, clear-cut idea of what Christianity means. . . . And all his thinking has been conscientiously and avowedly allied with the New Theology.[10]

An important segment of the social gospel, as we shall soon see, was a product of the theological liberalism known as the New Theology. However, to define the social gospel as liberalism is to miss the mark, for not all liberals were social gospelers, and not all social gospelers were liberal. The theology of Walter Rauschenbusch was rooted in evangelical piety. As we will see, "evangelical" and "liberal" were sometimes combined in ways that were then possible. Liberalism was attacked in the thirties, but even the critics distinguished between liberalism and the social gospel. The continuing contributions of social gospel theology should be kept in mind throughout the following chapters including the final essay by John C. Bennett.

4. *What were the points of connection and tension (if any) between the social gospel movement and the larger progressive movement?*

Historian Richard Hofstatder has characterized the progressive movement as "a phase in the history of the Protestant conscience, a latter-day Protestant revival."[11] Indeed, the revivalists-turned-social-crusaders of both the social gospel and social justice progressivism knew each other well, operated from many of the same premises, and employed similar strategies. This climate of mutuality was encouraged under the moral leadership of Presidents Theodore Roosevelt and Woodrow Wilson. One of Roosevelt's confidants was Lyman Abbott, longtime editor of the *Outlook* and successor to Henry Ward Beecher as minister of the Plymouth Congregational Church in Brooklyn. Upon his retirement from the White House, Roosevelt accepted a position as a contributing editor of the *Outlook* and continued his "bully pulpit" approach to politics through that popular weekly periodical. Woodrow Wilson, the son of a Presbyterian minister and an articulate layman whose Calvinistic theology very definitely influenced his progressive politics, brought to the White House the kind of Christian idealism associated with perhaps no other American President. An address by Wilson to a gathering of ministers is included below to illustrate these connections, as are several items by "T. R."

The social gospel never became an organized "movement."[12] Rather it was a network of movements operating in different contexts. Those individuals connected with its ideology worked through ongoing religious and secular organizations. Occasionally, they did establish study and action groups of their own—like C.A.I.L. and the Brotherhood of the Kingdom—but often they made common cause with others of a social justice orientation. Whether at the American Economic Association, Chautauqua, the Southern Sociological Congress, or political conventions, exponents of the social gospel shared the platform with other progressives.

They did have much in common. Their belief in the ultimate goodness of America, despite their insistent cry of crisis, meant that their reform instincts were for the most part moderate in conception and strategy. Together they were optimistic about their ability to harness the industrial machines and the social sciences for the good of the common life. Later critics would point out that progressives in general, including the social gospelers, were often better at diagnosing the ills of society than providing concrete and long-term remedies. The tendency of both movements was to place too much confidence in preachers and publicists rather than hard-nosed programs. To their credit, they were able to elicit the idealism and energy of some of the most able men and women in America at a time of transition when those efforts were needed most.

In the study that follows, it is important to be aware of possible points of tension between the social gospel and progressivism. The social gospel has sometimes been caricatured as simply mirroring the spirit of the times. This does an injustice to the diversity and complexity of the movement. The kingdom of God was not simply the American dream. Involved in the political process, social gospel leaders were sometimes more astute critics than other progressives because of their theological and ethical assumptions. A disproportionate share of the reformers concerned with race relations were allied to the social gospel despite much overt or silent racism.

These four questions, then, can help provide a way into the narrative, documents, and essays that follow. Other issues will arise as the story takes shape. Taken in its parts, this volume seeks to recapture and restate the meaning of a movement important for persons who might approach the study of the American experience from quite different disciplines and vantage points. Taken as a whole, the re-visioning of the social gospel can help us grapple with the overwhelming issues of our own day.

Notes

1. Carl Degler, *Out of Our Past: The Forces That Shaped Modern America* (New York: Harper & Row, 1950), 347.

2. Shailer Mathews, "Social Gospel," *A Dictionary of Religion and Ethics,* ed. Shailer Mathews and Gerald Birney Smith (New York, 1921), 416.

3. H. Richard Niebuhr, *The Kingdom of God in America* (New York: Harper & Row Torchbook, 1959), ix-x.

4. *The Social Gospel in America,* ed. Robert T. Handy (New York: Oxford University Press, 1966), 4.

5. Henry F. May, *Protestant Churches and Industrial America* (New York: Harper & Row, 1949; paperback ed., 1967), vii.

6. Donald B. Meyer, *The Protestant Search for Political Realism, 1919–1941* (Berkeley: University of California Press, 1960), 2–3.

7. Washington Gladden, *Recollections* (New York: Houghton Mifflin, 1909), 90–91.

8. Josiah Strong, *Our Country* (New York: American Home Missionary Society, 1885), 128.

9. Walter Rauschenbusch, *A Theology for the Social Gospel* (New York: Macmillan, 1917), 1.

10. John W. Buckham, *Progressive Religious Thought in America* (Boston: Houghton Mifflin, 1919), 222.

11. Richard Hofstatder, *The Age of Reform* (New York: Knopf, 1955), 152.

12. C. Howard Hopkins, *The Rise of the Social Gospel in American Protestantism, 1865–1915* (New Haven: Yale University Press, 1940, 319; a reprint edition of this work is planned for 1976–77.

I

Awakening the Church

Introduction

The rise of the social gospel precipitated renewal and reform on many fronts across America. A dominant evangelical tradition had long emphasized an individual salvation. Now the church was awakened to the possibilities of a social salvation as well. The call for a new social consciousness was not received without misunderstanding and controversy as men and women, clergy and lay alike, struggled to discern the meaning and strategy of the new movement. To some the social gospel seemed a departure from a more simple gospel, but to most of its adherents it was an extension and growth of the historic Christian faith.

The awakening of the church to a social gospel was the product of both the pressure of external events and the internal continuity of theological reflection and social action. The origins of the social gospel are, then, many and varied, ranging from Evangelicalism to liberalism and spawned by such crusades as Christian socialism and abolitionism. A movement that returned to the Old Testament prophets, it produced its own American prophets, who heralded a theology and a sociology of a present kingdom of God.

It is not possible to fix an exact chronology for the origin of the social gospel. Part I begins with the heritage of Evangelicalism not only because this was the personal heritage of many social gospel leaders but also because it is easy to forget their legacy when speaking of a movement that was often popularly thought of as liberal. Though evangelical theology and conservative politics are often equated, Timothy L. Smith presents a respected but controversial thesis that questions this assumption, at least as it relates to mid-nineteenth-century revivalism.

Evangelical social reform found a perfect vehicle after 1830 in the developing antislavery crusade. The system of slavery and the ideology of racial caste brought into being a whole cluster of abolitionist groups quite diverse in motivation, ideology, and tactics. Chapter 2, written for this volume by William B. Gravely, discusses the "Christian abolitionists," both as they were a distinctive part of the larger abolitionist movement and as they anticipated later social gospel ideology and strategy.

3

One option for churches awakening to a more highly developed social consciousness was what came to be called Christian socialism. If both sin and salvation were social (as well as personal), then system and structure needed to be changed as well as individuals. Christian socialism came to be an important force within the American social gospel movement, influencing many who could not accept socialism as a complete political system or ideology. The roots of Christian socialism in America are to be found in Europe and Great Britain, and will be discussed both in Part I and in Part IV. The Christian socialism that emanated from the Church of England is important in its own right, but is of special interest because of the way it helped transform the Episcopal Church in America from a conservative to a progressive church body.

Moved by the crosscurrents of thought and action in American life, a cadre of theologians and pastors began to articulate a theology adequate for a changing church. Called the "New Theology," it strove to maintain continuity with the past while setting forth a new emphasis that caused many to see it as a radical departure from traditional religion.

Part I concludes with a glimpse at Walter Rauschenbusch, the foremost theologian of the developed social gospel, whose theology was changed and shaped by an eleven-year pastorate in the Hell's Kitchen section of New York City. Rauschenbusch became a spokesman for a whole generation of social gospelers. His reputation sank during the thirties and forties, but appreciation of his contributions is being restored now, as we work through the various social and political crises of our own day.

1   Revivalism and Reform

The roots of the social gospel within the American soil are rich and diverse. As important as any, though sometimes overlooked, is the heritage of Protestant evangelicalism. Centered in the experience of the new birth in Christ, nourished by the recurring fires of revivalism, evangelical faith and piety were the seedbed of religious experience for many who would later be affiliated with the social gospel.

It is difficult for the contemporary American to appreciate the extent to which evangelical religion underlay the culture of nineteenth-century America. William G. McLoughlin has observed:

> The story of American Evangelicalism is the story of America itself in the years 1800 to 1900, for it was Evangelical religion which made Americans the most religious people in the world, molded them into a unified, pietistic-perfectionist nation, and spurred them on to those heights of social reform, missionary endeavor, and imperialistic expansionism which constitute the moving forces of our history in that century.[1]

For our purposes it is important to understand the ways in which evangelical religion, and particularly revivalism, nourished the impulse to social reform. "Awakenings" in America have always had social, political, and economic overtones and results. Like the Great Awakening of the eighteenth century and the Second Great Awakening at the dawn of the nineteenth century, the awakenings of the 1820's and 1830's resulted in yet more tangible structures for social reform. In these years Charles Grandison Finney, "the father of modern revivalism," encouraged converts to move from the personal regeneration of an "anxious bench" experience to the social mission of the growing antislavery crusade. In these same years a whole cluster of organizations promoting personal renewal, moral reform, and missionary advance grew up. They flourished in the atmosphere of Finney's revivals and the challenge of the opening up of the West. These societies emphasized action more than belief. They were rooted in the typical American ar-

5

rangement of "voluntaryism" in which individuals (not churches) joined together to support a common cause. Called from our vantage point the Evangelical United Front, these Bible, anti-slavery, peace, and dozens of other evangelical societies were the prototypes of similar reform organizations that would flourish a half-century later under the banner of the social gospel.[2]

The climax of the Evangelical United Front was the mid-1830's, but Timothy L. Smith has recovered the story of the continuing interaction between revivalism and reform in the quarter-century before the Civil War. Edwards and Finney were reared in the tradition of Calvinism, with its emphasis on election. But much of mid-nineteenth-century revivalism came to be dominated by an emphasis on perfectionism and holiness stemming from the Wesleyan tradition. Even as Finney was rejecting much of his Presbyterian heritage, it was the Methodists and Baptists who were winning the West.

The Evangelical Origins of Social Christianity

The rapid growth of concern with purely social issues such as poverty, workingmen's rights, the liquor traffic, slum housing, and racial bitterness is the chief feature distinguishing American religion after 1865 from that of the first half of the nineteenth century. Such matters in some cases supplanted entirely the earlier pre-occupation with salvation from personal sin and the life hereafter. Seminaries reorganized their programs to stress sociology. Institutional churches and social settlement work became prominent in the citiies. Crusades for the rights of oppressed groups of all sorts absorbed the energies of hundreds of clergymen.

The vanguard of the movement went far beyond the earlier Christian emphasis on almsgiving to a search for the causes of human suffering and a campaign to reconstruct social and economic relations upon a Christian pattern. At its height evangelicals like William Booth and Charles M. Sheldon stood as stanchly for reform as their more liberal brethren. Outstanding among the latter were Washington Gladden— Congregationalist pastor in Columbus, Ohio, and labor's fast friend— and Walter Rauschenbush, professor at the Baptist seminary in Rochester. Gladden's hymn, "O Master, Let Me Walk With Thee," hauntingly expresses the spiritual content of his many appeals in behalf of workingmen's rights. The same note of reference echoes in

Rauschenbush's *Prayers of the Social Awakening* and in his little book
on *The Social Principles of Jesus.*

The best-known recent works on the beginnings of social Christianity have leaned toward either an intellectual or a sociological interpretation and placed chief emphasis upon the events which followed the
Civil War. Pressure from urban maladjustments and industrial strife, the
challenge of Darwinian philosophy and the new psychology, and the influence of the optimistic and communitarian spirit of the age seemed to
Charles Howard Hopkins, Aaron I. Abell, Henry F. May, and James
Dombrowski the chief factors which turned Christian minds toward
social reconstruction. That humanitarian impulses flowed earlier from
hearts warmed at Finney's revival fires has not been forgotten, of
course. But for the past half-century church historians have assumed
that revivals and perfectionism declined in public favor after about
1842, the year in which Elder Jacob Knapp was banished from Boston
and the Oberlin preachers suffered widespread attacks for their "fanaticism." Thus scholars have eliminated these two forces from consideration as causes of the movement which seemed to emerge later on.

The discovery that the doctrine of sanctification and the methods
of mass evangelism played an increasingly important role in the program of the churches *after* 1842 compels a revaluation of their impact
on every facet of the contemporary religious scene. Here, then, is offered an evangelical explanation of the origins of the social gospel. . . .
Whatever may have been the role of other factors, the quest for perfection joined with compassion for poor and needy sinners and a rebirth of
millennial expectation to make popular Protestantism a mighty social
force long before the slavery conflict erupted into war.

In many ways, of course, the evangelists' preoccupation with personal religious experience could nurture an exclusively spiritual faith.
Their chief concern was to prepare men for another world, their most
earnest prayer for a miraculous "outpouring of the Holy Spirit" which
would break the shackles of human sin. Opposition to social evil was
often only an occasional skirmish in their war on personal wickedness.
Charles G. Finney, for example, inspired many an abolitionist. But he
never thought himself primarily a reformer. He composed his *Lectures
on Revivals* in 1834 partly to help Joshua Leavitt, editor of *The New
York Evangelist,* rescue that paper from the near ruin which Leavitt's
strong stand against slavery had brought upon it. Two decades later
Elder Jacob Knapp blamed only himself when a Louisville congregation
halted one of his campaigns upon learning that Knapp was about to
break his self-imposed silence on slavery. Though always an abolitionist,

he believed his first work was to save souls not free slaves. "I let all debatable subjects alone," James Caughey wrote from England in 1857; "have nothing to do with reformers as reformers, but as *soul-savers* I know all good men." A sincere revivalist had little choice when the alternative was to drive penitents from the place of prayer.

The violence of the slavery controversy only made the problem more difficult. True enough, a Baptist minister wrote, the aim of the Christian faith was "to revolutionize the world and bring all powers under its own sway." But had not Christ himself set an example of love and longsuffering toward the authors of oppression?

When right-wing Calvinists and Episcopalians accepted revival measures, they became the chief spokesmen for such spiritual conservatism. The editor of Boston's *Puritan Recorder* attempted in 1854 to show that past American awakenings had prospered in proportion to their "holiness," by which he meant the extent to which they "drew a wide line between politics and religion, between the interests of this world and of another." The Episcopal *Church Journal* attributed the success of lay leadership in the revival of 1858 to the public reaction against "Kansas and antislavery preachers" who had neglected spiritual tasks. That only their church's share of the awakening had begun under clerical auspices seemed to these editors proof that the people preferred a politically conservative ministry. Similarly, the pastoral address which Charles P. McIlvaine prepared for circulation on behalf of the board of Episcopal bishops in 1862 condemned Southerners for rebellion but not slavery and warned Northern Christians of the dangers which periods of public excitement bring to the life of the spirit. "Let not love of country make your love to God and your gracious Saviour less fervent," the address ran. "Immense as is the present earthly interest, it is only earthly."

But liberalism on social issues, not reaction, was the dominant note which evangelical preachers sounded before 1860. The most influential of them, from Albert Barnes and Samuel S. Schmucker to Edward Norris Kirk and Matthew Simpson, defined carefully the relationship between personal salvation and community improvement and never tired of glowing descriptions of the social and economic millennium which they believed revival Christianity would bring into existence. Even the doctrine of human depravity seemed to such men a demonstration of the solidarity of the race and the brotherhood of man, a crushing rebuke to "all contempt of even the vilest" of Adam's sons. That they thought individual regeneration a chief means of social reform does not set them apart from their postwar successors. As late as

1910, according to the foremost student of the subject, the central feature of Christian social method in America remained the dedication of person and resources to the will of God. Thus, Lyman Abbott and Josiah Strong would have agreed with the editor of the Baptist *Watchman and Reflector* who insisted in the year 1857 that legislation alone could not "reach down to the root of our social evils." For this, he wrote, "moral and Christian power must be invoked. . . . The great panacea is the gospel of Christ."

These later reformers might also have shared the same editor's enthusiasm for Frederic Dan Huntington's declaration before a Unitarian gathering planning a denominational tract society, that "the world's salvation consists in a spiritual redemption . . . and *not* in a mere natural development of the human powers according to natural laws." The books Unitarians circulated, Huntington said,

> must affirm the radical and essential distinction between morality and piety, insisting on the latter as the vital root of the former. They must recognize the offices of the Holy Spirit, the Comforter, in regenerating the soul, sanctifying it, flooding it with grace, and raising it to glory. And finally, they must fearlessly and unqualifiedly apply the principles and spirit of the Lord Jesus, not only to the ordinary labor and familiar relations of man's life in the world, but to all popular combinations of sin, organized iniquities, and public crimes, like intemperance, slavery, and war. . . .

In fact, if evangelicals insisted upon moral solutions to social questions, they never forgot that personal sin often had communal roots. Albert Barnes pointed in 1842 to the "evils of alliance, of compact, of confederation" characteristic of urban life, to "sins of common pursuit, where one man keeps another in countenance, or one man leads on the many to transgression." Sin is never solitary, he declared, nor can it be banished piecemeal from society.

> One sin is interlocked with others and is sustained by others. . . . The only power in the universe which can meet and overcome such combined evil is the power of the Spirit of God. There are evils of alliance and confederation in every city which can never be met but by a general revival of religion.

Fifteen years later *The Watchman's* editor, a leader in the crusade for just such a nation-wide awakening, reproved those who were taking

refuge from the gloomy social outlook in purely spiritual contemplation. True, he acknowledged, the slave power was gaining ground every
day. The American Republic, instead of being superseded by the kingdom of Christ "as the star of dawn is swallowed up in the perfect day,"
might have to be overturned in judgment before Christians could enjoy
millennial peace. But, declared this earnest Baptist, the triumph of the
gospel calls for its victory over all evil, not a mere deliverance of individual Christians from harm.

> It is something more than a gathering together of those who shall
> be saved in a future state, leaving the world to destruction; it con-
> templates the organization and supremacy of goodness in human
> society—the doing of God's will *on earth*—the coming of His
> Kingdom hither, as well as our going hence to it. . . . True, when
> his work in this respect is accomplished, we are taught that there
> will be new heavens and a new earth, in which all external circum-
> stances shall be conformed to the spiritual glory of that consum-
> mation. . . . Meanwhile, it is ours, not only to fit ourselves and
> others for a better world, but to labor to make this world better.

The growth of slavery could only be halted, the writer continued,
when Christians comprehended the infinite value which Christ had at-
tached to every human creature through his incarnation, sufferings, and
atoning death. Men must "learn to regard slavery as not merely the
denial of rights conferred in original creation, but as an outrage on the
nature which the Son of God was pleased to make the temple of His
divinity." For this reason, he believed that the growth of the "pure
spirit" of Christianity would be more effective against the extension of
the institution than a hundred legislative prohibitions. The latter were
indispensable, even as they were "altogether rightful." But if the church
of Christ were "more suffused with His spirit," their necessity would be
greatly diminished. "Oppression and violence could not with their darkness affront *that* light," he cried; "faith and love and purity would prevail, because vivified and directed by One who has all power, as He is to
have all dominion."

It is no wonder that when the intermittent and local awakenings
characteristic of the years after 1842 gave way in 1858 to a Pentecost
of seemingly miraculous proportions, revivalists were convinced that
the conquest of social and political evil was near at hand. For long
afterward they were apt to ascribe humanitarian progress to the force
of the gospel. As late as 1880 a Freewill Baptist minister predicted confidently that the faith which had "swept slavery from the earth, ele-

vated women from a state of bondage," and "weakened the grasp of despots" would ultimately triumph over every ill. "War will eventually cease," he cried. "The strong will foster the weak, capital befriend labor . . . and the spirit of mutual helpfulness pervade all the ranks of society."

What was needed to accomplish these ends was more and purer piety. Hence the importance of the fervor for Christian perfection which spread through the churches after 1835. All of the socially potent doctrines of revivalism reached white heat in the Oberlin and Wesleyan experience of sanctification—ethical seriousness, the call to full personal consecration, the belief in God's immanence, in his readiness to transform the present world through the outpoured Holy Ghost, and the exaltation of Christian love.

William Arthur most clearly expounded for nineteenth-century Methodists the social implications of their belief in deliverance from all sin and in entire consecration. In his book *The Tongue of Fire,* which appeared in a half-dozen editions in England and America after 1854, Arthur warned that the two most dangerous perversions of the gospel were to look upon it as "a salvation for the soul after it leaves the body, but no salvation from sin while there," and as "a means of forming a holy community in the world to come, but never in this."

> Nothing short of the general renewal of society ought to satisfy any soldier of Christ. . . . Much as Satan glories in his power over an individual, how much greater must be his glorying over a nation embodying, in its laws and usages, disobedience to God, wrong to man, and contamination to morals? To destroy all national holds of evil; to root sin out of institutions; to hold up to view the gospel ideal of a righteous nation . . . is one of the first duties of those whose position or mode of thought gives them any influence in general questions. In so doing they are at once glorifying the Redeemer, by displaying the benignity of his influence over human society, and removing hindrances to individual conversions, some of which act by direct incentive to vice, others by upholding a state of things the acknowledged basis of which is, "Forget God."
> Satan might be content to let Christianity turn over the subsoil, if he is in perpetuity to sow the surface with thorns and briers; but the gospel is come to renew the face of the earth.

Other Methodist perfectionists struck a similar note. The editor of *Zion's Herald* declared in 1854 that spirituality must be expressed in irreproachable morality and unceasing efforts to reform society, lest the "adversaries of Christ" be permitted to appear more interested in the welfare of mankind than the friends of the gospel. Every Christian should seek to overthrow slavery, intemperance, political corruption, and all other public vices. A few weeks later the same journal argued that only "entire self-devotion to Christ" could produce the systematic benevolence which was the hope of the poor. The way to avoid the sin of covetousness was "to subject our property, with ourselves, to the dominion of Christ." *The Guide to Holiness* printed in 1856 Finney's letter advising ministers "to inquire affectionately and particularly" into the political beliefs of their parishioners, "whether they are cleaving to a party without regard to principles," as well as "in what manner they demean themselves toward those who are in their employment.[3]

Smith's arguments, widely appreciated, have had lasting value, both as a starting point for various scholarly reinterpretations of nineteenth-century social and religious thought, and as an historical rationale and apologetic for contemporary evangelical activism (see Chapter 23). It is important to point out, however, that his thesis is not universally accepted. Smith argues that revivalism produced social reform. But it also produced social conservatism. Critics have asked whether Smith attributes to all evangelicals the virtues of a few social reformers. To be sure, revivalism and perfectionism were important to Methodists and Baptists, but many of the earliest social gospelers came from Congregational, Episcopal, and Unitarian backgrounds. Finally, and most important, was the reform impulse of antebellum revivalism really the same as the motivation and substance of the social gospel? The reader is encouraged to keep these questions in mind in studying the documents and essays that follow.

Notes

1. William G. McLoughlin, ed., *The American Evangelicals, 1800–1900* (New York: Harper & Row, 1968), 1. See also, Whitney R. Cross, *The Burned-Over District: The Social and Intellectual History of Enthusiastic Religion in Western New York, 1800–1850* (Ithaca: Cornell University Press, 1950); William G. McLoughlin, *Modern Revivalism: Charles Grandison Finney to Billy Graham* (New York: Ronald Press, 1959); and Bernard A. Weisberger, *They Gathered at the River: The Story of the Great Revivalists and Their Impact upon Religion in America* (Boston: Little, Brown, 1958).
2. For the story of the Evangelical United Front, see Charles I. Foster, *An*

Errand of Mercy: The Evangelical United Front, 1790–1837 (Chapel Hill: University of North Carolina Press, 1960). For an alternative thesis dealing with some of the same materials, see Clifford S. Griffin, *Their Brothers' Keepers: Moral Stewardship in the United States, 1800–1865* (New Brunswick, N.J.: Rutgers University Press, 1960).

3. Timothy L. Smith, *Revivalism and Social Reform in Mid-Nineteenth-Century America* (Nashville: Abingdon, 1957), 148–55. Copyright © 1957 by Abingdon Press. By permission.

2 Christian Abolitionism

In the tradition of social criticism and agitation in the United States, the abolitionist movement from 1830 to 1870 was a significant early development. The men and women who battled the economic and political system of chattel slavery and its ideological bulwark, racial caste, were pioneers in social reform. As they articulated an ethical critique of slavery, planned and implemented strategies to attack it, debated the relation of moral suasion to political action, and formed new voluntary associations as institutions for social change, they dealt with many of the issues which faced later reformers.

There was a wide range in kinds of abolitionist commitment, varying in intensity, consistency, and motivation. No one organization or individual is representative of such a diffuse movement. The connection of religion to abolitionism is similarly ambiguous. Some American churchmen, Protestant and Catholic, vigorously defended the enslavement of black people, proving that elements of the Christian religion could be appropriated to support human oppression.[1] Moreover, there was no single religious persuasion among abolitionists, despite the fact that most interacted, one way or another, with an overarching evangelical Protestant ethos. Among opponents of slavery were theologically conservative Protestants, liberal Unitarians and Transcendentalists, and pietistic revivalists.

Historians of abolitionism have devoted most attention to the liberal wing of the movement, associated with the career of William Lloyd Garrison and geographically dominant in New England. Most Garrisonians believed that antislavery organizations should include members with different religious, social, and political views. They tended to be radical in their social philosophy and comprehensive in their critique of mid-nineteenth-century American life. Their criticism extended to

Note: Chapter 2 is contributed by William B. Gravely, Associate Professor in the Department of Religion at the University of Denver. Dr. Gravely is the author of *Gilbert Haven, Methodist Abolitionist.*

questions of women's rights, pacifism, nonresistance, and religious faith as well as to the most blatant of the sins of society, slavery.[2]

Many abolitionists, however, rejected Garrison's brand of antislavery reform. They called themselves "Christian abolitionists" to distinguish their outlook from the more revolutionary, anti-institutional tendencies of the Garrisonians. They were not less vehement in their opposition to slavery and caste, but they saw themselves more as reformers within American religion and politics than as radicals who would subvert the social order and replace it with some new model. Like Garrisonian abolitionists they diagnosed the American political compromise over slavery as corrupt, but they refused to disavow politics. They also agreed with the Garrisonians in damning most religious organizations for their accommodation to racism and slavery, but they did not conclude that evangelical Protestantism, the dominant religious force in the nation, was entirely irredeemable. Hence, Christian abolitionists often withdrew from the popular denominations which tolerated slaveholders and their sympathizers, but these seceders in turn organized new churches and a series of alternative institutions in religion, education, and politics established on strict antislavery principles.

All abolitionists agreed on the basic contentions that slavery was a sin per se, that the system of bondage and not merely its attendant evils was immoral, that human equality was both a Christian and a democratic tenet and that slaves ought to be freed without expatriation or compensation to owners.[3] On these points Christian abolitionists parted company with proslavery churchmen, North and South, who justified American slavery by linking it with precedents in the Bible and ancient history. They also dissented from the nominal antislavery viewpoint of the majority of northern Protestants, who regretted the existence of slavery and hoped for its removal, but who refused to take direct action against an institution so deeply rooted in American social experience.

The assertion that slavery in principle was evil became the foundation for the Christian abolitionist's ethical critique of a complex social system. In 1842 the little band of pastors and laity of the Franckean Evangelical Lutheran Synod in New York State defined slavery as "the abhorrent principle of chattelship—the sinking into annihilation all the personal rights of man to himself or the products of his industry and his reduction to a thing."[4] No one truly comprehended American slavery, a convention of abolitionist Christians in 1850 declared, without perceiving the "chattel principle" as its essence.[5] All efforts, therefore, to ameliorate the condition of the slaves without also requiring emancipation undercut the moral demand for justice and, in the words of Free

Presbyterian George Gordon, treated the institution as "but an inno-
cent thing abused."[6]

Abolitionists were not, of course, unconcerned about the treatment of slaves. Again and again they described in morbid detail the
atrocities which accompanied the system. Occasionally they inferred
that all slaveholders were lecherous and sadistic. More often than not,
however, their condemnation focused on the immorality of the relationship itself, which gave slaveholders the power to separate families or
to violate bondswomen, whether or not that power was exercised. The
Vermont clergyman Silas McKeen recognized that "humane masters
may soften the hardships of slavery, and render the yoke less intolerable than it generally is; but," he proclaimed, "the nature of the institution, and its essential injustice, remain, even in their hands, the same."[7]

Anticipating the social gospel later in the century, Christian abolitionists extended the range of ethical responsibility beyond the con-
fines of a private morality to encompass the corporate nature of social
evil. They refused, therefore, to attribute "to the credit of the system,
what is due to the generosity and humanity of the master."[8] They
acknowledged how in subtle ways moral men became implicated in
social wrong. "The strength of the slave power," a committee of Methodist abolitionists stated in 1840, "consists in the countenance extended to the system by professedly good men."[9]

The ethical realism of Christian abolitionists was further borne out
in their awareness that slavery would never be uprooted without a fundamental transformation of the racial attitudes and practices of white
Americans. All narrowly sectional interpretations of the antislavery crusade fail to perceive that abolitionists were urging a national reformation of values and customs. Not every abolitionist was consistent on
this point, for some found it easier to concentrate on the sins of southern slaveholders than on racial injustice in northern churches and communities. Prior to the 1850's, however, anti-abolition backlash was so
pervasive throughout the nation that protest against slavery was almost
as relevant in the North, where such criticism was possible, as in the
South, where it was prohibited. Condemnation of black servitude,
therefore, was a criticism of national racial attitudes wherever it was
uttered.

The abolitionist effort to rally opinion against slavery did not fail
to censure racial discrimination, which, in the words of John W. Lewis,
a black Free Will Baptist, "every colored man of us has to feel and endure in almost every turn of life."[10] Among the pioneers of religious
protest against caste were Negro churchmen, who customarily belonged

to black denominations which originated partly to oppose the racism of white Christians. They were the first to notice when northern whites were inconsistent in their behavior or unwilling to act upon the principle of human equality. Black Presbyterian Theodore S. Wright, for example, told the New York State Antislavery Society in 1837, "It is an easy thing to ask about the vileness of slavery in the South, but . . . to treat the man of color in all circumstances as a man and brother—that is the test."[11]

Among those white abolitionist churchmen who met Wright's test was Lewis Tappan (whose letter to the Christian Anti-Slavery Convention concludes this chapter), a major antislavery organizer and financial supporter. During his career he fought segregation in churches, schools, and benevolent organizations. Once he was excommunicated from a Presbyterian church in New York City after he began a racially integrated antislavery society in the congregation. Alongside immediate abolition it sought "to elevate the character and condition of the people of color."[12] Judge William Jay, an Episcopalian and son of one of the country's founding fathers, advocated "the abolition of CASTE as well as of slavery," as did New England Methodist Gilbert Haven, who preached that racism was "the corner-stone of American slavery" and the special sin of white northerners.[13]

Despite an endemic paternalism, such men were egalitarians in principle and innovators of interracial association in practice. They founded and supported the academies and colleges which accepted black students before the Civil War—schools like Oberlin, Knox, Oneida Institute, Iberia. The New York Central College, whose president was the veteran Baptist abolitionist Cyrus P. Grosvenor, even had an integrated faculty and staff. At a time when most Americans refused civil and political rights to Negroes, Christian abolitionists spoke out for enfranchisement and equal opportunity and demanded protection for the lives, liberties, and properties of black persons. They challenged the popular Hamite myth of black inferiority, refuting eminent anthropologists who argued for the diverse origins of the human race as a scientific justification of white racism.

Abolitionism, however, was more than ideology, for it affected social behavior and structures. It was institutionalized in numerous voluntary associations for antislavery and anticaste reform. No single body represented the entire movement, despite the forty-year history of the American Anti-Slavery Society. By 1840 most Christian abolitionists had broken with that organization to join the American and Foreign Anti-Slavery Society, its successor the American Abolition Society, or the Church Anti-Slavery Society, which was formed in 1859. These national antislavery organizations, which depended heavily on regional, state, and local affiliates for support, required other agencies in the larger task of racial reform.

In terms of the organizational network of the antislavery crusade, Christian abolitionism exhibited four distinctive features. First, it challenged denominations which accommodated slavery. Adopting the principle, "no fellowship with slavery," abolitionist churchmen usually withdrew from the larger denominations to form new antislavery churches. This secessionist strategy accounted for the birth of several new denominations: the Wesleyan and the Free Methodists, the Free Presbyterians, three black Methodist groups (African Methodist Episcopal, African Methodist Episcopal, Zion, and Union American Methodist Episcopal churches), the American Baptist Missionary Convention composed of congregations of free Negroes, and an association of black Congregational and Presbyterian churches. There were also abolitionist churchmen whose tradition, as in the case of the Quakers, the United Brethren, and the Covenanters, had been consistently antislavery, or who chose to remain, as a prophetic remnant, in the major denominations. But a sectarian model of church reformation usually characterized Christian abolitionism. Its impact was felt in the American religious mainstream when abolitionists precipitated sectional divisions over slavery in Presbyterian, Baptist, and Methodist denominations beginning in the late 1830's.

A second component of Christian abolitionist organization was the establishment of an alternative system to the American Protestant benevolent empire. Attacking missionary, tract, and Bible societies which employed slaveholders and prohibited antislavery sentiment from their literature and proceedings, abolitionist churchmen formed the American Reform Tract and Book Society, and an interracial Union Missionary Society, which later merged into the more influential American Missionary Association. These agencies of an antislavery Christianity implemented the strategy of moral suasion which was directed toward shaping a social conscience against bondage.

Thirdly, Christian abolitionists sponsored denominational and ecumenical conventions to dramatize the "stain on the character of American Christianity" that must occur, as Congregationalist William Goodell put it, when "the Bible, the Church, and the ministry [are made] the handmaids of oppression."[14] A fully ecumenical abolitionist movement was never achieved, due to the power of denominationalism and antiabolitionism in the churches, but important conventions of antislavery

Protestants were held in Boston (1846), Cincinnati (1850), Chicago (1851), and Columbus, Ohio (1859).

Finally, Christian abolitionism had political significance. It joined moral suasion and ecclesiastical reformation to political action. As an organizational strategy, abolitionists circulated petitions to legislatures, undertook third-party campaigns, and engaged in court actions and civil disobedience, usually in conjunction with the capture of fugitive slaves. By supporting the Liberty, Free Soil, Radical Abolitionist, and Republican parties, most Christian abolitionists never voted for a winning national candidate until 1860, and in some cases not until 1864. But they refused to withdraw from the political struggle, remembering that an appeal to "non-interference with American slavery," as A. K. Moulton told the Free Will Baptist Anti-Slavery Society, required Christians to "forget every injunction of the gospel."[15] Ministers were obliged, the Cincinnati convention insisted, "to instruct their congregations in the duties of citizens, of voters, of legislators, and of administrative and judicial officers of civil government."[16] The struggle against slavery demanded that Christians "labor in the closet, at the family altar, in the community, at the polls, with prayer, and speech, and purse, and vote."[17]

Rooted in their formulation of a socially relevant religion, Christian abolitionists brought the tradition of a higher law to bear upon American morality with reference to slavery and thus subsumed national destiny and political authority under transcendent judgment. They sought to redefine the slogans and symbols of the democratic faith so as to end the contradiction of slavery in a free republic. In the end neither the moral nor the political strategy to abolish slavery triumphed. The system of black servitude met its fate only after four long years of war's carnage which left that gaunt figure in the White House musing whether the God of justice had not required that "all the wealth piled up by the bondman's two hundred and fifty years of unrequited toil shall be sunk, and . . . every drop of blood drawn with the lash, shall be paid by another drawn with the sword."[18] Abolitionist Christians were uniquely prepared to comprehend Abraham Lincoln's meaning, for they believed that "not until every fetter is broken will God's controversy with America come to an end."[19]

During the war and Reconstruction abolitionist churchmen continued the struggle for racial justice. They countered discrimination by supporting legislative measures and constitutional amendments designed to secure equal civil and political rights. As early as 1862 they embarked on an educational crusade for southern freedmen.[20] Ironically,

few Christian abolitionists knew fully what a radical revolution they
had envisioned when they made their commitment to overthrow slavery
and caste. Those who lived to see Reconstruction fail, however, learned
that slavery, but not racism, had been abolished and that the tradition
of racial Christianities—white and black—lived on in America.

The *Minutes* of the Christian Anti-Slavery Convention held in Cincinnati in 1850 contains a little known document written by a figure of
whom a recent, sympathetic biographer declares: "Lewis Tappan did
not contribute one memorable or thought-provoking pamphlet or article to the cause."[21] Even though Tappan is better known for his organizational contributions than his intellectual acumen, his letter to the
Cincinnati convention concisely summarizes the main emphases of
Christian abolitionism.

Born in 1788, Tappan was at mid-career when he became an abolitionist. With his brother Arthur, he was an early member of the American Anti-Slavery Society. After splitting with Garrison, he continued to
coordinate the activities of many white and black abolitionists. He frequently managed the treasuries of antislavery agencies and publications,
adding liberally from his own wealth earned in the credit-rating business
which later became the firm of Dun and Bradstreet. A founder of the
American Missionary Association, the American and Foreign
Slavery and American Abolition Societies, and Oberlin Institute,
Tappan also supported numerous local churches, missionaries, and benevolent causes. Due to age his career effectively terminated during the
Civil War, but for thirty years no abolitionist was more absorbed in trying to give form to a Christian vision of social reconstruction.

New York, April 13, 1850

Gentlemen: Did not the approaching anniversary of the *American and
Foreign Anti-Slavery Society* require my services here, I should gladly
accept your invitation to attend the Christian Anti-Slavery Convention,
to be held in Cincinnati, this month. . . .

The fact that out of fifteen gentlemen who signed the Call, twelve
were clergymen, representing eight different denominations of Christians, and that the Call has been responded to, as I learn, by nearly two
thousand persons, living in different parts of the country, is, of itself,
sufficient evidence that the time has fully arrived when such a Convention should be held. Tens of thousands of Christians, in the free States,
and a considerable number of the slave States, are, I doubt not,

anxiously and prayfully [*sic*] considering what is their duty, as members of the Church of Christ, with regard to American Slavery. . . .

The Church, at the North, generally believe that Slavery is a social, political, and moral evil; but they think, as do Northern politicians, that they have very little to do with it. "It is a Southern institution," say they, "and beyond the expression of individual opinions, we ought not to meddle with it." A small part of the Church, at the South, also, have the same opinion of slavery, and yet do not attempt much for its removal, while no inconsiderable part defend it as a Bible institution.

Very few, either at the South or North, except professed abolitionists, believe that slaveholding is a sin. What are called the abuses of the system, they allow is sinful; but they reject the statement that Slavery is a sin per se. Abolitionists, it is presumed, without exception, believe that the abuses of Slavery are inseparable from the system; that if an end should be put to these abuses, the system itself would cease. And many intelligent, and nominally Christian slaveholders, have acknowledged that Slavery cannot be maintained independently of these abuses, though, in such instances, they do not call them abuses, but necessary evils. There is no intelligent and honest man, it is believed, who has attentively considered the subject, but allows that the maintenance of Slavery in the country imperatively requires the exercise of force to the last extremity, and the prohibition of learning to read and write as a general rule, while the separation of families and the subjugation of the females in all respects to the wills of the slaveholders, are considered unavoidable concomitants.

When the proof is demanded that slaveholding, under all circumstances, is sinful, we need only to refer to Exodus, 21 chap. 16v . . . , where stealing, selling, and holding a man are put on a level, and in each case the penalty was the same—*death;* and to 1st Tim., 1st chap., 9 and 10 verses. . . . Even the General Assembly of the Presbyterian Church, in 1818, when that body was more free from party influences than it is at present, solemnly declared Slavery to be a sin against God. But now, ministers in that Church, and of other denominations, abound, who assert that Slavery, in the sense in which the term is generally understood, existed in the Old Testament times, and that Christ and his apostles did not denounce it.

In reply to such reasoners it may be said— 1. If slaveholding or manstealing is forbidden, both in the Old and New Testaments, as has been shown, texts that *seem* to allow it must be construed in accordance with, and not in opposition to the clear prohibitions. 2. Hebrew servitude, and servitude as it existed in the time of our Savior, were quite different from American Slavery. In the time of Moses, the heathen sold their services to the Jews for a limited period; and in the time of Christ, slaves were treated with only the same barbarity that their masters were allowed to exercise toward their own children, and the enslaved had then many privileges that are denied to slaves in modern times. 3. It is quite a different thing for men who profess to reverence God, to act in the nineteenth century of the Christian dispensation as those professing similar regard to the divine Being did 3000 or even 1800 years ago, either under the Mosaic or Christian dispensations, even if it can be proved, as it can not, that in those remote and semi-barbarous ages, slavery as known to this age existed.

Holding Slavery to be a social, political and moral evil, and also a sin *per se,* what is our duty in relation to it, as members of Churches, and disciples of the Lord Jesus Christ? Here I beg leave to state, as concisely as I can, some of the duties that in my judgment devolve upon all, and especially upon Christian abolitionists, in relation to the gigantic sin of American Slavery. And I do this with great deference to my brethren who meet with you in council to consider this important subject.

1. We should have a high standard of personal holiness. Reprovers, it has been said, should have clean hands. Therefore, in our domestic, social, business and religious relations, we ought scrupulously to conform to all the requirements of the gospel, and reflect in all our conduct the image of its Divine founder. In our tempers, modes of living, diligence in business, and moderation in the possession of property, we should be thorough and consistent Christians. So far as we can, we should promote, and endeavor to unite all the sincere followers of Christ in Church fellowship.

2. We ought not to continue in Church relations where we cannot have freedom of speech and action in regard to the subject of Slavery; where slaveholders are allowed to preach or administer the sacraments; where delegates are sent to ecclesiastical bodies that forbid freedom of speech and action on the subject of Slavery; where members are received, as a matter of course, from slaveholding Churches; where certificates are given to members to unite themselves with slaveholding members, as well as all other moral delinquents, on the gospel principle of leading them to repentance and reformation.

3. We ought not, I conceive, to continue in membership with any religious Society, Missionary, Bible, Tract, Temperance or Sunday School Association, where freedom of speech and action on the subject of Slavery does not exist, and where slaveholding is not viewed as a sin-

ful relation, and in all proper ways discountenanced as a social, political, and moral evil.

4. When Providence casts our lot where we cannot attend a congregation, which is free from the delinquencies above mentioned, we should, after faithful admonition and labor in vain with such Churches, associate with Christian brethren nearest to us in maintaining the worship of God, and religious instruction in a school-house, or other convenient place, until we are able to erect a Church edifice, have regular preaching and the administration of the ordinances of the Gospel. We should also unite with kindred minds in Missionary, Bible, Tract, Temperance and Sunday School labors, where anti-slavery associations of this character exist.

5. Neither ought we to continue in any political party that adopts slaveholders as candidates for office—that sanctions Slavery—that consents that the General Government should sanction, uphold or extend it—that does not put forth its energies to deliver the country from its extension and perpetuity—that does not, in every legitimate way, act on the principle, "Righteousness exalteth a nation, but sin is a reproach to any people."

6. Christian abolitionists should exercise the privilege of voting for civil rulers and representatives, but give their suffrages only for those who are known to be opposed to slavery, root and branch, and who are men of good moral character, and qualified to fill the offices for which they are designated.

7. We should see to it that our children are not instructed by pro-slavery teachers, either in the primary, academical, or theological seminaries, and that before leaving the parental roof they understand the doctrines of both the divine and civil governments in reference to the practical duties of life.

8. We should discourage our children from residing in Slave States for literary, professional, mercantile, agricultural, or mechanical purposes, and especially do all we can to restrain them from forming family or business connexions with slaveholders.

9. Northern merchants should instruct their attorneys on no account to take mortgages on slaves as security for debts, or on execution, as many have done, not excepting Christian abolitionists.

10. Northern Christians should not give money to the American Tract Society while it refuses to publish tracts on the sinfulness of American Slavery, nor to the American Sunday School Union while it drops from its catalogue, in compliance with Southern dictation, books containing definitions of American Slavery; nor to the American Home

Missionary Society while it sustains ministers to preach to slaveholding Churches with lips sealed as to the subject of Slavery, and admit slave-holders to Church privileges; nor to the Seaman's Friend Society so long as it manifests a want of sympathy for northern sailors imprisoned in southern ports merely on account of their complexion.

Such are some of the principles that should, I humbly conceive, guide every Christian abolitionist in the land. In a time of degeneracy, like the present, when members of Churches are hardly distinguishable in their social, political, and business relations, from men who make no profession of religion; when politicians are often in advance of profess-ing Christians in regard to political conduct; when ministers of the gos-pel are ignorant of or shrink from the inculcation of Bible truths on the subject of Slavery; when Slavery finds a sanctuary in the Church; when important ecclesiastical bodies treat abolitionism as the worst kind of heresy; when the benevolent and religious associations of the country are conducted, as well as the legislative bodies, under the influence of Slavery, it behooves all who believe in the great doctrine of the equality of man, in democratic principles of government, and in the impartial and holy freedom of the Gospel to maintain high and uncompromising principles, and to carry them out, fearlessly and consistently, into daily practice, at all hazards, but with Christian forbearance and meekness.

With Christian regard, I remain yours respectfully,

Lewis Tappan

Notes

1. The best historical analysis of racism and Christianity in America focuses on the South but always in dialogue with national developments. See H. Shelton Smith, *In His Image, But . . . : Racism in Southern Religion, 1780–1910* (Durham: Duke University Press, 1972).

2. Aileen S. Kraditor, *Means and Ends in American Abolitionism: Garrison and His Critics on Strategy and Tactics, 1834–1850* (New York: Pantheon, 1969).

3. An indispensable essay on abolitionist thought is Donald G. Mathews, "The Abolitionists on Slavery: The Critique behind the Social Movement," *Journal of Southern History,* 33 (May, 1967), 163–82.

4. Douglas C. Stange, "The One Hundred and Twenty-Fifth Anniversary of a Fraternal Appeal," *Concordia Historical Institute Quarterly,* 40 (1967), 43–47.

5. *The Minutes of the Christian Anti-Slavery Convention, Assembled April 17th–20th, 1850, Cincinnati, Ohio* (Cincinnati: Ben Franklin Book and Job Rooms, 1850), 25.

6. *Secession From a Pro-Slavery Church A Christian Duty: A Sermon* (Mercer, Pa.: Wm. F. Clark, 1860), 13.

7. *Scriptural Argument in Favor of Withdrawing Fellowship from Churches and Ecclesiastical Bodies Tolerating Slaveholding among Them* (New York: American and Foreign Anti-Slavery Society, 1848), 9.

8. *Secession From a Pro-Slavery Church,* 12.

9. *Zion's Watchman* (New York), October 31, 1840, as quoted in Mathews, 172.

10. John W. Lewis, *The Life, Labors and Travels of Elder Charles Bowles, of the Free Will Baptist Denomination. Together with an Essay on the Character and Condition of the African Race by the Same. . . .* (Watertown, N.Y.: Ingalls & Stowell's Steam Press, 1852), 247.

11. Carter G. Woodson, *Negro Orators and Their Orations* (Washington: Associated Publishers, 1925), 90.

12. *Proceedings of a Meeting to Form the Broadway Tabernacle Anti-Slavery Society, with the Constitution, &c. and Address to the Church* (New York: William S. Dorr, 1838), 7.

13. Jay, *An Address to the Anti-Slavery Christians of the United States* (New York: John A. Gray, 1852), 6; Haven, *National Sermons* (Boston: Lee and Shepard), 1869), 123–52.

14. *Slavery and Anti-Slavery: A History of the Great Struggle in Both Hemispheres: With a View of the Slavery Question in the United States* (3rd ed.; New York: William Goodell, 1855), 488.

15. *A Peep at the "Peculiar Institution," with Hints as to the Duty of Northern Christians and Citizens . . .* (Dover, N.H.: William Burr, 1848), 6–7.

16. *Minutes of the Christian Anti-Slavery Convention, 1850,* 19–20.

17. Haven, 22, 56.

18. Roy P. Basler, ed., *The Collected Works of Abraham Lincoln* (New Brunswick, N.J.: Rutgers University Press, 1953), VIII, 333.

19. Haven, xii.

20. James M. McPherson, *The Struggle for Equality: Abolitionists and the Negro in the Civil War and Reconstruction* (Princeton: Princeton University Press, 1964).

21. Bertram Wyatt-Brown, *Lewis Tappan and the Evangelical War against Slavery* (New York: Athenaeum, 1971), xiii.

3   Christian Socialism

The social gospel was basically an indigenous American movement, but at the same time it was part of a larger interest in social Christianity.[1] Of great importance for the United States were the work and writings of leading churchmen in Great Britain. A generation before the calamities of industrialism made their mark in America, early Victorian industrialism was wreaking havoc among the working people of British towns and cities. As the lower classes were losing their battle for the Charter in 1848, Frederick Denison Maurice, Charles Kingsley, and others came forward to champion their cause. Articulating an idealistic, nondoctrinaire Christian Socialism, Maurice's social theology and Kingsley's novels of social protest gained adherents on both sides of the Atlantic.

English Christian Socialism was mediated to this country through the Protestant Episcopal Church. This English influence was responsible in part for transforming what was a socially conservative church before the Civil War to one of the leading exponents of a social gospel. W. D. P. Bliss, an Episcopal priest, formed an American branch of the Society of Christian Socialists in Boston in 1889. As a publicist of the movement, Bliss edited *The Encyclopedia of Social Reform*. In this volume he delineated the contribution of English Christian Socialism.

The term was first employed by the little group of men who gathered around Maurice (whom they considered their master), Ludlow, and Kingsley in England in 1848. It was used by them to express their conviction that socialism was really but a historical development or manifestation of Christianity. If in practice they understood by socialism little more than the principle and practice of cooperation as opposed to economic competition, it must be remembered that socialism itself had not developed into that more precise economic thought which is understood by the word today. The first Christian Socialists were accurately and truly Socialists of their day and generation, only holding that socialism to be practical must be founded on the Fatherhood of God and Brotherhood in Jesus Christ. They spoke of socialism as "the 19th-century livery of Christianity," and Maurice wrote in a tract in 1850, when the term Christian Socialist was first decided upon, "that is the only title which will define our object and will commit us at once to the conflict we must engage in sooner or later with the unsocial Christians and the unchristian Socialists."

The year 1848 was a dark one for English working men. Bad harvests, heavy taxes, and the potato famine had brought to a head all their sufferings and wrongs. Ireland was on the verge of rebellion. There were riots in more than one English town. On April 10, there was an immense mass meeting at Kennington Common. London was thrown into intense excitement and fear. Two hundred thousand special constables were sworn in.

Meanwhile, two clergymen of the Church of England, F. D. Maurice and Charles Kingsley, with a young lawyer, J. M. Ludlow, had been growing more and more interested in social questions. Charles Kingsley now rushed down from his parish at Eversley, and meeting Ludlow at Maurice's house, it was decided to publish placards and spread them broadcast, sympathizing with the workmen, but urging restraint from violence, and the necessity of virtue and religion to make men fit for liberty. Charles Kingsley wrote all that night, and the next morning his address to the workmen of England, signed "A Working Parson," appeared on thousands of posters. A pouring rain and the energy of O'Connor prevented an outbreak.

It was now decided by the above three to publish a penny weekly, entitled *Politics for the People*. In these, in addition to Maurice, Kingsley, and Ludlow, we find articles by Archbishop Whately, Dr. Guy, French, Stanley, Osborn, and others—a rare galaxy of brilliant minds. Kingsley wrote in it the well-known articles signed "Parson Lot." . . . The first number appeared May 6, 1848. The paper, however, was discontinued after seventeen numbers for lack of support, although it attained a circulation of 2,000.

The little knot of writers, however, now including Thomas Hughes, held meetings all winter, meeting with many of the Chartist leaders, and starting night schools. It was at one of these conferences that Kingsley made his celebrated speech beginning, "I am a Church of England parson and a Chartist," in which he acknowledged the grievous wrongs of the workmen, but dissuaded them from violence.

A Mr. Mayhew at this time contributed to the London papers a series of articles on the sweating system, which called out Charles

Kingsley's burning and indignant tract on "Cheap Clothes and Nasty."
But Maurice from first to last remained its directing spirit. Ragged
schools were begun under their auspices, and "sanitary leagues" when
the cholera began to rage. Colonization was projected. "Let us devise a
Socialist home-colonization as soon as you please; provided only we
give it a ground to stand upon, the sooner, the better," said Mr.
Maurice, in a letter to Mr. Ludlow.

A cooperative institution, which was a practical embodiment of
their ideas, was started, being an association of tailors in Castle Street,
nearly opposite to the place where now stands the Cooperative Institution. This was in 1849. In 1850 a society for promoting working-men's
associations was formed, with Maurice for its president, and became the
nucleus or center of the cooperative movement. The fundamental principle of this society was "the practical application of Christianity to the
purposes of trade and industry."

In December, 1849, a dinner was held at Ludlow's, and a plan for
cooperative stores was discussed—and for the first time the term *Christian Socialism* was agreed upon. The name was favored by Maurice
largely under the influence of Ludlow, who had been in Paris and seen
there the *associations ouvriers,* and who had written to Maurice from
there that "socialism must be Christianized or it would shake Christianity to its foundation, precisely because it appealed to the higher and
not to the lower instincts of man." The Christian Socialists, now working under this name, started a periodical and also a cooperative store
under the leadership of Walter Cooper, the ex-Chartist.

Their periodical, *The Christian Socialist,* was edited by Ludlow,
but contributed to by all the members. The following, by Ludlow,
clearly expresses its ideas:

A new idea has gone abroad into the world: that socialism, the
latest born of the forces now at work in modern society, and
Christianity, the eldest born of those forces, are in their nature
not hostile, but akin to each other; or rather, that the one is but
the development, the outgrowth, the manifestation of the
other. . . . That Christianity, on the other hand, in this 19th century of ours, becomes in its turn chilly and helpless when stripped
of its social influences; or, in other words, when divorced from
socialism. . . . That if the Gospel speaks true, and 'ye cannot serve
God and Mammon,' it is wholly incompatible with a political
economy which proclaims self-interest to be the very pivot of
social action; . . . but that it is compatible with those theories or
systems which have for a common object to bind up into fellowship, and not to divide by selfishness and rivalry; to substitute fair

prices and living wages for a false cheapness, and starvation, its
child; and which have adopted for their watchwords *Association*
and *Exchange* instead of *Competition* and *Profit.*[2]

Mild as their socialism appears in retrospect, opposition was not long in
coming from the English establishment of that day. But, as Bliss points
out, antagonism only energized the new Christian Socialists to more
practical efforts.

Eventually Maurice was removed from his chair at King's College, and
very affecting is the address of condolence presented to him by those
workmen who had through him come to believe in the divine mission of
Christianity in saving society. But opposition and obloquy, so far from
discouraging the Christian Socialists, only acted as a spur to further exertion. "I am a revolutionist," says Kingsley in one of his letters. His
"Bible Radicalism" meant to go to the root of the matter, and to recover the true and original basis of Christian fellowship. At the same
time they all felt that if their work was to prosper they must put their
hand to the plow and give a practical demonstration of their theory.
Mr. E. Vansittart Neale provided the funds for the first attempts in cooperative production and the establishment of the central cooperative
agency. Many of the aristocracy and clergy wished to encourage the
promoters. Orders came flowing in, and the success attained induced
the promoters to open an "East-End Needle-Women's Workshop," and
an association of shoemakers. In course of time a number of productive
associations were formed in London and the provinces, principally in
the north. Out of this came an agitation for needed legislation and the
"Magna Charta of Cooperation," the Industrial and Provident Partner-
ships Bill of 1852.

The early Christian Socialists, too, worked much for popular education. This led to the establishment of the Working Men's College,
which was opened in 1854. Henceforth the Christian Socialism of
England of this period is lost in the cooperative movement developing
in the north of England. The London stores either failed or were swallowed by the larger movement. But the Christian Socialist thought
lived.

Says Professor Seligman: "These Christian Socialists were reformers in the fullest sense of the word. The kingdom of Christ was to them

no empty formula; they were thoroughly imbued with the belief that this kingdom, created through revelation, actually existed and was destined in time to subjugate all wickedness and misery. Society, according to them, is not to be made anew by arrangements, but is to be regenerated by 'finding the law and ground of its order and harmony, the only secret of its existence, in God.' " The Bible they considered the poor man's book, the voice of God against tyrants and humbugs. "Justice from God to those whom men despise," was to them the thought running through the Bible.

Men of such a stamp viewed with a sovereign disdain the social doctrines of the Manchester school. They wrote: "Of all narrow, conceited, hypocritical, anarchic, and atheistic schemes of the universe, the Cobden and Bright one is exactly the worst." Said Kingsley:

"I expect nothing from a public press which panders to popular Mammonism by scraps of politico-economic cant, and justifies the ignorant miser to himself by retailing Benthamite phrases which sound like scientific laws, while they are really nothing but the assertion of barren truisms. I expect nothing from the advocates of *laissez faire*—the pedants whose glory is in the shame of society, who arrogantly talk of economics as of a science so completely perfected, so universal and all-important that common humanity and morality, reason and religion must be pooh-poohed down, if they seem to interfere with its infallible conclusions, and yet revile as absurd and utopian, the slightest attempt to apply those conclusions to any practical purpose...."

"Competition," said Maurice, "is put forth as the law of the universe. That is a lie. The time is come to declare that it is a lie, by word and deed. I see no way but by associating for work instead of for strikes."[3]

Notes

1. The indigenity of the American social gospel movement has been questioned by William R. Hutchison in *Church History* 44 (Sept., 1975), 367–81. The authors of this book believe that Professor Hutchison has overlooked the contributions of revivalism (Chapter 1, above), of Populism and Progressivism (Chapters 15 and 16), of conservative and radical aspects of the movement, and of its vast sweep, including the South. However, the problem remains one of interest (though of minor importance) and opens many opportunities for further research.

2. W. D. P. Bliss, ed., *The Encyclopedia of Social Reform* (rev. ed.; New York: Funk and Wagnalls, 1908), 199.

3. Bliss, 199–200.

4   The New Theology

The principal stimulus to the socialization of American Protestantism in the 1880's was a movement of thought that called itself the "New Theology." Although it emanated in large part from Andover Theological Seminary, whose faculty inaugurated the *Andover Review* to disseminate its ideas, its most popular and widely read expositor was the Reverend Theodore Thornton Munger, pastor of the United Congregational Church on the New Haven Green, and biographer of Horace Bushnell, whose influence was obvious throughout Munger's writings.

In *The Freedom of Faith,* published in 1883, Munger set out to describe "some of the main features" of the new theology, not to formulate it, but to "express something of its spirit, and to give it so much of definite form" that it could no longer be criticized for vagueness. Beginning with what it was not, he disclaimed any intention of doing without theology or of discarding "the historic faith of the church." He recognized instead "a process of development." The movement did not reject specific doctrines nor was it iconoclastic. It intended to work within the existing churches, claiming "only that liberty whereunto all are called in the church of Christ."

On the positive side, the new theology claimed "a somewhat larger and broader use of the reason than has been accorded to theology" in the past. It sought to interpret the Bible in what Munger described as "a more natural way," rather than in the former "hard, formal, unsympathetic, and unimaginative way." It sought to "replace an excessive individuality by a truer view of the solidarity [or interrelatedness] of the race:"

It does not deny a real individuality, it does not predicate an absolute solidarity, but simply removes the emphasis from one to the other. It holds that every man must live a life of his own, build himself up into a full personality, and give an account of himself to God: but it also rec-

ognizes the blurred truth that man's life lies in its relations; that it is a
derived and shared life; that it is carried on and perfected under laws of
heredity and of the family and the nation; that while he is "himself
alone" he is also a son, a parent, a citizen, and an inseparable part of
the human race; that in origin and character and destiny he cannot be
regarded as standing in a sharp and utter individuality. It differs from
the Old Theology in a more thorough and consistent application of this
distinction. That holds to an absolute solidarity in evil, relieved by a
doctrine of election of individuals; this holds to a solidarity running
throughout the whole life of humanity in the world,—not an absolute
solidarity, but one modified by human freedom. It is not disposed
wholly to part company with the Old in respect to the "fall in Adam"
(when the Scriptures, on this point, are properly interpreted), and
hereditary evil, and the like; it sees in these conceptions substantial
truths, when freed from their excessiveness and their formal and cate-
gorical shapes, but it carries this solidarity into the whole life of man. If
it is a fallen world, it is also a redeemed world; if it is a lost world, it is a
saved world; the Christ is no less to it than Adam; the divine humanity
is no smaller than the Adamic humanity; the Spirit is as powerful and as
universal as sin; the links that bind the race to evil are correlated by
links equally strong binding it to righteousness. It goes, in a certain
manner, with the Old Theology in its views of common evil, but it di-
verges from it in its conceptions of the redemptive and delivering forces
by ascribing to them corresponding sweep. To repeat: it does not admit
that Christ is less to the race than Adam, that the Gospel is smaller than
evil; it does not consign mankind as a mass to a pit of common depravity, and leave it to emerge as individuals under some notion of election,
or by solitary choice, each one escaping as he can and according to his
"chance," but the greater part not escaping at all. It does not so read
revelation and history and life, finding in them all a corporate element,
"a moving altogether when it moves at all,"—an interweaving of life
with life that renders it impossible wholly to extricate the individual.
It allies itself with the thought of the present age and the best thought
of all ages, that mankind is moved by common forces, and follows common tendencies falling and rising together, partakers together in all
good and ill desert, verifying the phrase, "the life of humanity." It believes that the Spirit broods over the "evil world" as it brooded upon
the chaos of old; that humanity is charged with redemptive forces,
wrought into the soul and into the divine institutions of the family and
the nation, and whatever other relation binds man to man; and it believes that these forces are not in vain.

Still, it does not submerge the individual in the common life, nor free him from personal ill desert, nor take from him the crown of personal achievement and victory. It simply strives to recognize the duality of truth, and hold it well poised. It turns our attention to the corporate life of man here in the world,—an individual life, indeed, but springing from common roots, fed by a common life, watched over by one Father, inspired by one Spirit, and growing to one end; no man, no generation, being "made perfect" by itself. Hence its ethical emphasis; hence its recognition of the nation, and of the family, and of social and commercial life, as fields of the manifestation of God and of the operation of the Spirit; hence its readiness to ally itself with all movements for bettering the condition of mankind,—holding that human society itself is to be redeemed, and that the world itself, in its corporate capacity, is being reconciled to God; hence also an apparently secular tone, which is, however, but a widening of the field of the divine and spiritual.

Further, the new theology would recognize a "new relation to natural science," ignoring the "long apparent antagonism" between "the kingdoms of faith and of natural law." In contrast to the older modes of thought, the new movement offered "a wider study of man," finding its methods in "the every-day processes of humanity, rather than in formal logic," dealing with human life "as do poets and dramatists." Such a "full and direct look" at humanity would induce what Munger could call "the ethical habit of thought": the new theology sought "to recover spiritual processes from a magical to a moral conception." It would have a moral God, a "divine government truly moral, and a moral atonement."[1]

How the new theology led to a new ethics may be seen in the activities of Professor William Jewett Tucker of Andover Theological Seminary, one of the pioneers of social ethics in the theological curriculum and subsequently president of Dartmouth College. In 1889, Andrew Carnegie's essay *The Gospel of Wealth* attracted widespread attention throughout the English-speaking world, precipitating a debate on both sides of the Atlantic. This classic statement of Social Darwinism[2] prompted Tucker to review the issues in an extensive article in the *Andover Review* in 1891. In getting to "the heart of the matter," Tucker asked:

Why should there be this vast amount of wealth in the hands of the
few? The question is not, How shall private wealth be returned to the
public? but, Why should it exist in such bewildering amounts? Mr.
Carnegie's gospel is really a belated gospel. It comes too late for a social
remedy. What it does accomplish is to call attention to the fact of the
enormous surplus of private wealth. The honest and courageous endeav-
or of a millionaire to return his fortune to society, and his call to his
fellow-millionaires to do likewise, brings them, as a class, before the
public, and puts the public upon a reckoning of the volume of wealth in
their hands. Consciously or unconsciously, Mr. Carnegie has hit upon
the great object-lesson in our economic civilization. It is not pauperism,
conspicuous and grievous as that is, but the concentration of wealth.
The most striking, and in many ways the most startling, feature of the
economic situation is, not that the poor are growing poorer,—that I
doubt, except with those too low for computation,—but that the rich
are becoming so very rich. The question before us, be it remembered, is
not that of capital, or of corporate wealth, or of ordinary private
wealth, but of extreme riches in the hands of the few,—the enormous
concentration of wealth.[3]

Tucker replied to those who would ask What do you propose? by dis-
claiming the necessity for another proposal, it being the obligation of
those who teach to apply the ethical test to all social theories. In summary, he repeated that his purpose in analyzing Carnegie's thought had
been to call attention to "the moral significance of great fortunes" and
to "show the ethical bearing of the amassing of private wealth."

I have not cared to enter the field of the methods of social relief and reform. Methods belong to economists and legislators. The concern of
moral and religious teachers is with principles. They have to do legiti-
mately with the ethical factor which is put into, or which is left out of,
all proposed reforms. They are bound to test all theories which are offered in aid of society, and to test them all the more if they are offered
with moral earnestness and under religious names. They have the right
to ask of any new scheme whether it will leave society better or worse
in the end for its adoption. My criticism of Mr. Carnegie's scheme has

been that, to the degree in which it is organized and made the ruling method of adjusting wealth to society, it becomes a vast system of patronage, than which nothing can in the final issue create a more hopeless social condition. And further, that the assumption upon which it rests, that wealth is the inevitable possession of the few, and is best administered by them for the many, begs the whole question of economic justice now before society, and relegates it to the field of charity. But charity, as I have claimed, cannot solve the problems of the modern world. And the point is reached at which this claim is seen to be valid, whenever any scheme is proposed for the redistribution of wealth through charity, leaving the question of the original distribution of wealth unsettled, or settled only to the satisfaction of the few. What the ethical question of to-morrow in the economic world may be I know not. But the ethical question of to-day centres, I am sure, in the distribution rather than in the redistribution of wealth. I would hinder no man's gifts in the largest charity; I would withhold no honor from the giver; but I would accept no amount in charity as a measure of the present social need, or in settlement of the present economic demand.[4]

Notes

1. Theodore T. Munger, *The Freedom of Faith* (Boston: Houghton, 1883), ch. 1.

2. Richard Hofstadter, *Social Darwinism in American Thought, 1860–1915* (Philadelphia: University of Pennsylvania Press, 1945).

3. William Jewett Tucker, " 'The Gospel of Wealth,' " *Andover Review,* XV (June, 1891), 637–38.

4. Tucker, 645.

5   An American Prophet

Wherever the student of the social gospel turns, he confronts the name of Walter Rauschenbusch (1861–1918).[1] Not only did this unassuming professor of church history at a minor seminary set forth the "classic" social gospel most fully and persuasively, but he couched his message in terms that are surprisingly congenial to later generations. Although it is the purpose of this book to open unexplored or previously neglected aspects of the social gospel, Rauschenbusch must be included because of his preeminence.

His earliest memory was of draping the family front door in Rochester, New York, with crepe after President Lincoln's assassination. Rauschenbusch was educated in that city and in Germany; the seventh in an unbroken line of Lutheran and then German Baptist ministers, his inheritance of warm-hearted piety broke down under the intolerable situations and questions put to him by his first parishioners, the working-class members of a German Baptist congregation on the border of Hell's Kitchen in New York City, many of them "out of work, out of clothes, out of shoes, and out of hope."

A decade in this $600-a-year post brought the sensitive young pastor into dynamic contact with Edward Bellamy, author of *Looking Backward, 2000–1887,* and other reformers, but his chief debt was to Henry George, writer of the best-selling panacea *Progress and Poverty,* a threatening contender for the mayoralty of New York City in 1886, and himself a social gospeler in disguise.[2] Rauschenbusch read Marx and Tolstoi and during a sabbatical in Germany in 1891 met leading theologians and sociologists. He collaborated with a few friends to publish, for almost two years, a small paper called *For the Right*—"in the interests of the working people of New York City." To test their ideas and strategies Rauschenbusch and his friends formed a cell group they called the "Brotherhood of the Kingdom." It met regularly during the winter months and each summer held a week-long conference in the hills back of Newburgh, New York. There, within sight of the lordly Hudson, they could examine the confrontations of their time through prayer, meditation, and the sharp competition of ideas.[3]

In the early years of this fellowship, it planned to issue a manifesto. In all probability, Rauschenbusch was selected to produce the document, which was passed back and forth for criticism and editing among several of the brothers. For reasons unknown, it was shelved, to be recovered by an enterprising young scholar some seventy-five years later and published on the fiftieth anniversary of Rauschenbusch's death. Rauschenbusch wrote this "dangerous book" with "fear and trembling" when he was not yet thirty. Here is most of the first chapter.

Christianity is in its nature revolutionary. Its revolutionary character is apparent from the spiritual ancestry to which it traces its lineage. Jesus was the successor of the Old Testament prophets. The common people of his day discerned this kinship and whispered that he must be Elijah or Jeremiah or some other of the prophets. (Lk, 9, 19.) He himself repeatedly drew the parallel between the work and lot of the prophets and his own. Like the prophets he was rejected in his own country. (Matt. 13, 57.) Like the prophets he was to suffer at the hands of the wicked husbandmen. (Lk. 20, 4–18.) Like all the prophets he must perish at Jerusalem. (Lk. 13, 34–35.) His forerunner he calls a prophet, a second Elijah (Mk. 9, 11–13; Lk. 7, 26); and to his followers he predicts that like the prophets they will be slandered and persecuted (Matt. 5, 10–12), and at last like the prophets meet their death. (Matt. 23, 29–36.)

Now what were these prophets, to whose spirit and purpose Jesus felt so close a kinship, and whose lot he expected to share?

The prophets were the revolutionists of their age. They were dreamers of Utopias. They pictured an ideal state of society in which the poor should be judged with equity and the cry of the oppressed should no longer be heard; a time in which men would beat their idle swords into ploughshares and their spears into pruning hooks, for then the nations would learn war no more. (Isa. 2, 4.) No slight amelioration contented them, nothing but a change so radical that they dared to represent it as a repealing of the ancient and hallowed covenant and the construction of a new one. A proposal to abolish the Constitution of the United States would not seem as revolutionary to us as this proposal must have seemed to the contemporaries of the prophets.

They did not expect such a change to glide in without a struggle. A day of vengeance would have to precede it. It would be like a refiner's fire and like fullers' soap. (Mal. 3, 2.) The Lord would have a reckoning with those that oppressed the hireling in his wages, the widow, and the fatherless, and those that turned aside the stranger from his right. (Mal.

3, 5.) He would come upon the high ones and the kings of the earth, and gather them as prisoners are gathered in the dungeon, and shut them up in prison. (Isa. 24, 21–22.) For they had eaten up the vineyard, the spoil of the poor was in their houses; they had beaten God's people to pieces; they had ground the faces of the poor. (Isa. 3, 13–15.)

Nor were the prophets mere impractical dreamers and declaimers. They were men of action. They overthrew dynasties. They were popular agitators, tribunes of the people. They rebuked to their faces kings who had taken the plain man's wife or tricked him out of his ancestral holding.

These were the men whose successor Christ professed to be. This does not imply that he sanctioned all their actions or proposed to copy all their methods. But it does imply that of all the forces in the national history of Israel the prophets were the most worthy of his approval and most akin to his spirit.

The revolutionary character of Christ's work appears also from the elements in contemporary life to which he allied himself.

The Messianic hope, kindled and fanned by the prophets, was still glowing in the hearts of the people. When John the Baptist lifted up his voice by the Jordan, men were on the alert immediately, querying "whether haply he were the Messiah." (Lk. 3, 15.) The atmosphere of Palestine was surcharged with this electricity. When, in the synagogue at Nazareth, Jesus chose for his text that passage of Isaiah which tells of glad tidings to the poor, of release to the captives, of liberty to the bruised, and the acceptable year of the Lord, "the eyes of all in the synagogue were fastened upon him." The passage was universally understood to refer to the Messianic era. They were breathlessly eager to hear what attitude he would assume. And what was his attitude? He told them the time had now come: "To-day hath this scripture been fulfilled in your ears." (Lk. 4, 16–21.)

It is plain that the people counted him as their own. They were waiting to see him raise the standard of revolt and were ready to follow him as their king. (John 6, 14–15.) And in spite of all apparent disappointments to which he subjected them, they had their eye on him still. When at the very end he entered Jerusalem with something of public state, all their hopes revived and they hailed him as the Messiah coming to claim the Kingdom of his father David.

It is true that Christ steadfastly refused to fulfill their expectations. We shall discuss later on his reasons for doing so. Yet the fact remains that he did appeal to the Messianic hope. He found his followers among those in whom that hope was liveliest. He came so near to fulfilling the people's idea of the Messiah that they were always on the verge of expectation. To the Sadducean enemies of the Messianic movement he seemed, even at the end of his ministry, so closely connected with the movement that they regarded it as only a question of time when he would lead the revolt and plunge the nation into war with Rome. (John 11, 47–50.)

The contents of the Messianic hope of course varied. With some it was dyed in blood, with others it was irradiated by heaven. But this element was common to all who entertained it: they were weary of present conditions; they were longing for a radically different state of affairs; and they were sure that it would come and were ready to help it on. In other words, the Messianic hope was a revolutionary hope.

That this revolutionary element existed even among the most spiritually minded men and women is discernible from the recorded words of those choice souls among whom Jesus, by God's own appointment, spent his early years and by whom his thoughts were moulded. The hymns in the first two chapters of Luke, judged by internal evidence, express the Messianic hope before it had been modified by the teachings and the life of Jesus. Note the revolutionary tone:

> He hath shewed strength with his arm;
> He hath scattered the proud in the imagination of their heart.
> He hath put down princes from their thrones
> And hath exalted them of low degree.
> The hungry he hath filled with good things;
> And the rich he hath sent empty away. (Lk. 1, 51–53.)

Those were the thoughts of her whose blood ran in the veins of Jesus and who had the fashioning of his early years.

Zacharias blesses Jehovah for having raised up a horn of salvation,

> Salvation from our enemies, and from the hand of all that hate us;
> Granting to us,
> That we, being delivered out of the hands of our enemies
> Should serve him without fear
> In holiness and righteousness before him all our days. (Lk. 1, 71, 74–75.)

In these two songs the thought of the Messianic victory predominates, and Simeon thinks more of the conflict which shall precede it and which will bring about the prostration of some and the elevation of others. "Behold this child is set for the falling and the rising of many in Israel; and for a sign which is spoken against; yea and a sword shall pierce through thine own soul; that thoughts out of many hearts may be revealed." (Lk. 2, 34–35.) But in them all is the prophetic hope: a mighty uprising of Jehovah, a casting down of the powerful and wicked, and then peace and prosperity for the poor and righteous.

And when finally we turn to the man who Jesus himself has called the choicest fruit of all the past, we find the same revolutionary language.

> Make ye ready the way of the Lord!
> Make his paths straight!
> Every valley shall be filled
> And every mountain and hill shall be brought low;
> And the crooked shall become straight,
> And the rough way smooth. (Isa. 40, 3–4.)

Here is a general straightening out and leveling as a preparation for the coming of the Messiah. His advice to the people explains what he meant by straightening out the crooked ways and razing the high places: "He that hath two coats let him impart to him that hath none; and he that hath food let him do likewise." The abolition of social inequality, according to John, was the first step in the Messianic renewal. His conception of the Messiah's work is likewise expressed in flaming images of destruction and overthrowing: a dusty threshing-floor, a sifting of wheat and chaff, a consuming fire, a crashing down of rotten trees. The baptism of John, in which his preaching found its dramatic expression, was a revolutionary symbol. It was the baptism of repentance; a turning away from old ways and a consecration to the new; it was the rite of initiation into "the remnant" which would be prepared for the coming of the Messiah and fit for the new order of things to be ushered in by the Messianic judgment.

The revolutionary character of his work is expressly asserted by Christ. He had come to cast fire upon the earth, and he longed to see it kindled. He had come to hide a leaven in the world's trough of meal, and it would be in a ferment until the leaven had done its work.

He brought a new spirit and the new spirit would demand new forms of life. Men then as now had little discernment for the new spirit, but they raised a decided protest against the abolition of old forms and the evolution of new ones. He might bring new wine if he wished, but let him put it in the old vessels. But Jesus told them that they must not think that his young, bubbling wine could be bottled up in the old, cracked wine-skins, or that it would not suffice him reverently to patch bits of new cloth on the most shameless rents of the tattered garment wherewith society was seeking to cover its nakedness. A new spirit plus new forms and customs and institutions; that means revolution.

The change he was inaugurating was so radical, that after its consummation it would be found that the first had become last and the last first. Ideas now dominant would then be smiled over. Institutions now regarded as existing *jure divino* would then be recognized as having existed *jure diabolico*. Men now on top in society and state and church would go to the bottom, and many now despised and neglected would then be honored and would reign over the tribes of Israel. Such a reversal of values presupposes sweeping changes in the general conceptions and judgments prevalent in human society, and necessarily also in the social and political institutions in which these conceptions and judgments find their embodiment.

Jesus knew very well the difficulties of the work he had undertaken. He knew that those who have seats at the banquet where the old wine is served have little taste for the new. He knew that those who hold the places of power and privilege will seldom resign them without a struggle. He foresaw a terrible conflict, a division of humanity into hostile camps. A man would be set at variance with his father, and a daughter with her mother. Two in a household would be ranged against the other three. The strongest ties in the world would snap when they encountered this new force.

Jesus foresaw all this. If ever a heart was tender, surely it was his. Yet he did not shrink from precipitating the world into such a conflict. His was the revolutionary spirit, loving and inflexible.

Moreover his attitude became more revolutionary as he went on; his language grew sterner, his opposition to the powers that were more unyielding, until it grew plain that the most moral community of that age, and perhaps the most religious society of any age, was engaged in irreconcilable conflict with Jesus Christ, a conflict which could end only with the overthrow of one of the conflicting forces. We know that it did end with the apparent overthrow of the one and the actual overthrow of the other.

This interpretation of the tendency of Christ's work is borne out by the attitude of his contemporaries. Those who had anything to gain by a change followed him and heard him gladly. Those who had anything to lose by a change feared him. They feared him enough to hate him. They hated him enough to kill him. Self-interest is short-sighted, but its sight is marvelously keen for all that come within the range of its vision. When the chief priests and scribes and elders, the dignitaries of society as it then existed, combined to put him down at all hazard, they were not stabbing at shadows. They were closing with a deadly foe and they knew it. It was either his life or their privileges. They had no mind to be placed at the bottom in any overturning process of his.

In fact, if we consider what Christ's work really consisted in, we shall perceive that it could not but be revolutionary. He was sent by God, with his Father's thoughts and his Father's will in his heart, to make those thoughts known on earth and to secure obedience to that will.

Now if the world were lovingly doing God's will to the extent of its knowledge, and anxiously seeking more knowledge in order better to obey God, then Christ's work would have been educational and not revolutionary. With words of love he would have led his willing flock to the richer pastures and purer waters prepared for them. But that is not the state of the world. The crucifixion of Jesus gives the lie to that theory of life, and he that has eyes to see can see along the track of history a long line of Calvaries, where successive generations have sought to choke the Word of God calling them to righteousness. It has ever been easy for man to obey his lusts and hard to resist them. And the evil of centuries has found its proper expression and manufactured its fitting tools in the laws, the customs, the opinions and traditions prevailing in human society, so that an old man, who had seen much of life and yet loved mankind, sadly summed up his thoughts in the judgment: "The whole world is embedded in wickedness."

Now given such a world, and given a great Christ who comes to see God's will done on earth, and in the nature of the case, there must be a collision, an upheaval, a revolutionary movement which must last and be revolutionary until either the world is brought into submission or Christ is conquered and gives up his attempt.[4]

In 1897 Rauschenbusch was called back to Rochester to teach in the seminary. He now had a greater opportunity than as a pastor to read, write, and try out his ideas on students and faculty colleagues. He became known throughout the northern Baptist denomination and in reform and social gospel circles. By 1906 he was ready to present his ideas to a wider public, and the next year his first book, *Christianity and the Social Crisis,* appeared. It was an immediate success; it bore little resemblance to the then hidden document we have just seen. It established the Rochester professor as the primary spokesman of the rapidly spreading social gospel movement. Banqueted at an elegant New

York hotel on his return from a second sabbatical in Europe, he was now called upon for speeches the nation over. The Brotherhood considered disbanding, so adequately had Rauschenbusch proclaimed their stance.

Three years later he brought out his second book, *For God and the People,* a small collection of "prayers for the social awakening," which will be presented later, in Chapter 14. In 1912 there appeared *Christianizing the Social Order,* a detailed socialist critique of capitalism that was sufficiently "without a note of hatred" that he continued to be a welcome guest in the Rockefeller home. Here he insisted that social justice and economic democracy must be the solid foundation of what he envisioned as a "Christian" social order. During the First World War he wrote a small manual, *The Social Teachings of Jesus,* which proved to be the most widely circulated of his works, thousands of copies being used as study texts by the Y.M.C.A. service organizations in the armed forces. Rauschenbusch's last book, *A Theology for the Social Gospel,* to be discussed in Chapters 21 and 22, was the printed version of a series of lectures at the Yale Divinity School the year before his untimely death from cancer.

In the concluding chapter of *Christianity and the Social Crisis,* Rauschenbusch challenged young women and young men to "a new apostolate":

The first apostolate of Christianity was born from a deep fellow-feeling for social misery and from the consciousness of a great historical opportunity. Jesus saw the peasantry of Galilee following him about with their poverty and their diseases, like shepherdless sheep that have been scattered and harried by beasts of prey, and his heart had compassion on them. He felt that the harvest was ripe, but there were few to reap it. Past history had come to its culmination, but there were few who understood the situation and were prepared to cope with it. He bade his disciples to pray for laborers for the harvest, and then made them answer their own prayers by sending them out two by two to proclaim the kingdom of God. That was the beginning of the world-wide mission of Christianity.

The situation is repeated on a vaster scale to-day. If Jesus stood to-day amid our modern life, with that outlook on the condition of all humanity which observation and travel and the press would spread before him, and with the same heart of divine humanity beating in him, he would create a new apostolate to meet the new needs in a new harvesttime of history.

To any one who knows the sluggishness of humanity to good, the impregnable intrenchments of vested wrongs and the long reaches of time needed from one milestone of progress to the next, the task of setting up a Christian social order in this modern world of ours seems like a fair and futile dream. Yet in fact it is not one tithe as hopeless as when Jesus set out to do it. When he told his disciples, "Ye are the salt of the earth; ye are the light of the world," he expressed the consciousness of a great historic mission to the whole of humanity. Yet it was a Nazarene carpenter speaking to a group of Galilaean peasants and fishermen. Under the circumstances at that time it was an utterance of the most daring faith,—faith in himself, faith in them, faith in what he was putting into them, faith in faith. Jesus failed and was crucified, first his body by his enemies, and then his spirit by his friends; but that failure was so amazing a success that to-day it takes an effort on our part to realize that it required any faith on his part to inaugurate the kingdom of God and to send out his apostolate.

To-day, as Jesus looks out upon humanity, his spirit must leap to see the souls responsive to his call. They are sown broadcast through humanity, legions of them. The harvest-field is no longer deserted. All about us we hear the clang of the whetstone and the rush of the blades through the grain and the shout of the reapers. With all our faults and our slothfulness we modern men in many ways are more on a level with the real mind of Jesus than any generation that has gone before. If that first apostolate was able to remove mountains by the power of faith, such an apostolate as Christ could now summon might change the face of the earth.

The apostolate of a new age must do the work of the sower. When the sower goes forth to sow his seed, he goes with the certainty of partial failure and the knowledge that a long time of patience and of hazard will intervene before he can hope to see the result of his work and his venture. In sowing the truth a man may never see or trace the results. The more ideal his conceptions are, and the farther they move ahead of his time, the larger will be the percentage of apparent failure. But he can afford to wait. The powers of life are on his side. He is like a man who has scattered his seed and then goes off to sleep by night and work by day, and all the while the seed, by the inscrutable chemistry of life, lays hold of the ingredients of its environment and builds them up to its own growth. The mustard-seed becomes a tree. The leaven assimilates the meal by biological processes. The new life penetrates the old humanity and transforms it. Robert Owen was a sower. His coöperative communities failed. He was able to help only a small fraction of the workingmen of his day. But his moral enthusiasm and his ideas fertilized the finest and most self-sacrificing minds among the working classes. They cherished his ultimate hopes in private and worked for realizable ends in public. The Chartist movement was filled with his spirit. The most influential leaders of English unionism in its great period after the middle of the nineteenth century were Owenites. The Rochdale Pioneers were under his influence, and the great coöperative movement in England, an economic force of the first importance, grew in some measure out of the seed which Owen had scattered. Other men may own the present. The future belongs to the sower—provided he scatters seed and does not mistake the chaff for it which once was so essential to the seed and now is dead and useless.

It is inevitable that those who stand against conditions in which most men believe and by which the strongest profit, shall suffer for their stand. The little group of early Christian socialists in England, led by Maurice, Kingsley, and Hughes, now stand by common consent in the history of that generation as one of its finest products, but at that time they were bitterly assailed and misunderstood. Pastor Rudolf Todt, the first man in Germany who undertook to prove that the New Testament and the ethics of socialism have a close affinity, was almost unanimously attacked by the Church of Germany. But Jesus told his apostles at the outset that opposition would be part of their day's work. Christ equipped his Church with no legal rights to protect her; the only political right he gave his disciples was the right of being persecuted. It is part of the doctrine of vicarious atonement, which is fundamental in Christianity, that the prophetic souls must vindicate by their sufferings the truth they preach. . . . The championship of social justice is almost the only way left open to a Christian nowadays to gain the crown of martyrdom. Theological heretics are rarely persecuted now. The only rival of God is mammon, and it is only when his sacred name is blasphemed that men throw the Christians to the lions.

Even for the social heretics there is a generous readiness to listen which was unknown in the past. In our country that openness of mind is a product of our free intellectual life, our ingrained democracy, the denominational manifoldness of our religious life, and the spread of the Christian spirit. It has become an accepted doctrine among us that all great movements have obscure beginnings, and that belief tends to make men respectful toward anything that comes from some despised Nazareth. Unless a man forfeits respect by bitterness or lack of tact, he is accorded a large degree of tolerance, though he will always be made to feel the difference between himself and those who say the things that please the great.

The certainty of opposition constitutes a special call to the strong.

The ministry seems to have little attraction for the sons of rich men. It is not strange when one considers the enervating trials that beset a rich man in a pastorate. But here is a mission that ought to appeal to the rich young man if he has heroic stuff in him. His assured social standing would give him an influence with rich and poor alike which others attain but slowly if at all. The fear of being blacklisted for championing justice and mercy need have no terrors for him. To use his property as a coat of mail in fighting the battles of the weak would be the best way of obeying Christ's command to the rich young ruler to sell all and give it to the poor. When Mr. Roosevelt was still Police Commissioner in New York, he said to the young men of New York: "I would teach the young men that he who has not wealth owes his first duty to his family, but he who has means owes his to the State. It is ignoble to go on heaping up money. I would preach the doctrine of work to all, and to the men of wealth the doctrine of unremunerative work." The most "unremunerative work" is the work that draws opposition and animosity.

Mr. Roosevelt implies here that a man's duty to his family is the first and dominant duty, and that this exempts him in some measure from service to the larger public. It follows that the childless have a call to the dangerous work of the kingdom of God. A man and woman who are feeding and training young citizens are performing so immense and absorbing a service to the future that they might well be exempt from taxes to the State and from sacrificial service to the kingdom of God. If nevertheless so many of them assume these duties in addition, the childless man and woman will have to do heroic work in the trenches before they can rank on the same level. It is not fair to ask a man with children to give his time and strength as freely to public causes as if he had none. It is still more unfair to expect him to risk the bread and the prospects of his family in championing dangerous causes as freely as if he risked only himself. The childless people should adopt the whole coming generation of children and fight to make the world more habitable for them as for their own brood. The unmarried and the childless should enlist in the new apostolate and march on the forlorn hopes with Jesus Christ.

In asking for faith in the possibility of a new social order, we ask for no Utopian delusion. We know well that there is no perfection for man in this life: there is only growth toward perfection. In personal religion we look with seasoned suspicion at any one who claims to be holy and perfect, yet we always tell men to become holy and to seek perfection. We make it a duty to seek what is unattainable. We have the same paradox in the perfectibility of society. We shall never have a perfect social life, yet we must seek it with faith. We shall never abolish suffering. There will always be death and the empty chair and heart. There will always be the agony of love unreturned. Women will long for children and never press baby lips to their breast. Men will long for fame and miss it. Imperfect moral insight will work hurt in the best conceivable social order. The strong will always have the impulse to exert their strength, and no system can be devised which can keep them from crowding and jostling the weaker. Increased social refinement will bring increased sensitiveness to pain. An American may suffer as much distress through a social slight as a Russian peasant under the knout. At best there is always but an approximation to a perfect social order. The kingdom of God is always but coming.

But every approximation to it is worth while. Every step toward personal purity and peace, though it only makes the consciousness of imperfection more poignant, carries its own exceeding great reward, and everlasting pilgrimage toward the kingdom of God is better than contented stability in the tents of wickedness.

And sometimes the hot hope surges up that perhaps the long and slow climb may be ending. In the past the steps of our race toward progress have been short and feeble, and succeeded by long intervals of sloth and apathy. But is that necessarily to remain the rate of advance? In the intellectual life there has been an unprecedented leap forward during the last hundred years. Individually we are not more gifted than our grandfathers, but collectively we have wrought out more epoch-making discoveries and inventions in one century than the whole race in the untold centuries that have gone before. If the twentieth century could do for us in the control of social forces what the nineteenth did for us in the control of natural forces, our grandchildren would live in a society that would be justified in regarding our present social life as semi-barbarous. Since the Reformation began to free the mind and to direct the force of religion toward morality, there has been a perceptible increase of speed. Humanity is gaining in elasticity and capacity for change, and every gain in general intelligence, in organizing capacity, in physical and moral soundness, and especially in responsiveness to ideal motives, again increases the ability to advance without disastrous reactions. The swiftness of evolution in our own country proves the immense latent perfectibility in human nature.

Last May a miracle happened. At the beginning of the week the fruit trees bore brown and greenish buds. At the end of the week they were robed in bridal garments of blossom. But for weeks and months the sap had been rising and distending the cells and maturing the tissues which were half ready in the fall before. The swift unfolding was the culmination of a long process. Perhaps these nineteen centuries of

Christian influence have been a long preliminary stage of growth, and now the flower and fruit are almost here. If at this juncture we can rally sufficient religious faith and moral strength to snap the bonds of evil and turn the present unparalleled economic and intellectual resources of humanity to the harmonious development of a true social life, the generations yet unborn will mark this as that great day of the Lord for which the ages waited, and count us blessed for sharing in the apostolate that proclaimed it.[5]

Notes

1. D. R. Sharpe, *Walter Rauschenbusch* (New York: Macmillan, 1942), is a full-length biography. R. T. Handy, *The Social Gospel in America, 1870–1920* (New York: Oxford, 1966), 251–389, has a biographical sketch and extensive selections of Rauschenbusch's writing. C. H. Hopkins, *The Rise of the Social Gospel* (New Haven: Yale, 1940), ch. 13, is a summary of Rauschenbusch's career and ideas.

2. F. Niklason, "Henry George: Social Gospeller," *American Quarterly*, 22 (Fall, 1970), 649–64.

3. For the Brotherhood, see Chapter 8, below.

4. Walter Rauschenbusch, "The Righteousness of the Kingdom," edited from the typed manuscript; by permission of the American Baptist Historical Society.

5. Walter Rauschenbusch, *Christianity and the Social Crisis* (New York: Macmillan, 1907), 414–22.

II

The New Urban America

Introduction

The rise of the city is the most obvious fact of modern American history. Its effect upon the inherited religion of the nation was to burden it "to the breaking point," as Professor Aaron I. Abell wrote in *The Urban Impact on American Protestantism*.[1] The urban pattern of America had been laid out by 1860 but it was the filling-in of this configuration by 1915, when half the population lived in cities, that created the most serious stresses to which American society had yet been subjected.[2] The cities, which had begun as trade centers for an expanding agrarian society, were now the "storm centers" of a new industrial order, and as such the prime theatres of social maladjustment and unrest.[3] The social gospel came upon the stage when human and spiritual values were threatened.

One of the keenest participants in and observers of this drama was Charles Stelzle, *A Son of the Bowery*, as he called his autobiography.[4] Like Walter Rauschenbusch and Reinhold Niebuhr, Stelzle came to a social gospel stance while ministering to a working-class church, but unlike them, he did so after almost a decade as a journeyman machinist. In 1903 he appeared on the national scene as executive of the department of church and labor of the (Northern) Presbyterian Church, from which position he carried on for a decade a dual campaign to sensitize his denomination to the labor movement, and to convince workingmen that a socialized Christianity was friendly to them. In a lecture given at a midwestern university in 1908, he described "the spirit of social unrest" in which he was himself deeply involved. His words provide a more vivid introduction to this chapter than the authors could possibly paint:

Twenty-five years ago a famous French statesman said, "The social question is a fad upon which serious statesmen should waste no time." To-day no thinking man will deny that it is the most important question that confronts us. This is true largely because our leaders in Church and school and State have persistently closed their eyes to the signs of the times. The awakening interest in recent years has come none too soon. For already the horizon is dark with clouds of social unrest which may distill into blessed showers or break upon us in a storm of fury.

Nowhere is this truer than in our great centers of population. Like a great whirlpool, the city draws unto itself the elements which constitute the social unrest. The growth of the city is one of the wonders of modern times. We are accustomed to speak of the growth of cities only in connection with the development of our own new country, but this is a world phenomenon. The same elements which make the city here make it across the sea. The city is the product of the newer civilization. It is the outgrowth of modern economic and social conditions from which there is no turning back. Therefore the city will unquestionably dominate the nation. Whereas in 1800 only four per cent of the population of the United States lived in the city, to-day thirty-four per cent live in the town. Whereas in 1800 there were only six cities with a population of 8,000 in America, to-day there are six hundred such cities. In these cities there are found more than twenty-five million people. From 1890 to 1900 the total increase of population in the United States was twenty per cent. But during the same period the population of the cities increased thirty-seven per cent.

The factors which are developing the city will never disappear. The introduction of labor-saving machinery multiplies the efficiency of those who remain on the farm, but it fails to increase the eating capacity of the rest of the world. It is quite evident that with the decreased demand for manual labor on account of the use of machinery, the farmer is driven to the city where he can find employment in shops where not only agricultural implements are turned out, but every other conceivable object, for which the demands are almost unlimited. Notwithstanding the attempts of well-intentioned philanthropists to induce immigrants and other classes to move onto the land, these immigrants and working people persist in remaining in the city, not only for the reasons already given, but because while the country-bred man driven into the city finds it comparatively easy to adapt himself to city life, the city-bred man rarely adjusts himself to the ways of the country. Those who do go to the country are the ones who are comparatively free from the very thing that seems to make this step necessary. With the rapidly developing transportation facilities, the business man who makes his money in the city can easily make his home in the suburb. And usually he assumes no responsibility for the city's civic and religious life, often leaving it in the hands of the most unfit. Because of these changing conditions, and because in the cities are found every element which has tested the strength and the virility of the Church, and in some instances destroyed the very life of government which had given promise of permanence, it is not difficult to understand that we are facing forces which challenge us for supremacy in the great storm centers of population.

Furthermore, I would remind you that the city is peculiarly an industrial problem. The economic interpretation of history seems to explain the long series of events which have followed one another in the development of mankind. Other influences there have been which can not be catalogued under this study, but nevertheless the fundamental basis of the development has been economic and industrial. It has been pointed out that the life of primitive man was largely determined by certain economic factors—the discovery of fire, the invention of pottery, the domestication of animals, and the use of tools. We assign industrial names to the ages, as, the age of stone, the age of brass, the age of bronze, and the age of iron. We talk of the hunting and fishing, the pastoral and agricultural, the commercial and industrial stages of civilization. The early migrations, the abolition of slavery, the awakening of nations, the American and French Revolutions, and most of the wars of history were largely due to economic causes. There is to-day no great political question before the American people which is free from the economic factor. Nearly every law passed by the legislature, and nearly every governmental enterprise, has its economic aspect, if indeed it is not altogether economic in its nature.

But it is the human element in the city's life which must chiefly concern us. The filthy slum, the dark tenement, the unsanitary factory, the long hours of toil, the lack of a living wage, the back-breaking labor, the inability to pay doctors' bills in times of sickness, the poor and insufficient food, the lack of leisure, the swift approach of old age, the dismal future,—these weigh down the hearts and lives of multitudes in our cities. Many have almost forgotten how to smile. To laugh is a lost art. The look of care has come so often and for so long a period of time that it is now forever stamped upon their faces. The lines are deep and hard; their souls—their ethical souls—are all but lost. No hell in the future can be worse to them than the hell in which they now live. They fear death less than they fear sleep. Some indeed long for the summons, daring not to take their own lives.

To such what does it matter whether the doors of the Church are closed or open? What attraction has the flowery sermon or the polished

oration? What meaning have the Fatherhood of God and the brotherhood of man? Where is God? they ask; and What cares man? they say.
It is in meeting the needs of these that the Church will be severely
tested in coming days.[5]

Stelzle then analyzed more specifically the factors of immigration,
labor, socialism, and the reticence of the Protestant churches to face up
to these problems. In doing so, he pulled no punches in confronting the
issues as he saw them, much as did Josiah Strong, another "forgotten
man" of the social gospel, whose writings were among the most popular
of the great outpouring of analyses and panaceas of the era.

Notes

1. Aaron I. Abell, *The Urban Impact on American Protestantism, 1865–1900* (Cambridge: Harvard University Press, 1943), 3.

2. Blake McKelvey, *The Urbanization of America, 1860–1915* (New Brunswick: Rutgers University Press, 1963), is an unusually readable account.

3. Charles Stelzle, *Christianity's Storm Center: A Study of the Modern City* (New York: Revell, 1907).

4. Stelzle, *A Son of the Bowery* (New York: Doran, 1926).

5. The Merrick Lectures for 1907–8, *The Social Application of Religion* (Cincinnati–New York: Jennings and Graham, 1908), 13–17.

6 The City

Josiah Strong came of age during the latter third of the nineteenth century. He came into national prominence with the publication of *Our Country* in 1885 and remained an important public figure until his death in 1916. His career as a Congregational minister, religious publicist, social organizer, and ecumenical churchman made him central to the late nineteenth- and early twentieth-century Protestant scene in a fashion matched only by Washington Gladden and Walter Rauschenbusch. While called the forgotten man of the social gospel movement by historians, Strong was visible and central to his generation's search for new theologies and new social orders.

He began his career under the American (Congregational) Home Missionary Society in Cheyenne, Wyoming. Schooled at Lane Seminary, he had caught the vision of its founder, Lyman Beecher, and joined the crusade to Christianize the West. After two years he returned to Ohio to teach at Western Reserve College, pastor several churches, and lead the Ohio Home Missionary Society. His vivid style of reporting Christian prospects for Ohio brought him an invitation to revise and update the Society's edition of *Our Country: A Plea for Home Missions.*

In early 1885, while writing *Our Country,* Strong accepted the pastorate of the Central Congregational Church in Cincinnati. The shift was significant. He was moving from small-town America to urban America. Since *Our Country* was prepared under the auspices of the Missionary Society, whose activities historically were in the West, Strong framed his discussions largely in terms of the West's impact upon the nation. His real perception was that the city was the next great frontier of the nation. While writing the book, he planned and hosted the first religious conference in the country devoted exclusively to the problems of the city.[1] After less than two years in

Note: Chapter 6 is by Paul Toews, who teaches history at Pacific College, Fresno, California.

Cincinnati, he moved to New York City, where he remained for the rest of his life. Before the transition was complete, the home missionary from the West would become an emergent modern-day social worker in the city.

Strong's concern for the city reflected his understanding of the impact of late nineteenth-century changes. The country was moving from muscular energy to mechanical power, from individualism to collectivism, from farm to factory, and from the village to the city. The city was the site of the emerging civilization. Its fate would determine the fate of the nation and the world. Its styles and contours would shape the intellect, culture, and morality of the twentieth century. To evade the problems of the new urbanism was to be disengaged from the future. As General Secretary of the Evangelical Alliance for the United States from 1886 to 1898, and founder and president of the League for Social Service (later renamed the American Institute of Social Service) from 1898 to 1916, and in numerous writings he described the problems of the city and sought to bring to it the imperatives of social Christianity.[2]

His doomsday rhetoric about urban evils reached many. One historian has called Strong's *Our Country* "the *Uncle Tom's Cabin* of city reform."[3] Strong was no more responsible for urban reform than Mrs. Stowe was responsible for starting the Civil War. Yet he brought the demands of urban reform to the progressive era; reformers and social gospelers traveled in the same circles, shared the same rhetoric and urged the same programs. The essence of Strong's argument is contained in this selection from *Our Country:*

The city is the nerve center of our civilization. It is also the storm center. The fact, therefore, that it is growing much more rapidly than the whole population is full of significance. In 1790 one-thirtieth of the population of the United States lived in cities of 8,000 inhabitants and over; in 1800, one twenty-fifth; in 1810, and also in 1820, one-twentieth; in 1830, one-sixteenth; in 1840, one-twelfth; in 1850, one-eighth; in 1860, one-sixth; in 1870, a little over one-fifth; and in 1880, 22.5 per cent, or nearly one-fourth.

Continuing his generous use of statistics from the Tenth Census, Strong went on to point out:

From 1790 to 1880 the whole population increased twelve fold, the urban population eighty-six fold. From 1830 to 1880 the whole population increased a little less than four fold, the urban population thirteen fold. From 1870 to 1880 the whole population thirty per cent, the urban population forty per cent. During the half century preceding 1880, population in the city increased more than four times as rapidly as that of the village and country. In 1800 there were only six cities in the United States which had a population of 8,000 or more. In 1880 there were 286.

The city has become a serious menace to our civilization, because in it . . . each of the dangers we have discussed [Romanism, socialism, wealth, intemperance, immigration – except Mormonism] is enhanced, and all are focalized. It has a peculiar attraction for the immigrant. Our fifty principal cities contain 39.3 per cent of our entire German population, and 45.8 per cent of the Irish. Our ten larger cities contain only nine per cent of the entire population, but 23 per cent of the foreign. While a little less than one-third of the population of the United States is foreign by birth or parentage, sixty-two per cent of the population of Cincinnati are foreign, eighty-three per cent of New York, and ninety-one per cent of Chicago.

Because our cities are so largely foreign, Romanism finds in them its chief strength.

For the same reason the saloon, together with the intemperance and the liquor power which it represents, is multiplied in the city. East of the Mississippi there was, in 1880, one saloon to every 438 of the population; in Boston, one to every 329; in Cleveland, one to every 192; in Chicago, one to every 179; in New York, one to every 171; in Cincinnati, one to every 124. Of course the demoralizing and pauperizing power of the saloons and their debauching influence in politics increase with their numerical strength.

It is the city where wealth is massed; and here are the tangible evidences of it piled many stories high. Here the sway of Mammon is widest, and his worship the most constant and eager. Here are luxuries gathered – everything that dazzles the eye, or tempts the appetite; here is the most extravagant expenditure. Here, also, is the *congestion* of wealth the severest. Dives and Lazarus are brought face to face; here, in sharp contrast, are the *ennui* of surfeit and the desperation of starvation. The rich are richer, and the poor are poorer, in the city than elsewhere; and, as a rule, the greater the city, the greater are the riches of the rich and the poverty of the poor. Not only does the proportion of the poor increase with the growth of the city, but their condition becomes more wretched. . . .

Socialism not only centers in the city, but is almost confined to it; and the materials of its growth are multiplied with the growth of the city. Here is heaped the social dynamite; here roughs, gamblers, thieves, robbers, lawless and desperate men of all sorts, congregate; men who are ready on any pretext to raise riots for the purpose of destruction and plunder; here gather foreigners and wage-workers; here skepticism and irreligion abound; here inequality is the greatest and most obvious, and the contrast between opulence and penury the most striking; here is suffering the sorest. As the greatest wickedness in the world is to be found not among the cannibals of some far off coast, but in Christian lands where the light of truth is diffused and rejected, so the utmost depth of wretchedness exists not among savages, who have few wants, but in great cities, where, in the presence of plenty and of every luxury, men starve. Let a man become the owner of a home, and he is much less susceptible to socialistic propagandism. But real estate is so high in the city that it is almost impossible for a wage-worker to become a householder. . . .

We have seen how the dangerous elements of our civilization are each multiplied and all concentered in the city. Do we find there the conservative forces of society equally numerous and strong? Here are the tainted spots in the body-politic; where is the salt? In 1880 there was in the United States one Evangelical church organization to every 516 of the population. In Boston there is one church to every 1,600 of the population; in Chicago, one to 2,081; in New York, one to 2,468; in St. Louis, one to 2,800. The city, where the forces of evil are amassed and where the need of Christian influence is peculiarly great, is from one-third to one-fifth as well supplied with churches as the nation at large. And church accommodations in the city are growing more inadequate every year. . . .

If moral and religious influences are peculiarly weak at the point where our social explosives are gathered, what of city government? Are its strength and purity so exceptional as to insure the effective control of these dangerous elements? In the light of notorious facts, the question sounds satirical. It is commonly said in Europe, and sometimes acknowledged here, that the government of large cities in the United States is a failure.

Here Strong introduced a telling paragraph from Henry George's

Progress and Poverty, a book that powerfully influenced many
social gospelers:

In all the great American cities there is today as clearly defined a
ruling class as in the most aristocratic countries in the world. Its
members carry wards in their pockets, make up the slates for nomina-
ting conventions, distribute offices as they bargain together,
and—though they toil not, neither do they spin—wear the best of
raiment and spend money lavishly. They are men of power, whose
favor the ambitious must court, and whose vengeance he must avoid.
Who are these men? The wise, the good, the learned—men who have
earned the confidence of their fellow-citizens by the purity of their
lives, the splendor of their talents, their probity in public trusts, their
deep study of the problems of government? No; they are the gamblers,
saloon-keepers, pugilists, or worse, who have made a trade of controlling votes and of buying and selling offices and official acts.[4]

Strong then concluded:

Holding a municipal office in a large city almost impeaches a man's
character. Known integrity and competency hopelessly incapacitate a
man for any office in the gift of a city rabble. In a certain western
city, the administration of the mayor had convinced good citizens that
he gave constant aid and comfort to gamblers, thieves, saloon-keepers,
and all the worst element of society. He became a candidate for a
second term. The prominent men and press of both parties and the
ministry of all denominations united in a Citizens' League to defeat
him; but he was triumphantly returned to office by the "lewd fellows
of the baser sort." And now, after a desperate struggle on the part of
the better elements to defeat him, he has been re-elected to a third
term of office.

Popular government in the city is degenerating into government by
a "boss." During his visit to this country Herbert Spencer said: "You
retain the forms of freedom; but, so far as I can gather, there has been
a considerable loss of the substance. It is true that those who rule you
do not do it by means of retainers armed with swords; but they do it

through regiments of men armed with voting papers, who obey the word of command as loyally as did the dependents of the old feudal nobles, and who thus enable their leaders to override the general will, and make the community submit to their exactions as effectually as their prototypes of old. Manifestly those who framed your Constitution never dreamed that twenty thousand citizens would go to the polls led by a 'boss.'

As a rule, our largest cities are the worst governed. It is natural, therefore, to infer that, as our cities grow larger and more dangerous, the government will become more corrupt and control will pass more completely into the hands of those who themselves most need to be controlled. If we would appreciate the significance of these facts and tendencies, we must bear in mind that the disproportionate growth of the city is undoubtedly to continue, and the number of great cities is to be largely increased. The extraordinary growth of urban population during this century has not been at all peculiar to the United States. It is a characteristic of nineteenth century civilization.[5]

Such fears were always counterbalanced in the larger context of Christian optimism. Strong could dramatize the perils facing the country because of his ultimate assurance that they would be reformed. The great changes of his time were not aimless meanderings on the historical landscape. They were the signposts of God's new kingdom. The laws of social Christianity would triumph and set the social order to rights. Something he called "Christian patriotism," a disinterested devotion to the general welfare, would reform the city.

Almost thirty years later Strong could write optimistically in *Our World: The New World Life* that amidst the chaos of rapid urban growth there was still the promise of God's kingdom:

We have seen that the city will certainly and of necessity dominate the nation and the world; and we have seen the significance of this fact, that it means far more than political control. We have seen that the city will determine the physique, the intellect, the moral character, the destiny of the race.

The problem of the city, then, is the advance problem of the nation and of the world.

The modern city is the microcosm of the new civilization. It is in the city that the new industrial problem must be solved, for the city is the centre of industrial organization. It is in the city that the new race problem must be solved, because it is there that the races are forced into the closest competitive relations. It is in the city that the new problem of the relations of the individual and society must be solved, because there is the social organism most complex. It is in the city that the new problem of legislation must be solved, because there the readjustments required by the new civilization are most radical and most numerous.

Thus as the meridians of the earth radiate from one pole and focus in the other, so these great world problems of the new civilization spring from the industrial revolution and gather in the city. The problem of the city, therefore, is nothing less than the problem of civilization, the problem of building in the earth the New Jerusalem. It is the problem of society's actualizing its highest possibilities by living in harmony with the laws of its own being, thus realizing the new social ideal.

Does such a problem seem beyond all human power and possibility of solution? Not to those who believe in God and in the coming of his kingdom.

At the beginning of the Divine-human Book our first glimpse of man is in a garden. It is a paradise of perfect beauty, of perfect simplicity, of perfect innocence. It is a paradise of virtue unfallen because of virtue untried. We turn to the close of the book, and there we catch another glimpse of man in a perfect estate. We see in this vision not the beauty of innocence, but the beauty of holiness. We see not the unstable peace of virtue untried, but the established peace of virtue victorious.

In the first picture we see individualistic man; in the second we see socialized man. In the first we see man unfallen, sustaining right relations to his Creator. In the second we see man redeemed, sustaining right relations to his God and to his fellows.

The story of this marvellous human drama begins in the country; its denouement is in the city. The crown and consummation of our civilization—the full coming of the Kingdom of God on earth—is typified not by a garden, but by a city—a Holy City—into which shall enter nothing unclean, and nothing that maketh a lie.

Paradise lost was a garden; Paradise regained will be a city.[6]

Notes

1. *Discussions of the Inter-Denominational Congress in the Interest of City Evangelization, Held in Cincinnati, Dec. 7–11, 1885* (Cincinnati: The Congress, 1886).

2. Two of Strong's eleven books dealt specifically with the city: *The Twentieth Century City* (New York: Baker and Taylor, 1898) and *The Challenge of the City* (New York: Young People's Missionary Movement, 1907).

3. Henry F. May, *The Protestant Churches and Industrial America* (New York: Harper & Row, 1949), 116.

4. Henry George, *Progress and Poverty* (1879), 382.

5. Josiah Strong, *Our Country: Its Possible Future and Its Present Crisis* (New York: American Home Missionary Society, 1885), ch. 10.

6. Josiah Strong, *Our World: The New World Life* (Garden City: Doubleday, 1913), 282–83.

7   Justice for Labor

Although the theatre of social unrest was the new urban environment, the concern of early—and later—social gospelers was directed in large measure to the labor problem, especially after the eruption of the great social volcanoes of 1877, 1886, and 1894.[1] These—the nationwide railroad strike that followed years of depression in the seventies, the so-called Haymarket riot in Chicago, and the Pullman strike of 1894—shocked the nation and Protestant complacency far deeper than the comparable convulsions of the 1960's in Newark, Detroit, or Watts.

But in all of this the sensitivities of the religious reformers with whom we are concerned in this book were, as Stelzle told his Ohio Wesleyan audience, directed toward "the human element." Another great New Yorker, Henry Codman Potter, whose first biography was subtitled *The People's Friend*,[2] came into prominence as the originator of a social service program to the immigrants and workers who inundated his middle-class parish. When, at the height of the outcry over the Haymarket affair, the then Episcopal Bishop Potter issued an epistle to the clergy of that influential diocese entitled "The Laborer not a Commodity," the phrase entered the social gospel vocabulary:

Christianity brought into the world a new law of brotherhood, and both by precept and example taught men that they to whom has been committed the stewardship of exceptional gifts, whether of rank, wealth, learning or cleverness, are not to treat them as their own, but as a trust for the whole community. "Bear ye one another's burdens and so fulfil the law of Christ"; "Ye that are strong ought to bear the infirmities of the weak"; "Charge them that are rich in this world that they be ready to give, glad to distribute", these words and others like them did not mean the mere giving of doles and indiscriminate distribution of alms. It is not by gifts such as these that the wounds in the body-politic are to be healed, and the parted tendrils of a dissevered humanity bound together; and it is an open question whether municipal and institutional charity has not irritated as much as it has soothed or healed them.

What the laborer wants from his employer is fair and fraternal dealing, not alms-giving, and a recognition of his manhood rather than a condescension to his inferiority. And it is at this point that the outlook is most discouraging. The growth of wealth among us has issued not in binding men together but in driving them apart. The rich are farther from the poor, the employer from his workmen, capital from labor, now, than ever before. Too many know less and less how the poor live, and give little time, or none at all, to efforts to know. The wage of the laborer may be, doubtless in most cases it is, larger than it was thirty years ago; but his wants have grown more rapidly than his wages, and his opportunities for gratifying them are not more numerous, but less. He knows more about decent living, but his home is not often more decent, and daily grows more costly. His mental horizon has been widened, but fit food for it is no more accessible. Instincts and aspirations have been awakened in him which are certainly as honorable in him as in those more favorably situated, but wealth does little either to direct or to satisfy them. The manners of the poor, it is said, are more insolent and ungracious than of old to the rich, and this discourages efforts to know and serve them. I do not see why poverty should cringe to wealth, which is as often as otherwise an accidental distinction, and quite as often a condition unadorned by any especial moral or intellectual excellence. But we may be sure that the manners of the poor, if they be insolent, are learned from those of people whose opportunities should at least have taught them that no arrogance is more insufferable or unwarrantable than that of mere wealth. And if we are reaping today the fruits of these mutual hatreds between more and less favored classes, we may well own that the fault is not all on one side, and that it is time that we awaken to the need of sacrifices which can alone banish them.

These sacrifices are not so much of money as of ease, of self-indulgent ignorance, of contemptuous indifference, of conceited and shallow views of the relations of men to one another. A nation whose wealth and social leadership are in the hands of people who fancy that day after day, like those of old, they can "sit down to eat and drink and rise up to play," careless of those who earn the dividends that they spend, and pay the rents of the tenement-houses that they own, but too often never visit or inspect, has but one doom before it, and that the worst. We may cover the pages of our statute-books with laws regulating strikes, and inflicting severest penalties on those who organize resistance to the individual liberty whether of employer or workman; we may drill regiments and perfect our police; the safety and welfare of a state are not in these things, they are in the contentment and loyalty of its people. And these come by a different road. When capitalists and employers of labor have forever dismissed the fallacy, which may be true enough in the domain of political economy, but is essentially false in the domain of religion, *that labor and the laborer are alike a commodity,* to be bought and sold, employed or dismissed, paid or underpaid as the market shall decree; when the interest of workman and master shall have been owned by both as one, and the share of the laboring man shall be something more than a mere wage; when the principle of a joint interest, in what is produced, of all the brains and hands that go to produce it is wisely and generously recognized; when the well-being of our fellow-men, their homes and food, their pleasures and their higher moral and spiritual necessities, shall be seen to be matters concerning which we may not dare to say, "Am I my brother's keeper?" then, but not till then, may we hope to heal those grave social divisions concerning which there need to be among us all, as with Israel of old, "great searchings of heart."[3]

One of Charles Stelzle's goals was to build friendly relations between churches and labor unions. To this end he advocated the exchange of fraternal delegates between local unions or labor councils and ministerial associations. He evangelized at noon meetings in shops. Always glad to testify for his faith in the ideals of the trades union movement and his belief in Christ the Toiler, he told the annual convention of the American Federation of Labor in 1905 that he found very much in common between organized labor and the organized church and that there was "no reason why a man may not be a good trade unionist, be loyal to the pledge he has taken, and at the same time be a member of the church and a Christian." As a member of the International Association of Machinists he stood squarely for organized labor and confessed from the bottom of his heart his belief that the church was interested in child labor, tenement improvement, and comparable reforms: it hasn't done all it should have done, "but it seems to me," he concluded, that "the mission of the Church of Christ today is to consider the social and material needs of the people as well as their moral needs."[4]

Important as it may have seemed to address a national labor convention, Stelzle found a vastly greater audience of the rank and file of workingmen through syndicated sermonettes published in 250 labor papers across the country and presumably read by as many as three million persons. Here are two of them:

What Is Christianity?

The difference of opinion among men with regard to the nature of Christianity is due to the fact that it has to do with *life*. As life expands, our conception of all related subjects changes. We do not believe about anything just what we believed about it ten years ago—provided that we are living and growing. A row of fence posts placed alongside the road will remain the same for many years, or until they rot. But a row of trees planted in the same place will grow, and hence change, every day, because they are living.

The fact that men's opinions concerning Christianity undergo a change is nothing against it. It is rather in favor of Christianity and in favor of the men whose minds are expanding. For while the fundamental principles of men's characters are eternal, both are capable of infinite expansion. They cannot be limited to the ecclesiastical terminology of the theologian in the one case, nor to a narrow interpretation of life in the other.

Our conception of Christianity depends largely upon our peculiar natures or our previous environment. To the Russian Jew, Christianity means the brutality of Kieff or Kishenev. To others it means the Catholicism of South America or of some half-enlightened European country. To still others it means the Protestantism of a former generation or even the monstrosities that have grown round about it in our own day. But these are not fair illustrations of any of the churches or denominations involved. Organized labor demands that it shall be judged not by its worst characteristics, but by its best hopes and aspirations. By the same token, the Church must be judged not by its weakest but by its best output. We are discussing not the Church, but Christianity. We are quite ready to confess that the Church has not always truly represented Christianity.

Neither is "religion" Christianity. Some men are very religious, but they are not very good Christians. You have heard of men who have become insane because they had too much religion, but you never heard of a man who became insane because he had too much Christianity.

Christianity is not a scheme to increase the population of heaven. Its cardinal principle is that given by its founder "He that saveth his life shall lose it, and he that loseth his life (for the sake of his fellow men) shall find it." Its purpose for its followers is not to get to heaven, but to bring heaven down to earth. Principally, then, Christianity is a character and a life—the possession and the manifestation of the life and the spirit of Christ. Not essentially the life of the monk, or the "Pharisee," or the stoic, or the "Puritan." These may all be Christian in a very important sense, but they are abnormal. The healthy Christian life is lived in the world among men and is interested in their every-day affairs. It is lived at the primary and in the labor union. It is lived in the shop and in the office. There is nothing which concerns the well-being of men which can be alien to the Christian life. It does not involve a belief in an impossible dogma. It does not demand an absolute acceptance of the inspiration of the Bible. It asks merely that the man who wishes to become a Christian shall bring his life into conformity with the life and the purpose of Christ, and that he shall accept Christ as the governing power of his life, helping to carry out His will and plan for the redemption of the world.

Organized Labour and the Church

The editor of a Western socialist paper accuses me of trying to "swing workingmen into the church," and immediately he declares that I am insincere in my motives.

I do not expect to make every reader believe that I am perfectly sincere. I do not propose to try it; but there is nothing like plainly telling another man just what you believe and why you believe it.

Recently I declared with emphasis that I stand for organized labour, and I gave my reasons for this position. I'd like to know why it is inconsistent for a man to believe in both the trades union and the church; and if I believe in the church, why should I hesitate to tell men so and try to persuade them that it is a good thing, just as I would tell them that trades unionism is a good thing?

I do not think for a moment, that any sane workingman would believe me if I pretended that I do not care whether or not he is indifferent to the church, and that for which it stands.

And so I would say without fear of losing caste with my fellows, that just as I stand for organized labour, so I stand for the organized church. And just as I would persuade a man to identify himself with one, so I should seek to have him identify himself with the other, because, however they may differ in some of their methods, they have very much in common.

The pledge of the man who unites with the American Federation of Labour, commits him to—"the emancipation of our class from poverty, ignorance and selfishness; to be respectful in word and action to every woman; to be considerate to the widow and the orphan, the weak and the defenseless; and never to discriminate against a fellow worker on account of creed, colour or nationality. To defend freedom of thought, whether expressed by tongue or pen. To educate ourselves and our fellow worker in the history of the labour movement. We promise that we will never knowingly wrong a brother or see him wronged, if in our power to prevent it. We will endeavour to subordinate every selfish impulse to the task of elevating the material, intellectual and moral conditions of the entire labouring class."

Every Christian man and woman could subscribe to these principles. There is nothing in them that is contrary to the pledge of the man who joins the church. Need I be ashamed, therefore, of asking a man to identify himself with an organization which stands committed to these high purposes?

When the church was started two thousand years ago, it was organized by a company of workingmen. Its leader was a carpenter. When it spread to other cities, it was received most cordially by the workingmen who formed the great labour guilds of the day—the labour unions we would now call them.

I can see no reason why workingmen should not again rally around the church of Christ, accepting Him as their leader and their champion. I believe the day is approaching when this will come to pass; when with the power that can come alone from Him, the pledge of the unionist and the vow of the Christian, looking towards the complete emancipation of the whole body of workingmen, physical, mental and moral, will be lived out for the sake of our brother men.[5]

Notes

1. H. F. May, *The Protestant Churches and Industrial America* (New York: Harper & Row, 1949), 91–111.

2. Harriet A. Keyser, *Bishop Potter, the People's Friend* (New York: Whittaker, 1910), and George Hodges, *Henry Codman Potter, Seventh Bishop of New York* (New York: Macmillan, 1915).

3. *Christian Thought,* 4th ser. (1886), 289–91.

4. *Twenty-fifth Annual Convention of the American Federation of Labor, Pittsburgh, 1905* (Washington, D.C., 1905), 150–54.

5. Stelzle, *The Gospel of Labor* (Commission on the Church and Social Service of the Federal Council of Churches in America; New York: Revell, 1912), pp. 80–82, 98–101.

8   Movements toward the Kingdom

The social gospel was not only the utterances and activities of individuals; it was also group movement and organization. We have selected two of these to describe, largely because of their differences. The first, an Episcopal society, reflected a widespread, but far from universal, concern in that church body for a means to realize in action such ideals as those expressed in Bishop Potter's pastoral letter.

In many respects the most remarkable organization in the half century of social Chirstianity's growth, with the exception of the Federal Council of Churches, was the Church Association for the Advancement of the Interests of Labor. This Episcopal society not only typified the advanced social thought of that communion but was a specific example of the transfer of British experience to America through the medium of Anglican influence. "C.A.I.L." [pronounced "cail"] came into being in New York City in 1887 as an attempt to translate into action a deep-seated belief that as a part of her universal ministry to mankind the church had a genuine concern in the welfare of those involved in industry. The Association's constitution set forth certain fundamental principles:

> The Church Association for the Advancement of the Interests of Labor, believing that the clergy and the laity of the Church should become personally interested in the social questions now being agitated, should inform themselves of the nature of the issues presented, and should be prepared to act as the necessities of the day may demand, sets forth the following principles and methods of work for its members:
>
> Principles
>
> 1. It is the essence of the teachings of Jesus Christ that God is the Father of all men and that all men are brothers.

2. God is the sole possessor of the Earth and its fulness; Man is but the steward of God's bounties.

3. Labor being the exercise of body, mind and spirit in the broadening and elevating of human life, it is the duty of every man to labor diligently.

4. Labor, as thus defined, should be the standard of social worth.

5. When the divinely intended opportunity to labor is given to all men, one great cause of the present widespread suffering and destitution will be removed.

Methods

1. Prayer.

2. Sermons, setting forth the teachings of the gospel as the guide to the solution of every question involved in the interests of Labor.

3. The proper use of the press and the circulation of tracts as occasion may require.

4. Lectures and addresses on occasions when the interests of Labor may be advanced.

5. The encouragement by precept and example of a conscientious use of the ballot.

Special Duties

It shall be the duty of each member to take, or read, at least one journal devoted to the interests of labor.

It shall be the duty of each member to devote a certain portion of his time to study of the social questions of the day in the light of the Incarnation.

Collect

O Lord Jesus Christ, who didst glorify labor by Thy life of toil, bless, we beseech Thee, the efforts of our Society, that we may both rejoice to work with Thee, and may also strive to open to all our brothers and sisters the way to honest labor, and secure to them the fruits of their toil; Who with the Father and the Holy Ghost livest and reignest one God, world without end. Amen.[1]

Under the leadership of such men as Bishops Frederic Dan Huntington and Henry Codman Potter, the Association soon spread across the country and was often accepted by labor as a friendly ally, as examples of its activities indicate. In 1890 three sizable mass meetings were held at which labor's problems and their solutions were discussed. That year the group endorsed the efforts of the Working Women's Society of New York toward the improvement of the status of women and children workers in retail stores, and it recommended successfully to the diocese of New York that its printing be given only to firms paying standard wages. C.A.I.L. instituted in Episcopal churches the first observance of Labor Sunday in America, also in 1890. In 1893 a plan for mediation in labor difficulties was proposed to Bishop Potter. The resulting impartial committee served for many years and Potter's name became a symbol for fair judgments. The next year sweatshop and tenement committees were formed to agitate against those evils by various means such as posters and other forms of propaganda. In 1895 was begun the publication of *Hammer and Pen,* a rather remarkable quarterly that dealt frankly with strikes, legislation, and general reform news. A sort of subsidiary of C.A.I.L. was the Actors' Church Alliance, organized in 1899 to support the efforts of the Actors' Society for one day of rest in seven. Actually pursuing a broader program, by 1905 the Alliance had enlisted Episcopal ministers in more than four hundred towns and cities as "chaplains" to traveling actors.

Local chapters of C.A.I.L. frequently stimulated their parishes to useful social services. That in St. Michael's Church of New York, for example, held meetings for the discussion of such matters as the single tax, woman suffrage, prison reform, tenements, sweatshops, and other phases of the labor problem. This chapter had three standing committees: that on tenements inspected all buildings in the parish and reported violations of the law; the labor-organization group—chaired by a member of the bricklayers' union—acted for justice in controversies; and a sweatshop committee published a "white list" of clothing firms that paid living wages and treated employees fairly.

C.A.I.L. was active for forty years. With its sister organization the Church Social Union it was instrumental in securing the adoption of social-service measures by the General Convention of the Episcopal Church. . . . It voluntarily disbanded in 1926 when a secretary for industrial relations was made a regular member of the staff of the denomination's Department of Christian Social Service.[2]

The Brotherhood of the Kingdom, which grew out of the fellowship of Walter Rauschenbusch and a group of young Baptist preachers in New York City and Philadelphia, first met in 1892 but had its real beginning in a summer retreat the next year at the hilltop home of one of the members, Leighton Williams, at Marlborough, New York. The papers read at this first session were "so helpful and inspiring" that the group planned an annual meeting at which there would be intellectual stimulation, meditation, prayer, and worship; for twenty years the brothers brought "the problems of the world" to this hospitable hilltop, expanding their ecumenical fellowship over the years to include most of the men and women associated with the social gospel—both well known and today unknown.

At the first gathering in August, 1893, a statement was adopted setting forth the "Spirit and Aims of the Brotherhood," an interesting contrast to C.A.I.L.'s constitution:

Organization

The Spirit of God is moving men in our generation toward a better understanding of the idea of the Kingdom of God on earth. Obeying the thought of our Master, and trusting in the power and guidance of the Spirit, we form ourselves into a Brotherhood of the Kingdom, in order to re-establish this idea in the thought of the church, and to assist in its practical realization in the world.

Aims

The aims of the Brotherhood shall be carried into effect by the following means:

1. Every member shall by personal life exemplify obedience to the ethics of Jesus.

2. Every member shall propagate the thoughts of Jesus to the limits of his or her ability, in private conversation, by correspondence, and through pulpit, platform and press.

3. Every member shall lay special stress on the social aims of Christianity, and shall endeavor to make Christ's teaching concerning wealth operative in the church.

4. On the other hand, each member shall take pains to keep in contact with the common people, and to infuse the religious spirit into the efforts for social amelioration.

5. The members shall seek to strengthen the bond of Brotherhood by frequent meetings for prayer and discussion, by correspondence, exchange of articles written, etc.

6. Regular reports shall be made of the work done by members, in such manner as the Executive Committee may appoint.

7. The members shall seek to procure for one another opportunities for public propaganda.

8. If necessary, they shall give their support to one another in the public defense of the truth, and shall jealously guard the freedom of discussion for any man who is impelled by love the truth to utter his thoughts.[3]

It had been intended to publish the papers read at the first conference but instead certain ones were printed as pamphlets from time to time. We believe that Rauschenbusch's *Righteousness of the Kingdom,* (Chapter 5, above) was hammered out on the anvil of Brotherhood discussion and was originally intended as a manifesto by the group.[4]

The Brotherhood's interests were about equally divided between social, ethical, and theological concerns. . . . The papers read at the first meeting were mostly occupied with the kingdom idea. While this interest was predominant in the earlier conferences, during its life the Brotherhood discussed practically every significant social problem that was arousing popular interest in those days. The land question and the single tax, retail trade, politics, socialism, labor, the home, corporations, direct legislation, and the municipal problem were all dealt with. On a few occasions the Brotherhood acted in a corporate way to protest specific wrongs or to challenge the churches with their social duties. The conference of 1897 addressed a resolution of sympathy to the striking coal miners. We have neither the call nor the information to sit in judgment on present conditions, this statement read, but "we hold this to be self-evident, that men are entitled to a fair living wage, and it seems to be generally conceded that the miners have been pressed down beyond the level of decency and humanity." Such things concern us all, and we add our voice to the universal protest, holding especially that "the tendency to give capital a first lien on the proceeds of industry" is unethical. "A fair wage to the worker should come first," the resolution concluded, "and interest and dividends second, for life is more than property." An outstandingly important theme was that of Christian union. The social teachings of the Bible, the lives of great reformers and of Christian saints were studied and discussed, notably the seventh Earl of Shaftesbury and St. Francis of Assisi. Louise Seymour Houghton, translator of Sabatier's *Life of St. Francis,* became an enthusiastic member of the Brotherhood, and even built a summer home at Marlborough.

The fellowship's wide range of interests was well exemplified in the program for the conference of 1898, at which three series of papers were presented. The first of these, dealing with various aspects of liberty, analyzed political, industrial, and social liberty; the second group included sketches of four social prophets: Lammenais, Tolstoi, Mazzini, and Wycliffe; the third series was on Biblical topics, presenting in turn

"The New Testament's Line of Approach to Social Ethics," "The Social Ideas of Paul," and "The Prophetic Office of the Pulpit." Other papers given at this conference were: "The Prophets of Israel as Social Leaders," "The Rural Population and the Social Movement," trade unions in New York, the social work of the church, and a review of Sidney and Beatrice Webb's *Industrial Democracy*.

But all these interests were viewed in the light of the religious ideal of the kingdom of God. It cannot be too forcibly pointed out that the Brotherhood of the Kingdom, like the widespread social gospel movement of which it was a vital part, was fundamentally religious. The first principle upon which the fellowship had been founded was, as Williams wrote, that of discipleship to Jesus rather than loyalty to a creed. The second basic idea was that of brotherhood rather than a hard and fast organization. But the third, and by far the most important principle, was the kingdom idea itself. This was at once a theological and a social ideal, a theme for study, and a focus for worship. . . .

The Kingdom is, however, in a real sense yet to come. The present order is not divine. God does not sanction the feast of Dives and the starvation of Lazarus. That a social system shall prevail in which one man, by financiering and speculation, can become the controller of millions of dollars and thousands of lives; that able bodied young men shall walk the streets in desperation looking for a job—these things are no part of the kingdom. At this point the practical aim of the Brotherhood was brought into play: it is one of our special tasks, declared Rauschenbusch at the conference of 1895, "to wed Christianity and the social movement, infusing the power of religion into social efforts, and helping religion to find its ethical outcome in the transformation of social conditions." This belief was phrased in a corporate way by the Brotherhood in 1908, when, in an address to the churches of the United States, it declared that the kingdom idea "is adequate for continuous reconstructions because it is of the same structure, laws, ideals, principles and life as the Kingdom of God in Heaven or in any kind of colony of the universal kingdom. To it is given the task of extending its rule until the consummation would be achieved through agencies resident in humanity: slowly but surely the gospel of the crucified Nazarene is penetrating the heathenisms of the earth. The effort to advance the kingdom is not a hopeless struggle. The Kingdom ideal has been the potency of countless revolutions in the past and contains the prophecy of more to come. "The only hope for the world is in the Gospel of the Kingdom, with its crucified Savior, its law of love, its doctrine of brotherhood, its passion for righteousness, and its message of peace."

All these aspirations of the Brotherhood were summed up in an oft-quoted phrase of Rauschenbusch in his leaflet *The Brotherhood of the Kingdom:*

> We desire to see the Kingdom of God once more the great object of Christian preaching; the inspiration of Christian hymnology; the foundation of systematic theology; the enduring motive of evangelistic and missionary work; the religious inspiration of social work and the object to which a Christian man surrenders his life, and in that surrender saves it to eternal life; the common object in which all religious bodies find their unity; the great synthesis in which the regeneration of the spirit, the enlightenment of the intellect, the development of the body, the reform of political life, the sanctification of industrial life, and all that concerns the redemption of humanity shall be embraced.

To the accomplishment of these aims the Brotherhood worked quietly and steadily. It made no concerted effort to secure members or to propagate its beliefs other than by word of mouth, through friendship and fellowship, by means of sermons, magazine articles, the circulation of essays in pamphlet form, and through the books written by individuals. "The extension of the Brotherhood is not the extension of an organization," declared a speaker at the conference of 1897, "but the dissemination of the idea of the kingdom of God for which we stand. We seek in all ways to make the idea of the kingdom which we cherish the common property of all of God's people." To this end several series of tracts were printed and the proceedings of the annual conferences were published, although not every year. From August, 1907, until January, 1909, the Rev. W. H. Gardner of New Haven, a member of the Brotherhood, attempted the publication of a magazine entitled *The Kingdom,* dedicated to the propagation of the fellowship's ideal. Several branches were established, notably in Rochester, in Boston, and in New York. The New York group centered around Leighton Williams at Amity Church; it carried on various activities of which we unfortunately have no records. The Boston chapter, of which E. Tallmadge Root was the leading spirit, was formed about 1914 and lapsed in 1932. It included among its members George W. Coleman, sponsor of the Ford Hall Forums, the Rev. O. P. Gifford, Woodman Bradbury, and Roger W. Babson.

The Rochester chapter appears to have been formed not long after Walter Rauschenbusch returned to his home city in 1897. It held monthly meetings given to devotions and discussion and was, doubtless, one of the influences that led Rauschenbusch to write his *Prayers of the Social Awakening.* It prepared a list of social gospel topics on which its members offered to speak. One of these circulars described the organization as consisting of men and women who "believe in the application of Christian principles and forces to the wider social life of humanity" and who hold the basic aim of Christianity to be "the establishment of the Kingdom of God on earth," a process involving not only the conversion of individuals but "the Christianizing of all human relations." Members of the local group . . . offered to speak on such subjects as the kingdom ideal, socialism, child labor, social problems and related themes. Perhaps the experience of Carl A. Daniel was typical; "Professor Rauschenbusch and I," he wrote years afterward, "appeared before the Labor Lyceum of Rochester a few times discussing problems of labor from the Christian point of view and experienced some bitter criticisms."

The world at large came to know of the ideals of the Brotherhood chiefly through the published writings of its members. The first book to attract a wide audience was Samuel Zane Batten's *The New Citizenship,* which won a $600 prize from the American Sunday School Union in 1898. In it Batten declared that "the Kingdom of God is all-inclusive and comprehends every interest and relation and activity of man." The next year three significant essays by members appeared: *The Republic of Man,* by Nathaniel Schmidt; an exegetical study entitled *The Kingdom,* by George Dana Boardman; and a treatment of the Biblical ethics of wealth by E. Tallmadge Root, *"The Profit of the Many."* In 1905, Schmidt's scholarly treatise, *The Prophet of Nazareth,* came from the press.

But by all odds the most important writings by members of the Brotherhood were those of Walter Rauschenbusch, whose epochal book, *Christianity and the Social Crisis,* appearing in 1907, made its author at once the acknowledged leader of American social Christianity and soon acquainted the Protestant world with the basic tenets for which the Brotherhood had long labored. In this book, as in his later works, Rauschenbusch stated the social gospel in terms of the realization of the kingdom ideal—the kingdom ideal that had been the subject of so many Brotherhood papers and discussions. Indeed, the appearance of *Christianity and the Social Crisis* was a sort of crisis for the Brotherhood. When the conference of 1907 met, it considered disbanding the organization, so well had Rauschenbusch's book stated its aims. The favorable reception given the work seemed to vindicate the fellowship's efforts "to establish the social nature of Christianity." We have contended for the kingdom ideal, declared Leighton Williams in a paper at that conference, and we have assailed the present social order as essentially unrighteous and contrary to the will of God. We have maintained that it is the duty of Christians to interest themselves in social questions. Quoting Frederick Denison Maurice, he asserted that the Brotherhood had opposed both "unsocial Christians and unchristian socialists" and had been disliked and feared by both. The group had nevertheless held its ground for fifteen years and was perhaps the oldest organization of its kind in the country. And now, he said, we may point to Rauschenbusch's book with pride "as a finished exposition of our opinions and thank him most heartily for it." But, continued Williams, there is still a vast work to do. And so the Brotherhood continued in its quiet way to meet each summer on the consecrated hilltop overlooking the Hudson, although with an increasing sense of a completed task. In 1909 Rauschenbusch wrote in the Visitors' Book:

> Only where mind touches mind does the mind do its best work. Where love and confidence draw back the bars and bolts of caution and distrust thought passes easily from heart to heart, and finds ready lodgment. So we grow. . . . God bless this hill-top temple of the spirit. . . . May it do for others in the future what it did for me in the past.

When the Northern Baptist Convention first met in 1908, Samuel Zane Batten and several other members of the Brotherhood began what was to be a significant work in organizing its social service activities. The kingdom ideal played a large part in the subsequent reports of this body, and in the ideology expressed in the study courses it developed. In 1909 Batten produced another book, *The Christian State.* In 1911, now a professor in Des Moines College and Chairman of the Convention's Social Service Commission, he wrote *The Social Task of Christianity,* which was subtitled "A summons to the new crusade." In 1911 also William Newton Clarke published a book entitled *The Ideal of Jesus,* in which he declared that "the kingdom of God is the embodiment of the ideal of Jesus," a position that had received less explicit sanction in his earlier works. The next year came the second of Rauschenbusch's great books, *Christianizing the Social Order,* although in *For God and the People,* published in 1910, the kingdom ideal had played a large part in these "Prayers of the social awakening." In *Christianizing the Social Order,* Rauschenbusch paid tribute to the Brotherhood. It has been too unselfish to become large, he said, but it was a powerful stimulus in those early days of isolation. Of all the ideas we tried to work out, there is not one but has become a recognized and commanding issue. Of the men who trusted to the inner voice and the outer call, he continued, a number have risen to positions of acknowledged leadership, a fact attributable to the all-inclusive conception of Christianity that they adopted having set them large tasks, "unified their otherwise scattered interests, inspired them with religious joy, compelled them to fight for God, and so made strong men of them."[5]

A recent full-length study of the Brotherhood makes Leighton Williams its prime mover, and shows how the evangelical piety from an earlier time, such as is described by Timothy L. Smith in Chapter 1, above, mediated to the group through Williams' father, provided the Brotherhood's chief motivating power.[6] Another fresh insight into the dynamics of the Brotherhood is the influence of the English Non-Conformist minister Richard Heath, whose book *The Captive City of God, or, The Churches seen in the Light of the Democratic Ideal,* was of profound importance in shaping Walter Rauschenbusch's ideas.[7]

Notes

1. The constitution of C.A.I.L. was often printed in its literature.

2. C. H. Hopkins, *Rise of the Social Gospel* (New Haven: Yale University Press, 1940), 150–52. See also the biographies of Potter in note 2 of Chapter 7, above, and Spencer Miller and Joseph F. Fletcher, *The Church and Industry* (New York: Longmans, Green, 1930), ch. 4.

3. "The Spirit and Aims of the Brotherhood" was frequently printed in their literature.

4. See a review of *The Righteousness of the Kingdom,* C. H. Hopkins, in the *Union Theological Seminary Quarterly Review* (New York), Winter, 1969, 211–13.

5. Hopkins, *Rise of the Social Gospel,* 131–34, and "Walter Rauschenbusch and the Brotherhood of the Kingdom," *Church History,* 6 (June, 1938), 138–56.

6. A full-length study of the Brotherhood is Frederic M. Hudson, 'The Reign of the New Humanity': A Study of the Background, History, and Influence of the Brotherhood of the Kingdom (unpub. Ph.D. diss., Columbia University, 1968; Xerox–University Microfilm #71-22438).

7. Richard Heath, *The Captive City of God* (London: Fifield, 1904).

9   Voices from the New South

The assumption has often been made that during the first decade of the new century no whites in the New South were concerned with the reform impulse now building to a climax in the North. For a long time this error was part of one of the larger oversights in American history, namely that Progressivism had not been present in the South. To properly appreciate the role of Progressivism one must distinguish between the political and humanitarian thrusts of the movement. It is true that political Progressivism, offering relief to political injustices via such means as the direct primary, initiative, and referendum, as well as business regulation, was at work below the Mason-Dixon line. More recent historical studies have shown, furthermore, that humanitarian reform, dealing with such issues as child labor, education, health, prisons, agriculture, and race, was also present as a countermovement to the prevailing structure and ethos of white southern society.[1]

Even as attention has focused recently on the social justice side of Progressivism, there has been an historical lag in examining a corollary assumption that the social gospel was absent from the southern scene. Aaron I. Abell and Henry F. May did not consider the South in their studies of the social gospel. If the social gospel is defined narrowly, as a determined response to industrial problems, it is now apparent that the south took important strides in industrialization in the closing years of the century, which were accompanied by many of the problems known in the North. If the social gospel is defined more widely, as a particular kind of response to a whole variety of social problems in a changing society, then problems more particularly southern, such as farm tenancy, illiteracy, the convict-lease system, and race relations, need to be considered also.

Recently the influence of the social gospel in the South has begun to be reassessed. John L. Eighmy did his primary work on the southern denomination most renowned for its conservative social stance, the Southern Baptists.[2] Surveying the spectrum of Protestant thought in the South, Eighmy concludes: "for all the admitted resistance to religious liberalism, the new Protestant thought, especially the social gospel, exerted important influences within southern church life." His career shortened by his recent untimely death, the following 1969 essay is the first reporting of his findings.

The social gospel was one of the most productive intellectual movements to originate from American Protestantism. Essentially, the new religious ideology of the late nineteenth century brought the ethical element of Christianity to bear upon the unprecedented problems of social adjustment caused by the rise of an industrial society. It inspired an outpouring of social criticism and reform activity unequalled in the nation's religious experience. The urban-centered problems of slums, crime, political corruption and industrial strife turned progressive-minded churchmen to the mission of social uplift. . . .

Students of social Christianity have treated the movement almost exclusively as the Protestant response to the industrialization of the North. This generally accepted definition of the social gospel almost precludes any consideration of social Christianity in the less industrialized South. . . .

That historians would assume that liberalism failed to penetrate Southern religion is understandable. The region has a long history of resistance to change in matters of the mind and spirit. The South produced no pioneers in social Christianity or nationally recognized spokesmen for the cause in later years. Certainly, the New Theology owed nothing to Southern intellects. Ecumenism found its inspiration elsewhere. It has been easy to conclude that the region's ruralness and cultural conservatism barred those religious ideas associated with social reform in the North. For many, indeed, the Southern Protestant has become the stock Mencken figure: provincial hardshell, enemy of the flesh, heaven-bound defender of the faith. But the figure is a stereotype, overdrawn and unfair. It is the contention of this paper that, for all the admitted resistance to religious liberalism, the new Protestant thought, especially the social gospel, exerted important influences within Southern church life.

We might begin our examination by considering, in the Southern context, the definition of the social gospel as the Protestant response to industrial ills. It is true that Southern industrial development never equalled that of the North, but from the 1880's onward substantial growth in textiles, tobacco, wood products and various minerals began to alter the fundamental character of the region's economy. During these years, the South consciously adopted as its own the industrial standards of the North. The New South evangelists successfully promoted industrialization as a public and private venture, invited investments of local and outside capital, and generally preached the success goals of the business world. If there is a causal relationship between industrialization and social religion, one might expect to find some forms of social Christianity in the South by the turn of the century.

But whatever the degree of industrial growth, the consideration of practical Christianity, particularly in the South, should not be confined to those reforms directed at urban ills and a business economy. The region's long-standing problems of illiteracy, farm tenancy and racial discrimination were in themselves sufficient cause for an aroused social conscience. It was, in fact, the recognition of these chronic problems along with those arising from new Southern industry that produced widespread social criticism, resembling in many of its assumptions, methods, and objectives the ideology of the social gospel.

The campaigns for social betterment drew heavily upon the South's religious resources, even though these crusades usually were conducted under the more secular banner of Progressivism. . . . Some of the best known features of the movement—initiative, referendum, direct primary and business regulation—won approval in Southern states prior to their better known adoption in the North. But Southern Progressivism went beyond democratic reforms and attacks on big business. The leaders, perhaps more so than their Northern counterparts, came from the ranks of the middle class and professional people. They urged the respectable citizens to join the cause of social improvement. The movement made a strong appeal to the moral responsibility of the favored classes. The Reverend Edgar Gardner Murphy challenged the people of "intelligence and property" to exhibit the "real spirit of *noblesse oblige*" by accepting their duty as the natural leaders in uplifting the disenfranchised masses of both races.

An important characteristic of Southern reform was the broad range of causes it embraced—causes which, by reason of the humanitarian zeal with which they were promoted, became something of a counterpart to the social gospel in the North. Southern Progressives worked through the Prison Reform Association to secure, along with other improvements, the abolition of the convict-lease system by 1919 in every state except Alabama. Public health advocates, encouraged by new medical discoveries, initiated a campaign against the regional maladies of hookworm, pellagra and malaria. State health boards, some new and others rejuvenated, began effective programs in every state. Rockefeller philanthropy went far in eradicating the hookworm disease among the rural poor.

In agriculture, Charles H. Otken, a Mississippi Baptist minister, combined Populist ardor with muckraker reporting to expose the evils of the crop-lien system; farm editor Clarence Poe preached a gospel of self-help through education, cooperation and scientific agriculture; Seaman A. Knapp, Southern agent for the Department of Agriculture and adviser to the General Education Board's farm program, devised the demonstration method on farmer-owned fields; and Charles S. Barrett of the Farmers' Union worked for production controls and farm co-operatives.

In education, men of the cloth joined statesmen and schoolmen in the work of upgrading institutions of learning. The movement doubled per capita tax support between 1900 and 1917 and attracted millions from Northern philanthropists. In the Conference on Education, financed by New York merchant Robert Curtis Ogden, ministers were as numerous as educators. This organization at its inception, more-over, was dedicated to Christian education, although it later became a propaganda agency for public school needs. The closely related General Education Board, a Rockefeller foundation, gave more than one hundred million dollars to Southern education by 1921.

The place that religion of the practical sort occupied in Southern Progressivism was much in evidence in the movement against child labor. The two ministers who led this fight devoted their careers to social causes. Although best known as an opponent of child labor, Edgar Gardner Murphy also took time from his parish ministry to work for better education and racial justice. In 1900 Murphy and his fellow Montgomery ministers founded the Alabama Child Labor Committee, the first such organization in the nation. After securing legislation in that state, Murphy established the National Child Labor Committee. The continuation of this work was placed in the hands of Alexander J. McKelway, a Presbyterian minister and editor who, after reading of Murphy's efforts against the mill owners, had used the columns of the *Presbyterian Standard* to support a North Carolina child labor law. Largely because of McKelway's leadership and the backing of the American Federation of Labor, every Southern state had an age-and-hour law by 1912.

Southern churches made their most direct contribution to Progressivism through the prohibition movement. Unfortunately, the "noble experiment" has sometimes been regarded as the work of pious fanatics and political opportunists who made a sham of the progressive-reform tradition. However misguided they might have been, most of the prohibitionists operated from a deep belief that the liquor establishment was an enemy of social progress and humane values. Certainly the teetotalers were concerned about personal morality, but their case for prohibition rested on the *social* evils allegedly caused by strong drink. If the drys were naive and utopian in their reliance on legislation, such was the character of much Progressivism. If they were reacting to a changing American culture, or to a "status revolution" to use Richard Hofstadter's phrase, their motivation was not unlike that of many who patronized reform causes. The fact remains, as James Timberlake has recently emphasized, that prohibition was an authentic part of Progressivism. Most important for this study, prohibition led Southern churches to affirm a social responsibility that in future years would not be restricted to the temperance issue . . .

Southern Progressivism advanced many reforms by engaging in organized promotion and agitation such as the League employed. Conferences and crusades, specialized agencies and publications rallied public sentiment and pressured lawmakers in behalf of a host of causes: penal reform, public health, child labor laws, better schools and improved agriculture. None of these movements won the massive church support that prohibition enjoyed. However, all of them found some backing among the more enlightened lay and clerical leadership.

Perhaps the best demonstration of conspicuous clerical involvement in the broad range of social reform was the work of the Southern Sociological Congress. The Congress itself illustrated something of the scope and character of Southern Progressivism. The idea for the organization was that of social worker Kate Barnard, commissioner of charities and corrections in Oklahoma. Miss Barnard found a sympathizer in the reform governor of Tennessee, Ben Hooper, who had built a public career on the issues of prohibition, prison reform, and ridding the state of machine politics. In 1912 Hooper issued the initial call for the Congress and served as its first president. Some 700 ministers, educators, social workers, and heads of health, penal and welfare institutions assembled in Nashville for a four day meeting featuring sessions on child welfare, courts and prisons, public health, organized charities, racial problems and the social mission of the church.

The Sociological Congress met annually until 1919. The organization sought to unite public officials and professionals in a broad program of social uplift in which the South's "better citizens" would effect improvements along moderate lines. As one of the first steps toward self-improvement, the Congress sought to break down Southern isolationism. Governor Hooper, in an address to the first conference, called for a "new patriotism in the South," meaning that a national outlook should replace the region's preoccupation with its tragic past. Although the Congress dealt with regional problems, they were viewed as part of larger national issues. Recognizing that the South was already being nationalized economically, the Congress challenged the region to reach national standards in social welfare services. Although the organization encouraged criticism, even by non-Southerners who frequently addressed the sessions, a mood of optimism prevailed in all the meetings. Speeches and reports sounded the note of crisis but not despair. The delegates generally believed that the South, having just entered the industrial age, stood at the threshold of great social advancement. Such optimism resembled the Progressive spirit elsewhere in the nation, as did the emphasis on urban problems, there being no sessions at any conference on rural problems. The reliance on political remedies for social ills also followed the Progressive formula.

Besides revealing a vital Progressivism, the work of the Congress showed the prominent place of religion in Southern reform and more particularly the unmistakable influence of the social gospel. More than one-fourth of the officers and participants in the organization were ministers, many noted for their interest in social causes. Vice-President John E. White, an Atlanta Baptist pastor, had earned distinction as a dry crusader, an advocate of better race relations, and a promoter of mission work among the mountain people. The Presbyterian cleric Alexander McKelway of the National Child Labor Committee chaired the Committee on Child Welfare and presided over the second conference. The forceful General Secretary for the Congress, James E. McCulloch, was a Methodist minister, principal of a training school for social workers and an enthusiast for the institutional church. John A. Rice, whose Fort Worth church offered an institutional-type program, headed the Committee on the Church and Social Service.

Non-Southerners who addressed the Congress included leading social gospel spokesmen. Samuel Zane Batten, chairman of the Northern Baptist Social Service Commission, lectured on the church's duty to Christianize society. Walter Rauschenbusch, generally regarded as the greatest social gospel prophet, discussed the recently adopted Social Creed of the Federal Council of Churches. Charles S. Macfarland, executive-secretary for the Federal Council, addressed the Congress on four occasions, pleading for church unity in the work of social reconstruction. Graham Taylor, seminary professor and founder of a Chicago settlement house, spoke on the professional training of social workers.

The presence of the nation's foremost social gospelers and ecumenists helped establish the Congress as a kind of rallying point for social Christianity. Men of the South viewed the task of the Congress as the promotion of "civic righteousness." They challenged their churches to develop a "social ministry" and frequently employed religious appeals in behalf of reform programs. Congress secretary McCulloch commented on the "moral earnestness" of the participants. "Every word," he reported, "breathed of prayer and social justice." Each annual meeting gave program space to the Committee on the Church and Social Service.

The most striking parallel to the social gospel movement was the Social Program officially adopted by the Congress. This statement of purpose sounded very much like the Social Creed of the Federal Council of Churches. Because of its attention to sectional problems, the Social Program may be rightly considered as a distinctly Southern version of the social gospel. It addressed the region's special ills: the convict-lease system, racial injustice and educational backwardness. On the other hand, the declaration, except in its opposition to child labor, did not deal with labor problems, the issue of primary concern to the social gospel spokesmen in the more industrialized North. The remaining objectives were improved juvenile courts and reformatories, better care of defectives, uniform marriage laws, and the suppression of alcoholism and prostitution. The statement concluded with an appeal for the "closest cooperation between the church and all the social agencies" to secure these goals.

The Southern Sociological Congress effectively expressed the common hopes of a large number of socially concerned leaders who believed that the churches were essential and natural allies in any movement for social betterment. The churches themselves were quite aware of the current emphasis on social religion in America. Reactions to the new ideology ranged widely. Some churchmen were extremely skeptical, others responded with qualified approval, and still others with enthusiastic endorsement. Opponents argued that social reconstruction was based on the faulty theological principle of "regeneration through environment," a radical doctrine that could lead the church away from its primary mission of individual conversion. Moreover, the social gospel confused the church's spiritual functions with the work of secular institutions, especially the state.

Although objections to the new gospel were commonplace, they were seldom unequivocal. Many critics who by reason of their evangelical faith doubted that institutional forms of evil could be eradicated by an act of the collective will nevertheless admitted that the church had been too narrow, too individualistic, and too irrelevant to social ills. Such critics endorsed the declared objectives of social Christianity, but they expressed grave fears that the movement would make social regeneration the primary business of the church. Sensing the ambiguity of their position, they often seized upon the argument, almost in desperation it appears, that social gospel ends could best be achieved as the natural fruit of the individual regeneration. . . .

We have surveyed Southern Progressivism with attention to its religious elements in the hope of dispelling the notion that the region's church life was thoroughly in the grip of religious and political fundamentalism. The social gospel ideology broke the conservative solidarity of nineteenth century Southern religion, much as it did in the North. Churchmen of the New South became more receptive to outside ideas, more responsive to social ills and more involved in the Protestant search for secular relevance. To state the point differently, religious developments in the South, as elsewhere, were not isolated from the general trends in American culture. Although still aware of its sectional identity a half century after Appomattox, the land of Dixie consciously identified itself with a national reform era. Its churches conceded that secular goals were proper religious concerns. They accredited the work of social betterment as a kingdom enterprise and thus embraced the central idea of social Christianity.[3]

Central to Eighmy's overview was the career of Episcopalian Edgar Gardner Murphy, a pioneer reformer in child labor, education, and race relations. Even as the South has not until now been included in the story of the social gospel, just so Murphy has not been ranked among the social gospelers. But he deserves to be. As a parish priest in Kingston, New York, Chillicothe, Ohio, and Montgomery, Alabama, as organizer of the Southern Society for the Promotion of the Study of Race Conditions and Problems in the South, and as Executive Secretary of the Southern Education Board, Murphy exhibited a social consciousness that brought him national attention.[4]

Like many social gospelers Murphy did not confine the leaven of the Kingdom of God to the institutional church. Resigning from his duties at St. John's parish in Montgomery to become Executive Secretary of the Southern Education Board, Murphy told the church vestry that this was "my best response to God's will, and to the needs of our church and our country." Within fifteen months he formally resigned from the Episcopal ministry, but his letter to his bishop made it clear that his own sense of ministry would continue now freed from misunderstandings that stemmed from society's ideas about the

nature and role of the minister. H. Shelton Smith sums up his career
with the observation, "In reality, Murphy was a preacher of what was
then called the social gospel."[5]

In 1901 Murphy assumed the leadership in founding the Alabama
Child Labor Committee, the first such committee in the nation.
Alabama had enacted a law to regulate child labor in 1887, but it was
repealed in 1894. Between 1890 and 1900 there was a 386 percent
increase in children under sixteen in the Alabama mills so that by 1900
they represented one-fourth of the rapidly growing textile work force.
As the ministry of St. John's reached out to the West End of
Montgomery, Murphy came into first-hand contact with the institutional evils created by the presence of child labor and the corollary absence
of educational facilities. Marshaling support for the presentation of
child labor laws in the state legislature, Murphy discovered that efforts
to block various bills were being led by northern mill owners. Writing
on behalf of the Alabama Child Labor Committee, Murphy addressed
the following pamphlet to the people and press of New England.
Written about Alabama, privately printed and distributed free, this and
subsequent pamphlets were used in many states facing similar problems.

Child Labor in Alabama: An Appeal to the People and Press of New England

Addressing ourselves to the public conscience of those historic localities
from which so much of good has come to our common country, we ask
your help in relation to the increasing evils of child labor in the South.

Our responsibility is more directly concerned with the State of
Alabama. It is not a responsibility which we would in any sense evade.
We would not excuse the apathy of large numbers of our own people,
though that apathy is partly due to their inexperience in relation to the
conditions of manufacture. The problems presented by the factory are
new to us. Nor would we forget or condone the indifference of certain
of our legislators.

Frightened by the threat that reforms would be followed by the
alienation of capital and by the withdrawal of investments, they have
hesitated to grant what the people have not demanded. Primarily, therefore, the guilt of this economic and social wrong must lie at our own
doors. To the conditions of the problem here we are addressing ourselves with all the forces at our command. If we bring this appeal to
New England, it is not because Alabama would shift the blame, but be-

cause we confidently believe that, if you know the truth, New England will share the task.

For the responsibility is also yours. Such protective legislation as we once had was repealed by the Legislature as a concession to the demands of the representatives of a mill, recently removed from the East and operated here by Massachusetts capital. While the proportion of the children under twelve in our Northern and Southern mills is approximately the same, yet in the mills representing Northern investments, the actual number of such children employed is twice as great as the number found in the mills controlled by Southern capital. In the struggle for reform legislation before the last Legislature, the friends of the Child Labor Bill were twice given a hearing before committees. In both cases the bill was killed in committee. In each instance the most aggressive and effective opposition came from the salaried representative of Massachusetts investments; and, at the second hearing, this representative appeared alone, as the chosen spokesman of all the forces of resistance.

That one or two of these mills should be provided with library, natatorium, gymnasium, and other incidents of a spectacular philanthropy, may not obscure the fact that they are supporting a system under which hundreds of our little children are denied the most elementary opportunities for health and happiness; a system representing the condition of compulsory ignorance; a system which destroys the efficiency of our future operatives by sapping the vitalities of youth, and which—by imposing upon the tender heart of the child an environment of whirling and deafening machinery, together with the burdens of sustained and unnatural labor—has made a school of experience disastrous alike to both capacity and character.

But we know that the argument of this question is, with the people of New England, unnecessary; and, in the space permitted us, impossible. We will gladly send our literature to those who may be interested.

Of the press we earnestly request the publication of this appeal. If the answer to it should be attempted, we ask that such statements may be forwarded to this committee for consideration and reply.

We shall be grateful to those who may wish to aid us financially in the conduct of our work. But we especially ask for something far more valuable to any righteous cause than contributions to its treasury. We pray for the awakening of public interest, and for the quickening of that public conscience which recognizes, through the unity and integrity of our national life, the unity of our responsibility for the welfare of all the people. We believe that Massachusetts, having defended her own children from a cruel and unnecessary industrial system, will question

the heartless policy with which her capital is using and is striving to per-
petuate the defenselessness of the children of the South. This capital is
doing here what it dare not do at home.

Realizing, with all the peoples of the Christ, that the protection of
the little child means the preservation of everything that is worth preserving, and believing that our fellow-countrymen of the North and
East will unite with us in attempting to check this exploitation of childhood for the creation of dividends, we earnestly ask your interest and
your aid.

October 1, A. D. 1901.

> EDGAR GARDNER MURPHY, Rector of St.
>   John's   Episcopal   Church,   Montgomery
> THOMAS G. JONES, Ex-Governor of Alabama
> LUCIEN V. LATASTE, Montgomery
> J. H. PHILLIPS, Superintendent of Schools, Bir-
>   mingham
> JOHN CRAFT, Member of the Legislature, Mobile
> A. J. REILLY, Member of the Legislature, Ensley
>   *Executive Committee for Alabama*[6]

This pamphlet, as others, elicited many replies to Murphy and the Committee. Often the replies complained against the motives of the reformers, who were variously depicted as naive idealists, labor agitators, or
sectional rabblerousers. One such correspondent was Horace S. Sears,
Treasurer of the West Point Manufacturing Company of Langdale,
Alabama. In concluding a rather vituperative letter, Sears paints an idyl-
lic picture of life around the mill.

Turning from the appeal of the executive committee, a picture arises
before me of the peaceful, happy mill settlement at Langdale, with its
pretty church filled to the doors on Sundays with an attentive, God-
fearing congregation, with its large and enthusiastic Sunday-school,
with its fine school and kindergarten department, with its well-selected
library of over 1,000 volumes, with its pleasant reading room open
every week-day evening, with its assembly hall often filled with an audience attracted by a programme of the debating club, or the literary society, or the entertainment committee, with its streets lighted by elec-

tricity, and with the mill agent and his beloved wife going in and out among the homes of the people, participating in all their joys and sorrows; and knowing that this is typical of many another manufacturing village in the South, especially of those under Northern management or controlled by Northern capital, I rub my eyes and wonder whether the animus of this appeal of the executive committee is that of ignorance, or of mischievous labor agitation, or of sectional hatred, which we had hoped was long since deservedly laid away in its grave-clothes.[7]

Murphy replies by setting the child labor issue within the larger context of religious and humanitarian values.

In attempting to arrive at the "animus" of the appeal of our Committee, Mr. Sears seems inclined to attribute our statement to "ignorance," or to "mischievous labor agitation," or to "sectional hatred." Sectional hatred! And which is the more likely to induce that malignant and excuseless passion—the spectacle of the attitude of the South toward the capital of Massachusetts, or the attitude of the capital of Massachusetts toward the little children of the South? The fact that these are white children, and that Massachusetts—always solicitous for the Negro—should be largely indifferent to the fate of our white children, does not relieve the situation. Suppose the conditions were reversed, and that the mills of Southern men were full of Negro children under twelve—how quickly and how justly New England would ring with denunciation!

The fundamental principle of our appeal is not that Alabama is guiltless, or that gentlemen like Mr. Nichols and Mr. Sears are intentionally brutal. That would be unjust to them and unjust to our own sense of right and truth. Our elementary contention is, simply, that the common conscience will hold, and should hold, the capital of Massachusetts to the moral and economic standards of Massachusetts. Both Mr. Nichols and Mr. Sears have admitted that the employment of little children is "wrong" from an economic and a humanitarian standpoint. Neither gentleman has told us, and no single representative of New England investments in Alabama has yet told us, that he is ready to join us to right this wrong by direct and effective legislation.

But the appeal of our Committee has not been without response.

We care to indulge in no recriminations for the past. We have prayed that, in our approaching struggle, New England will stand with us and not against us, for we have no intention whatever of seeing her investments here embarrassed by complex and oppressive labor legislation. Our motives can not long be misunderstood. For the large and generous response which has come to us from the New England press, and from the masses of the people of New England, we are sincerely grateful. I close this letter with an expression which has just reached me. It is a telegram from Seth Low, the Mayor-elect of Greater New York, in reference to our bill now pending before the Legislature of the State of Georgia. It reflects what we believe will be the real, the ultimate, response of the North to the appeal of the South. It is as follows:—

To the Rev. Edgar Gardner Murphy, Montgomery, Alabama:
    I am heartily glad to throw whatever influence I can exert, in favor of protective legislation for the children of Georgia, strictly defining the permitted age and hours of labor in factories, on lines of similar legislation in Massachusetts and New York. Georgia ought to profit by the experience of other States. She ought not to pay for her own experience with the lives of her children. I say this as one having indirectly an interest in the Massachusetts mills in Georgia.—*Seth Low*

That is statesmanship, that is religion, that is intersectional fraternity, and that is "Education."[8]

The most significant corporate forum in the South for discussion of reform issues was the Southern Sociological Congress. A scan of the Congress programs from 1912 through 1919 reveals something of the breadth of southern Progressivism. Eighmy discusses the Congress at some length, and he is correct in pointing up "the unmistakable influence of the social gospel." This is seen clearly in both ideology and personnel. The ideology is expressed in the statement of purpose adopted by the Congress. It sounds very much like the Social Creed of the Federal Council of Churches, to be discussed in Chapter 18.

The Social Program of the Congress

The Southern Sociological Congress stands:

For the abolition of convict lease and contract systems, and for the adoption of modern principles of prison reform.

For the extension and improvement of juvenile courts and juvenile reformatories.

For the proper care and treatment of defectives, the blind, the deaf, the insane, the epileptic, and the feeble-minded.

For the recognition of the relation of alcoholism to disease, to crime, to pauperism, and to vice, and for the adoption of appropriate preventive measures.

For the adoption of uniform laws of the highest standards concerning marriage and divorce.

For the adoption of the uniform law on vital statistics.

For the abolition of child labor by the enactment of the uniform child labor law.

For the enactment of school attendance laws, that the reproach of the greatest degree of illiteracy may be removed from our section.

For the suppression of prostitution.

For the solving of the race question in a spirit of helpfulness to the negro and of equal justice to both races.

For the closest co-operation between the Church and all social agencies for the securing of these results.[9]

The Southern Sociological Congress became a platform in these years for both the veterans of the social gospel—Walter Rauschenbusch, Graham Taylor, Samuel Zane Batten, and others—and less well-known, younger persons of similar persuasion. One such man was Willis D. Weatherford, a student secretary of the Y.M.C.A. with responsibility for fourteen southern states. At the 1914 S.S.C. meetings in Memphis, as Chairman of the Committee on Organization, Weatherford became embroiled in a controversy involving Negro delegates and visitors. The National Conference on Charities and Corrections was also meeting in Memphis at the same time. On the first evening of joint meetings at the Orpheum Theatre, blacks were not segregated in the usual manner, but sat on the main floor with the white delegates. The next morning a group of Memphis businessmen protested against this arrangement to the owner of the theatre and to the two organizations. At the next night's meeting, at the direction of the N.C.C.C., blacks were strictly segregated and as a consequence walked out. The following morning, Weatherford stated that blacks would not be segregated for the evening meeting, but the local committee and the owner of the theatre would not agree to this. Weatherford thereupon moved the evening session to the First Methodist Church. The meeting was subsequently attended by the largest gathering of the Congress. This action won for Weatherford, already a courageous voice in the area of race relations, new friends in the black community.[10]

Weatherford addressed the Memphis Congress in the section dealing with race. Entitling his remarks "Religion, the Common Basis of Cooperation," Weatherford wanted the delegates to know that religion was the foundation of his own hope and strategy for amelioration of the race issue.

Now the basis of this conviction is distinctly religious. We are coming to have a greater confidence in the negro because we are coming to have a greater confidence in all humanity. We are coming to appreciate, as men never before in the history of the world appreciated, that personality is sacred, it is valuable, it is Godlike. We are coming to feel that in every human being there is the image of God. It may be distorted, the likeness may be blurred, but essentially the image is there. We are coming to feel about humanity as Jesus felt, that all are capable of becoming true sons and daughters of an eternal father. When this conception once takes hold it is profound and far-reaching. It at once means that I cannot despise my neighbor, white or colored; it means that I must actively help all those who are my neighbors—and in Jesus' splendid teachings my neighbor is he who has the deepest need.[11]

Weatherford went on to delineate the particular understanding of religion that would be helpful for the present situation.

There is another phase of religious development in the South which is significant in relation to this race problem. We are fast getting away from religion as creed or as a mechanical system. We are coming to feel more and more that religion is life and life is relationship. To be religious is to be rightly related to all persons, God and men. Or to put it differently, to be religious is to be a friendly son of God and a brotherly friend of men. Life and religion are not therefore simply orthodoxy:

some of the most deeply prejudiced people I have ever met were theologically so sound that they were all sound. No! life and religion are right relationship toward all persons. And when we say all persons we mean *all.* We mean a real democracy. Many people talk about democracy who cannot call the first letter in the alphabet of democratic life. They have scarcely seen the faintest far-off glimmerings of the ideal. Real democracy is treating *every man* as if he had value in himself. It is recognizing the essential sacredness of all persons. It is adjusting yourself into right relations with all men. This is real democracy, a more genuine democracy than Jefferson ever thought or dreamed. And that kind of democracy can be built on nothing else save a deep religious conviction that God dwells in every man. The religion which fails to base itself deep on personal relationship can avail nothing in bridging the chasm between diverged races.[12]

Like so many of the social gospelers, Weatherford was aware of the need to change both persons and institutions. Religion for him was not to be confused with "superficial humanitarianism or philanthropy," but was a religion of the Bible. Painfully aware of how the Bible had been used to repress social reform, and blacks in particular, Weatherford called for a biblical religion free to pervade and transform southern society.

It ought still further to be said that the religion of the Bible and this religion alone has the transforming power to take the ignorant, the degraded, the weak, and make them into intelligent, respectable, and aggressive characters. It is only through the transforming power of this religion that the potential sacredness in each human soul can be brought into concrete reality. This is the foundation of our new hope and our new coöperation in the South. We are seeing all about us men and women snatched from the very jaws of death—moral, social, intellectual death—men and women lifted out of the slums, the back alleys, the horrible tenement houses—and by this mysterious power made into new and vital souls, ready to bear their share in the work of the world. It is this that gives us hope.

I know not how much emphasis the remainder of the country may put on the bearing of religion in the bettering of social conditions, but this I do know: that here in the South, where our great social problem is a problem of attitude toward persons of a different race, a different color, and a different heritage, there is only one thing that is far-reaching enough, only one thing profound enough, only one thing dynamic enough to make us all into a common humanity, and that is religion. No superficial humanitarianism or philanthropy will do this.

Our problem is a problem of attitude both for colored and white. The white man must come to believe in and trust the negro, and the negro must come to believe in and trust the white man. And this trust and confidence can alone rest on the fact of transformed lives—and religion alone transforms life. We will have confidence in each other only because our father, God, has had sufficient access to our hearts, that white and colored alike shall have been transformed into a society of brotherly men. This our religion is set to do, and, although the process is slow and painful, and not a few have become weary of waiting, I believe the process is surely going forward, and white and colored alike are being transformed into more Godlike men and women.

It is therefore most fitting that in a conference on social conditions this religious basis of coöperation between the races should be given prominence. Here, and only here, can a deep note of optimism be struck; for it is this religion of the Bible alone which gives a motive big enough and true enough to float our lives out of the shallows of pessimism and prejudice into the great sea of mutual confidence, cooperation, and brotherhood.

It is my deep and abiding conviction that although our problems may be great and the strain at times hard to bear, nevertheless we are making real progress. And if our problems are ever solved, it will be because the spirit of Jesus so pervades us all that the white man will trust the colored man and the colored man sincerely believe in the white man, and both together unite with God in working out a truer and a grander destiny. Our motto is "Brotherhood." If you are with us, come on.[13]

Notes

1. For the progressive movement in the South, see C. Vann Woodward, *Origins of the New South* (Baton Rouge: Louisiana State University Press, 1951), 371–95; Arthur S. Link, "The Progressive Movement in the South, 1870–1914," *North Carolina Historical Review,* 23 (April, 1946), 172–205; Anne Firor Scott, "Progressive Winds from the South, 1906–1913," *Journal of Southern History,* 29 (Feb., 1963), 53–70; and Herbert J. Doherty, Jr., "Voices of Protest from the

New South, 1875–1910," *Mississippi Valley Historical Review,* 42 (June, 1955), 45–66.

2. John Lee Eighmy, *Churches in Cultural Captivity: A History of the Social Attitudes of Southern Baptists* (Knoxville: University of Tennessee Press, 1972).

3. John Lee Eighmy, "Religious Liberalism in the South during the Progressive Era," *Church History,* 38 (Sept., 1969), 359–72. By permission.

4. See Hugh C. Bailey, *Edgar Gardner Murphy, Gentle Progressive* (Coral Gables, Fla.: University of Miami Press, 1968).

5. H. Shelton Smith, *In His Image, But* . . . (Durham, N.C.: Duke University Press, 1972), 285.

6. Edgar Gardner Murphy, *Child Labor in Alabama: An Appeal to the People and Press of New England* (Montgomery, Ala.: privately printed, 1901), 3–6.

7. *Child Labor in Alabama,* 26–27.

8. *Child Labor in Alabama,* 36–38.

9. *The Call of the New South,* ed. James E. McCulloch (Nashville: Southern Sociological Congress, 1912), 9. For the story of the Southern Sociological Congress, see E. Charles Chatfield, "The Southern Sociological Congress: Organization of Uplift," *Tennessee Historical Quarterly,* 19 (Dec., 1960), 328–47; and "The Southern Sociological Congress: Rationale of Uplift," *Tennessee Historical Quarterly,* 19 (March, 1961), 51–64.

10. For a popular biography of Weatherford, see Wilma Dykeman, *Prophet of Plenty: The First Ninety Years of W. D. Weatherford* (Knoxville: University of Tennessee Press, 1966). Dykeman states that Weatherford acted to desegregate completely the seating arrangements (75–77). John Joel Culley, "Muted Trumpets: Four Efforts to Better Southern Race Relations, 1900–1915" (unpub. Ph.D. diss., University of Virginia, 1967), modifies this, citing local newspapers, to say that blacks still sat separately, but at the same level as whites and in sections previously reserved for whites.

11. Willis D. Weatherford, "Religion, the Common Basis of Co-operation," *Battling for Social Betterment,* ed. James E. McCulloch (Nashville: Southern Sociological Congress, 1914), 184–85.

12. Weatherford, 186.

13. Weatherford, 187–88.

III

Neglected Reforms and Reformers

Introduction

The social gospel was a call for action. And the center of its concern was the issues arising out of the city and the factory. To what extent, though, did these activists also deal with other reform issues in changing America? One of the fruits of re-visioning the social gospel has been the renovation of reforms long neglected or forgotten. Part III suggests three such topics of reform—race, women, and imperialism—but many others are being rediscovered or await further investigation.

There are diverse reasons why some reforms and reformers have been muted. It is important to acknowledge at the outset that the critical nature of certain issues—for example, race—was not appreciated during the height of the social gospel era. Having said that, we must also acknowledge that later climates of opinion have played a part in sensitizing us to the contours of such issues whenever and wherever they did exist in earlier periods of American life. Abell and May both completed their studies of the social gospel in the 1940's, when the scope of opinion was not focused on racial reform. The civil rights activities of the 1960's, on the other hand, encouraged new research into earlier episodes of racial strife and reform.

On the basis of this new research a number of observations can be made. First, it is apparent that the commitment to or substance of various reforms cannot be measured simply by the attention they received from the contemporary press or public. Washington Gladden is not a forgotten reformer, but his commitment to racial reform is not remembered in the same way as his commitment to labor and municipal reform. The particular Gladden sermon published here for the first time has been forgotten, not published in its own day perhaps because it was not deemed sufficiently noteworthy. From our perspective, this sermon is of considerable interest, particularly as it focuses on the ideologies of Booker T. Washington and W. E. B. Du Bois.

Secondly, certain historical caricatures now need revising in the light of more complete investigations. Josiah Strong is one American leader who comes readily to mind when turn-of-the-century imperialism

101

is recalled. It might seem that Strong deserved most of the barbs subsequently hurled at the ideology at the heart of his 1885 study, *Our Country*. That this is not the full story is the burden of the essay and selection contributed by Paul Toews. Having recently completed a study of Strong, Toews asks us to re-examine Strong's discussion of the possibilities of a new international order in the light of the implications of a kingdom theology.

Thirdly, we still need a clearer appreciation of the contributions of women reformers if we are fully to renovate the social gospel story. That renovation should concentrate both on women who participated in the full range of reform activities and, in particular, on women and men involved in the women's issue. Many women and many issues were part of the rise of the social gospel. Jane Addams is the best-known woman reformer associated with the social gospel, but Vida D. Scudder, Anna Howard Shaw, Lucy Hammond, and many others also took part in the movement. We chose Frances Willard as the subject for Chapter 12 because, though she was once one of the best-known Americans, she has been allowed to slip from memory even as one of the causes she championed—temperance—seems to be part of a bygone era. Her story deserves to be told again if only by way of illustrating how the temperance movement became a vehicle for what is today an issue of very great import—the women's issue.

10   The Souls of Black Folk

Washington Gladden has been called "the father of the social gospel."
His wide-ranging ministry spanned six decades between the Civil War
and World War I. Not usually thought of as a man involved in the
"Negro question," Gladden was actually interested in the race issue all
his life. A central vehicle of his involvement was the oldest and
strongest of the church groups working for the education of the freedmen, the American Missionary Association. Having supported A.M.A.
educational activities since the earliest years of Reconstruction, at the
beginning of the twentieth century Gladden was elected to the
presidency of the association. In this position he was vitally involved
in the continuing discussion within the A.M.A. about the nature and
purpose of education for blacks, just as this discussion was becoming
a debate on a larger scale between various spokesmen within the black
community.

By the 1890's the leading voice within the black community belonged to Booker T. Washington. Shortly after Gladden's election as
President of the American Missionary Association, he commented in
a sermon, "Few men of whatever color are better entitled to the
gratitude and honor of Americans than Booker T. Washington." This
viewpoint remained unchanged until a series of experiences on a trip
to the South profoundly challenged and then redirected Gladden's
thinking.

In 1903, Gladden was invited to give the baccalaureate sermon at
Atlanta University, address the university's eighth conference on
Negro problems, and preach at the First Congregational Church, a black
congregation. The conference for "The Study of Negro Problems"
chose the Negro Church as its subject in 1903. The conference organizer was W. E. B. Du Bois, at that time a younger professor at Atlanta
University, a school of A.M.A. origin. During the days in Atlanta
many people and events made a deep impression on Gladden, but it
was Du Bois who made the most lasting imprint. Du Bois was just at
this time developing his own ideas about education, economics, and

politics, and calling for a positive demand for full black manhood instead of a posture of accommodation. He expressed these ideas forcefully in a short volume of essays that had just been published, *The Souls of Black Folk*. Containing a critical essay on Booker T. Washington, *The Souls of Black Folk* helped crystalize anti-Tuskegee sentiment while at the same time continuing to establish Du Bois and his ideas as viable alternatives in what would quickly escalate into a power struggle within the black community. Du Bois gave a copy of his book to Gladden, and on the train trip home its pages consumed his interest, so much so that *The Souls of Black Folk* formed the basis of his sermon the next Sunday in Columbus, Ohio.

"Some Impressions Gained during a Visit to the Southern United States" was indeed a remarkable sermon, and what follows are the concluding sections from it. Gladden here attempted to understand the admittedly strident voice of W. E. B. Du Bois at a time when most of Gladden's counterparts, Lyman Abbott, editor of the *Outlook*, for example, were critical if not hostile to Du Bois. Although Gladden had long championed industrial education, which its adherents said would result in economic advancement, he here indicates an apprehension that the Negro's economic plight was directly related to his political status. What is more, Gladden was aware that prejudice was such a primitive but complex phenomenon that it would be naive to think that educational or economic advancement would easily overcome it. Here is the gist of the sermon:

I turned away from this promising Congress with keen regret—the more so as four or five white citizens of Atlanta had appeared at the morning session; but I bore with me in my satchel a book which I was eager to open, and all that sultry afternoon as the swift limited express plunged through the red cuts, or swung around the low hills, or rushed through the narrow valleys of Western South Carolina and North Carolina these pages held me fast. I shall never disassociate the appeal of this notable book from that flying panorama. *The Souls of Black Folk*,—that is the book's name, and its author is Professor Du Bois of Atlanta,—a graduate of Fisk, and afterward a graduate and prize winner of Harvard,—a student at the University of Berlin,—having in his veins the blood of a French planter of Jamaica and a Dutch burgher of New York, and a captive woman from Africa,—himself a native of the Housatonic valley of Massachusetts. Professor Du Bois is, perhaps, the most cultivated man among the American Negroes; his is a highly organized, sensitive, practical nature, albeit his mind is thoroughly trained and his investigations of the race problem evince a genuine scientific habit. This book is a series of sketches and studies, sometimes historical, sometimes descriptive, sometimes analytical, sometimes biographical. I cannot undertake to tell you about it. I only wish to reflect, very briefly, the impression which it has made upon my own mind. I have read in the *Outlook* a review of it, comparing it with Booker Washington's books, greatly to its disparagement. I hope that none of you will accept that judgment until you have read *The Souls of Black Folk.* The account of the book there given is not, I think, a fair account. I do not wish to depreciate, in the slightest degree, the words of Booker Washington; but this book gives a complementary view which we must get and hold firmly if we wish to grasp the whole truth of this burning question.

It is easy to charge hypersensitiveness and morbidity upon the author of this book, but I try to put myself in his place and I cannot bring myself to censure him! He is accused of being ashamed of his race; I do not think that this is true; but the fact that his race is in a position of inferiority, and that the prevailing sentiment of large portions of the country means to keep it there, is a fact which he cannot ignore. Imagine yourself living in a civilization whose overwhelming sentiment puts you into a lower value of being and means to keep you there; do you think you could help making that sentiment a pretty large part of your own consciousness? "It is a peculiar sensation," says this Negro, "this double-consciousness, this sense of always looking at one's self through the eyes of others, of measuring one's soul by the tape of a world that looks on in amused contempt and pity. One ever feels his two-ness,—an American, a Negro; two souls, two thoughts, two unreconciled strivings; two warring ideals in one dark body, whose dogged strength alone keeps it from being torn asunder."

The history of the American Negro is the history of this strife,— this longing to attain self-conscious manhood, to merge his double self into a better and truer self. In this merging he wishes neither of the older selves to be lost. He would not Africanize America, for America has too much to teach the world and Africa. He would not bleach his Negro soul in a flood of white Americanism, for he knows that Negro blood has a message for the world. He simply wishes to make it possible for a man to be both a Negro and an American, without being cursed and spit upon by his fellows, without having the doors of Opportunity closed roughly in his face.[1]

That psychological experience I can dimly understand, and I do not think it altogether morbid. I can see how the environment which helps a white man to come to unity with himself, tends to force upon the black man a divided consciousness. It must be a great disadvantage; a serious handicap to him in all his intellectual and moral progress. We may tell him to ignore all this, not to care for what others think of him, to respect himself, and it is well, doubtless, for him to say all these things to himself; but I think that *we* have surrounded him with a social obfuscation which is somewhat stifling or rather heartless when we exhort him to take deep breaths and not mind it. It seems to me that our first business is to do what we can to purify the atmosphere which he must breathe.

I cannot follow Professor Du Bois through the discipline of this pathetic and appealing book. I want you all to read it. It will give you, I think, a deeper insight into the real human elements of the race problem than anything that has yet been written. It will show you something of what is hidden from the careless eye in *The Souls of Black Folk,* and what we all ought to be able to discern.

In these last few years, several things have happened to the Negro in this country with which we cannot as a nation afford to be too well content. In the first place he has been, in a large portion of the South, practically disfranchised: I do not object to the disfranchisement of ignorance and criminality: I would be quite ready to see the suffrage limited to those who were qualified to exercise it; but when one law is made for black men and another for white men, the injustice is so glaring that it cannot endure.... The iniquitous legislation by which the Negro has been shut out of political privilege will have to be repealed or modified, so as to open and keep open before him the door of hope for full citizenship.

In the second place there has been a tendency to disparage the higher education of the Negro and to put the emphasis of his need wholly on individual education and economic efficiency. That, I am sure is a mistake, surely a mistake of proportion. Doubtless he does need the manual training, the ego-winning faculty, but he needs more than this, and he needs it now. The Negro man, no more than the white man, can live by bread alone.... Booker Washington puts much emphasis upon the development of economic efficiency among the Negroes. That is, indeed, a crying need. But you will find, if you read the Du Bois book, that his political degradation has much to do with his economic inefficiency. In large sections of the South today he is in a condition of practical peonage. His loss of political power has resulted in conditions little better than slavery.

Nor can we be too confident that mere material thrift would give him the freedom and respect which are needful to his manhood. Mr. Washington emphasizes the argument that if the Negro will but succeed in a material way all doors will be open to him. But that is not quite certain! The history of the Jews is evidence enough that industry and thrift do not disown race prejudice. The worst offence of the Jew in Europe today is his economic efficiency. It is for his industry and thrift that he is hated; the Russian priesthood stirs up the populace against him because he works and saves and prospers. I fear that Mr. Washington is putting too much weight on economic efficiency as the solvent of race prejudice.

All that Booker Washington is doing we may heartily rejoice in; but there are other things that must not be left undone. These other things, I believe are becoming increasingly clear to many southern men. Mr. Proctor[2] asked me what the outcome of this race problem was going to be. I told him that it was going to be liberty and opportunity and manhood for the Negro; and that the help which he needed was going to come largely through the awakened moral sentiment of the Christian people of the South. It is impossible that these millions of white Christians should shut out of their minds and hearts the great ideas of human brotherhood which are accumulating in human thought, which envelop them like an atmosphere, and which are changing, everywhere, the spiritual climate. It is impossible that they should resist the altruistic understanding of this faith.[3]

In April, 1908, a remarkable meeting took place in Atlanta. Three white men and four black men met together for six hours to discuss the racial situation in the South and how it might be improved. All agreed that a major source of amelioration could be the young white college students populating the resurgent southern colleges and universities. Walter R. Lambuth, Missionary Secretary of the Methodist Episcopal Church, South, suggested that a book be written that would inform and challenge the college generation about the present racial situation in the South. All were agreed that the man who had called the meeting, Willis D. Weatherford, should be the author.

The fruit of Weatherford's research and personal experience appeared in 1910 as *Negro Life in the South*. By 1912 over 10,000 copies of the book had been studied by college men and women in the South, the number increasing to 30,000 copies used by nearly 50,000 students by 1916. The success of the venture was not simply in the

printing of such a volume, but in the fact that it was discussed and applied according to a strategy carefully worked out by Weatherford,
who was the Y.M.C.A. Student Secretary for colleges in the South and
Southwest. Weatherford had actually tried out the first draft of the
book on a summer college conference in North Carolina in 1909. He
was amazed to find that of the five seminars being offered, over half
the members of the conference signed up for the first attempt at talking about what was advertised as "The Negro Problem."

In 1911 reports poured in of the book's success. William L.
Poteat, President of Wake Forest, reported that 207 students were
enrolled in study groups. The University of Virginia, the home of
the first Y.M.C.A. student association, communicated that more men
were enrolled than ever before in a mission study. At Washington and
Lee University in Virginia, a young student named Francis Pickens
Miller was involved in the student Y.M.C.A. when Weatherford's book
was published. Miller would one day succeed John R. Mott as
General Secretary of the World Student Christian Federation. In
1949, he would make a courageous but losing bid for Governor of
Virginia, running on a platform that was remarkable for its progressive attitude towards blacks. In a recently published memoir, Miller
tells what caused a change in his thinking about the Negro:

> It was in one of these [YMCA] groups that I first began to take a
> serious interest in our race problem. I collected a number of
> students who were willing to discuss together a little book en-
> titled *The Negro in the South* that had just been written by W. D.
> Weatherford, the student Y.M.C.A. secretary for the southern
> region. What he said set in motion trains of thought and action
> which profoundly influenced my attitudes.[4]

For seven years Weatherford had talked and listened to both
whites and blacks in his travels as Student Secretary. The most lasting
impression of these years became the theme of *Negro Life in the
South*, stated in italics on the last page, "It is not the negro that is on
trial before the world, but it is we, we white men of the South." In
this pioneer work, the first textbook in the field, Weatherford was
cognizant of the range of attitudes held by both whites and blacks.
In the beginning of the study he spoke a word in defense of the
South's past conduct. However, the tone changed quickly as he
challenged the usual southern argument that the white man in the
South knew more about and could therefore better solve the race
question.

Our Ignorance of the Facts

My first answer to why we should study this question is, that we, as Southern college men, are woefully ignorant of the facts. It has been said hundreds of times in print and from the platform that this question cannot be handled by the Northern man, because he is hundreds of miles removed from the scene of action, and does not know the facts. I believe that most of the Northern men are coming to accept the truth of this statement, and most of the best informed negroes, such as Booker T. Washington, are saying plainly that the North does not and cannot know, at least under present conditions, the real race problem. With this first statement, there is always coupled the second, that the Southern white man does know and can therefore solve the Southern race question. I deliberately challenge this statement. I feel perfectly sure that we, as Southern white men, know much more of real negro life than men of other sections can possibly know; I feel sure also of the fact that the best and more broad minded men of the South are more intensely interested in this question than men in any other section can possibly be; and I further feel sure that this question, if ever solved, must be solved by the broad minded Southern men leading the way and calling to their aid the broad minded and philanthropic men of all the nation. But do we as Southern men know the negro?

Knowledge of Servant Class Only

We know the negro as a hired servant in our homes. We know Aunt Mary, who cooks our meals, who waits on our table or acts as housemaid in our homes. We know John, the butler, or the coachman, or the gardener. We know the day laborer who cleans the street or hauls the coal, or runs the grocery wagon. We know one or two negro men who, because of more intelligence, have positions as mail carriers, and perhaps we know half a dozen negroes who, because of skill and hard work, have entered the list of skilled employment. But all of these we know only in their work. We do not know their thought; we do not know their religious life; we do not know their home life.

The Church, the Home, the School

Probably the three best indices of the real character of a people are their religion, their schools and their homes. Of the religious life of the negro, we, as Southern men, know almost nothing. Most of us have not visited half a dozen negro churches in our lives, and then only as onlookers, rather than attempting to enter into the spirit of the service

and trying to find its real message. Neither have we studied their school
life. We have passed the negro school house every day of our lives, have
seen the negro college perched on the hill, but never have we visited
these places more than once or twice to see what was actually going on
in them. It has never occurred to most of us that these school buildings
have anything of interest for us, and nine cases out of ten we do not
know the negro preacher or the negro teacher who presides over the
nearest church or school. Neither do we know the home life of the
negro. I have again and again asked groups of college men how many
negro homes they had ever entered. I have rarely ever found men who
had been in more than two or three or half a score at the most. Even
where men have gone into negro homes, they have been of the poorer
type. It has been the home of the washwoman, the cook or the servant
man. The real life of the negro we do not know. There is much justice,
though it hurts us as Southern men to admit it, in the statement of Ray
Stannard Baker, after his careful and, on the whole, fair minded observations of conditions in the South:

"But, curiously enough, I found that these men rarely knew anything about the better class of negroes—those who were in business, or
in independent occupations, those who owned their own homes. They
did come into contact with the servant negro, the field hand, the common laborer, who make up, of course, the great mass of the race. On
the other hand, the best class of negroes did not know the higher class
of white people, and based their suspicion and hatred upon the acts of
the poorer sort of whites, with whom they naturally come into contact.
The best elements of the two races are as far apart as if they lived in
different continents; and that is one of the chief causes of the growing
danger in the Southern situation. It is a striking fact that one of the
first—almost instinctive—efforts at reconstruction after the Atlanta riot
was to bring the best element of both races together, so that they
might, by becoming acquainted and gaining confidence in each other,
allay suspicion and bring influence to bear on the lawless elements of
both white people and colored."

It is not fair to judge a race by its weaker exponents alone, neither
is it fair to judge a race simply by one aspect of its life. We must know
its whole life before we can claim to know the race. If we are to have a
right to speak with any authority on this race question, and if we are to
have our proper share in bringing about a true race adjustment, we will
need to study with care all the essential activities of this race. To what
other group of men can this appeal be so fairly made, and from what

other group of men should there be such ready response as from college men?[5]

In the final chapter of *Negro Life in the South*, Weatherford encourages his readers to translate their new knowledge into action. He reminds them, however, that any social awakening has its roots in an ideological awakening. After identifying three elements of that awakening, Weatherford challenges his readers with what, for him, is the real question for race relations.

What Can We Do?

Present Social Awakening

Ours may be characterized as a sociological age. Men are thinking today in terms of social life. It would be safe to say that more books dealing with social questions have come from the press within the last twenty-five years than in all the previous centuries of the world's history. There is a widespread awakening to the facts of all humanity and a consequent interest in them. One would scarcely dare to say that this is a wholly modern movement, for it has its roots deep in the soil of the past, but its flower can hardly be said to have burst into bloom until this present generation.

World Unity

At least three elements—each of which have had much accentuation during the last decade—have entered into this growing social consciousness. First of these may be mentioned the principle of a spiritual monism. Slowly, but surely, philosophy has been moving away from the various forms of dualism, until it now proclaims a unifying element in the universe, into which all forces and all beings are caught up and knit into one complete whole. Behind the forces of nature there is a supreme force; behind the lives of the universe, there is a supreme life; and these blend into a complete and perfect personality, whom Christians call God. Such seems to be the decided tendency of science and philosophy.

Sacredness of the Individual

The second element is but a corollary of the first—the growing sacredness of the individual. If all life is unified in one supreme life, each individual is enhanced in value because it is a part of the all inclusive and the universal. It partakes of the divine nature, and is to be judged not by what it possesses, but by what it is and by that to which it is related. This thought is as old as the book of Job, for there the writer says: If I have despised the cause of my man-servant or of my maid-servant, when they contended with me; what then shall I do when God riseth up? And when he visiteth, what shall I answer him? Did not he that made me in the womb make him? And did not one fashion us in the womb? Job 31:13-15. This was the supreme teaching of Jesus Christ—out of which grew His universal sympathy—but, strange to say, the Christian Church is just coming to realize the tremendous meaning of this conception.

Social Responsibility

Growing out of these two is the third element of modern social ideals, namely, the sense of responsibility which one man feels for the well-being of all other men. If there is one supreme person—a Father God; if each individual is caught up into that Godhood and so becomes sacred; then, each man is brother to his neighbor, just because they are both alike sons of God—and every true brother must be interested in, and, so far as his power extends, responsible for, the welfare of every other brother in this universal household. Such, it seems to me, is the real meaning of this new social awakening. . . .

The Real Question

Now, the real point of the race question is not *shall we have social intermingling—but shall we recognize that the other man has a soul, is a real human personality*—in spite of the fact that he often lives on a back alley, wears poor clothes, uses a broken language, and has a black skin. I have sometimes felt that we really do not believe the negro is possessed of human personality.

This fact came to me with intensity some years ago as I was riding on a Pullman car through Alabama. We stopped rather long at some small station, and I noted, without asking the cause, that a very large crowd of colored people were gathered on the station platform. After the train had started again, a traveling man, who had gone out to see what was wrong, returned to the car, and was asked by his companion the cause of the delay. "Oh, nothing," replied the drummer, "one 'nigger' shot another, and they were loading the wounded one on to carry him to the nearest town with a hospital." Then and there it dawned upon me that we really did not appreciate the sacredness of humanity, provided that humanity be clothed in a dark skin.

Professor DuBois describes in beautiful and heart-searching English the death of his own baby boy. He tells how dark the day seemed to him as the carriages rolled along through the crowded streets of Atlanta behind the hearse, which carried the lifeless form of the child, as dear to him as life. As the crowd parted for a moment to let the procession pass, some one inquired who it was that had died. Professor Du Bois heard the reply as it broke in upon his saddened heart—"Just 'niggers.' " Do you wonder that he is sometimes bitter?[6]

Notes

1. W. E. B. Du Bois, *The Souls of Black Folk* (Chicago: A. C. McClurg, 1903), 16.

2. Henry H. Proctor was pastor of the First Congregational Church of Atlanta, a black congregation. The next year, when Gladden was elected Moderator of the National Council of Congregational Churches, he would honor Proctor and the black community by appointing the Atlanta minister as Assistant Moderator.

3. Washington Gladden, Sermon, "Some Impressions Gained during a Visit to the Southern United States," May 31, 1903, Washington Gladden Papers, Ohio Historical Society, Columbus, Ohio. This sermon is preserved in the original handwritten manuscript. Certain words were transcribed from the longhand only tentatively and with great difficulty.

4. Francis Pickens Miller, *Man from the Valley* (Chapel Hill: University of North Carolina Press, 1971), 18–19.

5. Willis D. Weatherford, *Negro Life in the South* (New York: Association Press, 1910), 3–7.

6. Weatherford, 149–51, 151–53. For an example of a study outline of the race problem, see Josiah Strong, "The Race Question" (Studies in the Gospel of the Kingdom), *Homiletic Review*, 58 (Aug., 1909), 122–29. These lessons were also published separately in *The Gospel of the Kingdom.*

11   The Imperialism
of Righteousness

While devoting most of their energy to reform activity within the boundaries of the national state, the social gospelers never lost sight of the universal dream inherent in their kingdom theology. Reform of the nation only presaged international reform. This dream of global justice has frequently been seen by historians as a cloak for the less idealistic economic and political expansion of a burgeoning industrial economy. Josiah Strong's *Our Country* is often cited as prime evidence of the presence of vulgar imperialism. That interpretation, however, misrepresents the full range of his ideas and the tradition in which he stood. Strong's internationalism was tied to his vision of the coming kingdom of God and his understanding of the role of nations in ushering in that kingdom. From the general proposition that nations are purposive agents in God's historical drama he deduced a special role for the United States. This nation had a special providential part to play in realizing the kingdom. The nation was more than a nation. It was the chosen instrument to move the world toward solidarity and righteousness.

Our Country was not intended to be a reasoned apology for American expansion. From Strong's point of view the purpose of the entire book was to arouse Christians to embrace the work of purifying the nation internally. By suggesting the nation's international destiny, Strong hoped to awaken nationalism, not internationalism. Much as he later would invoke nationalistic sentiments to encourage internationalism, he was now using a heightened sense of international destiny to gain greater commitment to national reform. The American adoption of the world was present in Strong's thought in 1885, but his preoccupation at that time was with the Christian community's involvement with the nation. His sustained call for American expansion came in 1900 with the publication of *Expansion under New World Conditions.*

The new world conditions were a mixture of national greatness and

Note: Chapter 11 is by Paul Toews, who also contributed Chapter 6, above.

114

the emerging industrial order. They required renunciation of that form of traditional American isolation which had become negative, a myth which Washington's Farewell Address, as an example, had helped to foster. Isolation, a noble dream in an earlier century, now imposed unwarranted limitations on the nation's destiny. All great peoples—the Greeks, Romans, and Hebrews—developed centrifugal tendencies that were essential to the fulfillment of their high missions. America now faced a comparable decision.

Strong understood industrialism as irreversibly altering the trends of history. Before the nineteenth century, history was marked by diversity and isolation. Industrial economics and technological communications could now produce oneness and interdependence. Routine issues of the industrial society had come to be international issues. The world would become integrated and internationalized just as the national economy had. Strong found this gratifying because the new interdependency foreshadowed the global unity of the kingdom of God. To the degree that economic and political expansion accelerated this new universalism they were altruistic. The trend was economically inevitable and religiously productive.

Given the realities of international dependence, Strong saw several alternatives that the nation could adopt. It might retain the illusion that isolation was possible. That would disregard the new realities. It might embrace the European style of internationalism, which was unscrupulous and ambitious imperialism. That was too profane. The nation selected by God for a special destiny would need to combine globalism with spirituality. This country would bring to the new political and economic interdependency a fresh universal consciousness based on Christian ethics. Since this was the most Christian nation, its obligations to internationalism were obvious. Other peoples, by reason of their religious failures, were not equipped to inaugurate the enlightened Christian conscience.

This interplay of nationalism and internationalism which shaped Strong's view of the nation's global mission carried within it the potential for considerable subversion. His pleas were for the expansion of Christian idealism. His own international activities were humanitarian. He produced a dazzling vision of the "imperialism of righteousness," but with few safeguards. Strong failed to see that the cloak of righteous internationalism carried within it the seeds of sordid and selfish imperialism. The Spanish-American War revealed the flaw. He wanted the nation to be a moral force in the world. He accepted and welcomed imperial possessions in order to discharge the nation's obligation to itself and others. Apparently only by being an imperial power could it be a moral force. The "imperialism of righteousness" could easily decay into the "righteousness of imperialism."[1] Strong, however, seemed unaware of the danger. He saw himself as a Christian soldier marching into the kingdom.

This selection is from Strong's *Expansion under New World Conditions,* published in 1900—just after the Spanish-American War:

This world life is something greater than national life, and world good, therefore, is something higher than national good, and must take precedence of it, if they conflict. Local, and even national, interests must be sacrified, if need be, to universal interests. Or rather, world interests will prove to be the best criterion by which to judge of national interests, and it will ultimately be seen that he serves his country best who serves the world best, because the well-being of the member is found to depend on the health or well-being of the life of which it is a part.

Of course this world conscience is as yet feeble, because the world life is as yet in its infancy. But this world life, as we have seen, is real, and its further development cannot be reasonably doubted. Increasing communication and commerce will certainly render relations between the nations more intimate and complex, and as these relations become closer, friction will necessarily increase unless they are right relations. Thus a world life necessitates a world conscience which, as far as possible, shall hold the nations to an ethical standard common to the world.

Of course a Christian nation can adopt for its own standard nothing less than Christian ethics. A government cannot justly be called Christian unless it is controlled by Christian principles. "The state ought to be," as Milton said, "but as one huge Christian personage, one mighty growth or stature of an honest man."

It goes without saying that no state has as yet realized Milton's ideal, but has not the time come to adopt and confess that ideal? And is there not precisely here a sacred obligation and a noble opportunity for our nation?

God winnowed Europe for the seeds of civil and religious liberty with which to sow America, and kept this soil virgin until that seed could be developed, selected, and transported, that the new experiment in self-government might be tried under the most favorable conditions; and the success of democracy here has compelled the princes of Europe to reckon with the peoples of Europe.

Again has Providence prepared the world for an upward step, and for a new experiment to be tried under the most favorable conditions. The time has come for a new political philosophy and ethics which will meet the new world conditions and satisfy the claims of the new world life. On entering into the politics of the world it will be practicable for this nation to set up a new standard of national obligation that will be consonant with the individual conscience, and to adopt political ethics which will not outrage Christian ethics.

We are not called to take this step as a weakling, compelled to follow the lead of stronger nations in adopting the selfish and therefore immoral standards which have been consecrated by precedent and hallowed by time. That call comes to us in the recognized might of our manhood. Conscious of our strength, we may bind ourselves with the law of right and justice, aye, and of benevolence too, without being charged with weakness or fear. Unbound by habit and untrammeled by precedent in world politics, we may set for ourselves a new standard of national obligation which shall recognize the new world life, of which national life is a part, and which the nation is bound to serve with a purity of purpose for which it will be held answerable at the bar of the world conscience.

Let this nation prove the practicability of righteousness in international affairs, let it demonstrate that the recognition of world interests as supreme is the farthest-sighted wisdom, the highest statesmanship, the purest patriotism, and other nations will at length be compelled to follow our example and to accept the same political ethics. . . .

If we love justice for ourselves, but not for others, it is ourselves we love, not justice. If we love liberty for ourselves, and not for all the world, we love it as a selfish luxury, not as a principle.

It is heathenish to measure obligation by proximity or by blood-relationship. Christian ethics declares that whoever is found wounded on the Jericho road is our neighbor, and our neighbor is to be loved not only as a brother, but as ourselves. Moral obligation cannot be computed from a genealogical chart, nor measured with a yardstick. Duty does not, like gravitation, vary inversely as the square of the distance.

All this does not mean that the Anglo-Saxon race should become a Don Quixote, riding atilt at every windmill on the world's horizon, "but it does mean the consciousness in ourselves and the declaration to others that our national sympathies are everywhere on the side of justice, freedom, and education; it does mean the natural self-consciousness that in this respect our spirit and that of the people of Great Britain are one; and it does mean that the enemies of justice, freedom, and education the world over must hereafter reckon with America and Great Britain as the open, avowed, and courageous friends of these inalienable rights of humanity."

Such a world policy as is urged is not only justified, but required, by the new world life on which we have entered. True enough it is unprecedented, but so are the new world conditions which demand it. The wise words of Emerson, true when written, are peculiarly applicable today: "We live in a new and exceptional age. America is another word for opportunity. Our whole history appears like a last effort of Divine Providence in behalf of the human race; and a literal, slavish following of precedents, as by a justice of the peace, is not for those who at this hour lead the destinies of this people." Conservatism demands precedents; progress creates them. The first precedent is always unprecedented. The world moves.

It is time to dismiss "the craven fear of being great," to recognize the place in the world which God has given us, and to accept the responsibilities which it devolves upon us in behalf of Christian civilization.[2]

Notes

1. E. Berkeley Tompkins, *Anti-Imperialism in the United States: The Great Debate, 1890–1920* (Philadelphia: University of Pennsylvania Press, 1970), 11. For other views of Strong, see James Eldin Reed, "American Foreign Policy, The Politics of Missions and Josiah Strong, 1890–1900," *Church History* 41 (June, 1972), 230–45, and Dorothea R. Muller, "Josiah Strong and American Nationalism," *Journal of American History* 53 (Dec., 1966), 487–503.

2. Josiah Strong, *Expansion under New World Conditions* (New York: Baker and Taylor, 1900), ch. 9, "A New World Policy," 269–74.

12 Christian Women and Politics

For women, religion has always been a force both for repression and for liberation. If Elizabeth Cady Stanton, first president of the National American Woman Suffrage Association, was compelled to denounce the Bible and most clergymen, other leaders, most notably Frances E. Willard and Anna Howard Shaw,[1] were animated by a religious faith of wide-ranging social dimensions. Most interesting, from the standpoint of contemporary perspectives, is the often-forgotten story of the impetus given to the women's movement in the late nineteenth century by the Women's Christian Temperance Union, "the greatest women's organization of the century."[2]

In recapturing the dynamism of the early women's movement the modern reader must deal with the popular picture of the W.C.T.U. Because of this imagery—moralizing Puritans invading the privacy of other peoples' social habits—Frances E. Willard became forgotten until the renaissance of the women's movement in our own day. The details of Willard's life were once well known to nearly all schoolchildren. Remembered in stone in our nation's capital, the victim of hagiography after her death, she was, according to Sidney Ahlstrom, "the single most impressive reformer to have worked within the context of the evangelical churches."[3] A member of the Knights of Labor, increasingly open to the aims of Christian Socialism, she attacked the liquor trade not as a prude but as an early progressive armed with the insight that "demon rum" was a major factor contributing to the wretched existence of the poor in changing America.

Temperance had been part of the reform energies of the Evangelical United Front. Before the Civil War, thirteen northern and western states had emulated the initiative of Maine in passing various dry laws, but shortly after the war only Maine remained among the "drys." The renewal of the movement was brought about through what has become known as the Women's Revolution, a remarkable series of demonstrations and pray-ins. Begun in Hillsboro, Ohio, on December 24, 1873, and soon to spread throughout Ohio and to neighboring states, the tactics used call to mind similar strategies invoked eighty years later on behalf of another righteous cause. In hearing again Willard recount these episodes we catch something of the passion and idiom of the movement.

Thus have I tried to set forth the sequel of that modern Pentecost called the "Women's Crusade." That women should thus dare was the wonder after they had so long endured, while the manner of their doing left us who looked on, bewildered between laughter and tears. Woman-like, they took their knitting, their zephyr work or their embroidery, and simply swarmed into the drink-shops, seated themselves, and watched the proceedings. Usually they came in a long procession from their rendezvous at some church where they had held morning prayer-meeting; entered the saloon with kind faces, and the sweet songs of church and home upon their lips, while some Madonna-like leader with the Gospel in her looks, took her stand beside the bar, and gently asked if she might read God's word and offer prayer.

Women gave of their best during the two months of that wonderful uprising. All other engagements were laid aside; elegant women of society walked beside quiet women of home, school and shop, in the strange processions that soon lined the chief streets, not only of nearly every town and village in the state that was its birthplace, but of leading cities there and elsewhere; and voices trained in Paris and Berlin sang "Rock of Ages, cleft for me," in the malodorous air of liquor-rooms and beer-halls. Meanwhile, where were the men who patronized these places? Thousands of them signed the pledge these women brought, and accepted their invitation to go back with them to the churches, whose doors, for once, stood open all day long; others slunk out of sight, and a few cursed the women openly; but even of these it might be said, that those who came to curse remained to pray. Soon the saloon-keepers surrendered in large numbers, the statement being made by a well-known observer that the liquor traffic was temporarily driven out of two hundred and fifty towns and villages in Ohio and the adjoining states, to which the Temperance Crusade extended. There are photographs extant representing the stirring scenes when, amid the ringing of church-bells, the contents of every barrel, cask and bottle in a saloon were sent gurgling into the gutter, the owner insisting that women's hands alone should do this work, perhaps with some dim thought in his muddled head of the poetic justice due to the Nemesis he thus invoked.

And so it came about that soft and often jeweled hands grasped axe and hammer, while the whole town assembled to rejoice in this new fashion of exorcising the evil spirits. In Cincinnati, a city long dominated by the liquor trade, a procession of women, including the wives of leading pastors, was arrested and locked up in jail; in Cleveland, dogs were set on the crusaders, and in a single instance, a blunderbuss was pointed at them, while in several places, they were smoked out, or had the hose turned on them. But the arrested women marched through the streets singing, and held a temperance meeting in the prison; the one assailed by dogs laid her hands upon their heads and prayed; and the group menaced by a gun marched up to its mouth singing, "Never be afraid to work for Jesus." The annals of heroism have few pages so bright as the annals of that strange crusade, spreading as if by magic, through all the Northern States, across the sea and to the Orient itself. Everywhere it went, the attendance at church increased incalculably, and the crime record was in like manner shortened. Men say there was a spirit in the air such as they never knew before; a sense of God and of human brotherhood.

The W.C.T.U. was organized in 1874, and Willard, who had recently resigned as Dean of Women at Northwestern University, was appointed one of the first officers. Early on she became embroiled in a dispute between the "conservatives" and "liberals" within the organization, the issue being whether the temperance union should focus on the single issue of prohibition or campaign broadly for reform issues important to the women's movement. Backing away from the "conservative" viewpoint, Willard resigned in 1877 and worked for a while with evangelist Dwight L. Moody. In 1881 she won the presidency of the W.C.T.U., signaling not simply a personal triumph but a victory for the "liberal" outlook. With renewed energy she pushed the W.C.T.U. into the middle of the newly organized Prohibition party. A culmination of many of her efforts was the party convention of 1888. According to Willard, "the presence of the new school in politics and of women as an active power in public affairs to a degree before undreamed of, mark it as a sort of moral watershed."[4] Partly through her own adroit use of pressure politics a platform was constructed that, beginning with the temperance issue, championed suffrage and related reform issues.

The Prohibition party, in national convention assembled, acknowledging Almighty God as the source of all power in government, do hereby declare:

1. That the manufacture, importation, exportation, transportation, and sale of alcoholic beverages should be made public crimes, and prohibited as such.

2. That such prohibition must be secured through amendments of our national and state constitutions, enforced by adequate laws adequately supported by administrative authority; and to this end the organization of the Prohibition party is imperatively demanded in state and nation.

3. That any form of license, taxation, or regulation of the liquor traffic is contrary to good government; that any party which supports regulation, license, or tax enters into alliance with such traffic, and becomes the actual foe of the state's welfare; and that we arraign the Republican and Democratic parties for their persistent attitude in favor of the licensed iniquity, whereby they oppose the demand of the people for prohibition, and, through open complicity with the liquor crime, defeat the enforcement of law.

4. For the immediate abolition of the internal revenue system whereby our national government is deriving support from our greatest national vice.

5. That, an adequate public revenue being necessary, it may properly be raised by import duties, and by an equitable assessment upon the property and legitimate business of the country, but import duties should be so reduced that no surplus shall be accumulated in the treasury, and that the burdens of taxation shall be removed from foods, clothing, and other comforts and necessaries of life.

6. That the right of suffrage rests on no mere accident of race, color, sex, or nationality, and that where, from any cause, it has been withheld from citizens who are of suitable age and mentally and morally qualified for the exercise of an intelligent ballot, it should be restored by the people through the legislatures of the several states, on such educational basis as they may deem wise.

7. That civil service appointments for all civil offices chiefly clerical in their duties, should be based upon moral, intellectual, and physical qualifications, and not upon party service or party necessity.

8. For the abolition of polygamy and the establishment of uniform laws governing marriage and divorce.

9. For prohibiting all combinations of capital to control and to increase the cost of products for popular consumption.

10. For the preservation and defense of the Sabbath as a civil institution, without oppressing any who religiously observe the same on any other day than the first day of the week.

11. That arbitration is the Christian, wise, and economic method of settling national differences, and that the same method should, by judicious legislation, be applied to the settlement of disputes between large bodies of employés and employers. That the abolition of the saloon would remove burdens, moral, physical, pecuniary, and social, which now oppress labor and rob it of its earnings, and would prove to be the wise and successful way of promoting labor reform, and that we invite labor and capital to unite with us for the accomplishment thereof. That monopoly in land is a wrong to the people, and that the public land should be reserved to actual settlers, and that men and women should receive equal wages for equal work.

12. That our immigration laws should be so enforced as to prevent the introduction into our country of all convicts, inmates of other dependent institutions, and all others physically incapacitated for self-support, and that no person should have the ballot in any state who is not a citizen of the United States. [5]

Even as elsewhere the social gospel reached out to the emerging labor movement, Willard forged an alliance with the Knights of Labor. Founded in 1869, under the leadership of Terrence V. Powderly, who was elected General Master Workman in 1879, the Knights grew in membership from a few thousand to 730,000 in 1886. In 1887 Willard was given membership in the Knights of Labor. Her biographer, Mary Earhart, describes Willard's support of the labor movement as part of her continuous intellectual and social awakening.

Her open espousal of labor, despite the adverse public opinion of the day, was a logical step in the intellectual development of Frances Willard. She had shown socialistic tendencies before her association with the Knights. The Prohibition party platforms of 1884 and 1888, to which she not only thoroughly subscribed but whose policies she had helped to formulate, were tinged with socialistic theories. The root of her socialism was probably lodged in western political thought, which called for government control of railroads, an income tax, a national banking system, and other approaches toward state socialism. She merely carried state regulation further to the left than the rank and file of westerners. The Knights were considered extreme in their views, especially by the people of the East. No Socialist party had yet been organized, so that most people along the seaboard were shocked by such radicalism, some of which has since been included in our democratic creed. The American free-land policy, of course, was socialistic, although rarely regarded in this light.[6]

Despite growing criticism of her increasingly radical positions, Willard nevertheless linked the temperance, labor, and women's movements.

As a result of her inquiries, she found Terence V. Powderly, the General Master Workman, a stalwart supporter not only of the temperance cause but also of the purity program. She appealed to him and his loyal order to help with the petitions she was securing for Congress in the interest of better protection of girls. With his promising assurance of support on the purity petitions, she promptly added the labor movement to the activities of the Union, notwithstanding some trenchant criticism of this course within her own ranks. His splendid co-operation in this matter created a bond of friendship between them and between the two organizations. Thereafter, representative women of the Union frequently appeared on the platform of the Knights at their annual meetings. And Frances Willard always commended the Knights for their stand on suffrage, temperance, and equality of women in labor. She even was initiated into the order in 1887.

To carry along her cohorts of the Union it was essential to establish the bridgehead between temperance and labor. This was not difficult. Obviously, men addicted to drink were not the best workmen or the best husbands and fathers. Powderly himself was a total abstainer and adjured his Knights to be likewise. So the link was forged between factory, home, and temperance. The two organizations held similar views regarding the need for a Sunday closing law. The Union had long advocated the Sabbath as a day of rest. Frequently, temperance leaders presented petitions to local and national legislative bodies praying for bills to close shops and amusements on this day. The Knights likewise petitioned legislative bodies for a Sunday closing law. Although their motivation may have differed somewhat, the two organizations were well joined in this objective. So pleased was the leader of the Union to have labor's support on this issue that she was even willing to help the workingman secure the Saturday half-holiday and glibly told her followers how this would aid in the dedication of Sunday. She said: "Our department of Sabbath Observance may well co-operate with the Knights of Labor in securing the Saturday half-holiday that is sure to come, and which will do more than any other one measure to change the Sabbath from a day of recreation to a day of rest and worship."

The co-operation of the Union with the Knights of Labor, however, was not a one-sided advantage. Labor benefited too. Miss Willard by this time dominated a large body of liberal-minded, churchgoing, philanthropic, and third-party constituents. Her influence probably extended to several million people. For two decades the press of the land eagerly carried her views on politics, morals, and religion. Support of such a national figure was no small triumph for the nascent labor movement.[7]

Thus it was that Frances Willard molded the temperance movement in such a way that it became a vehicle for suffrage and related issues of the women's movement. She was increasingly liberal on social issues, but "beneath her zeal was the burning evangelical faith which she had always communicated with such unparalleled effectiveness."[8] She left a balanced heritage for others to build on.

Her greatest contribution in politics was that she opened the way for women to participate in party deliberations. By raising the Prohibition party to a potential third-party threat she dramatically emphasized the importance of women in party politics. With her graphic success before their eyes, the Republicans hastened to open their ranks to a few key women. Miss Willard was also significant in politics, in that she made thousands of women politically minded who had never before even realized the function of a party. Woman in politics, therefore, dates from Frances Willard's alliance with the Prohibition party. This activity, however, was more significant as a part of the wide-sweeping woman's movement than it was as a special contribution to politics.

The work of Frances Willard as reformer was so closely linked with that of the whole woman's movement that one was an integral part of the other. But her two outstanding reforms were the compulsory study of temperance in the public schools, which was adopted in practically every state and territory by the end of the century, and the drive on social purity, which induced state after state to revise its laws raising the age of consent to sixteen and eighteen, where before it had ranged from eight in the more backward states to fourteen in the more enlightened. So far as temperance was concerned, she was the first to show the relationship of the saloon and the home, which was so effective in enlisting the women by the hundreds of thousands on the side of prohibition. The impact of such a force was largely lost for temperance, as has been pointed out, through the diffusion of energy into many channels. Its effectiveness, therefore, was not for prohibition but as cohesion for the organization itself. "Temperance" was the binding force which drew and held this multitude of women together for a quarter of a century.[9]

Notes

1. Anna Howard Shaw, the first woman ordained in the Methodist Protestant Church and for nearly twelve years President of the National American Woman Suffrage Association, is claimed by a recent biographer as an authentic representative of the social gospel movement. See Ralph W. Spencer, "Anna Howard Shaw," *Methodist History*, 13 (Jan., 1975), 33–50.

2. Sydney E. Ahlstrom, *A Religious History of the American People* (New Haven: Yale University Press, 1972), 868. Two studies of the woman's rights movement are Eleanor Flexner, *Century of Struggle: The Woman's Rights Movement in the United States* (Cambridge, Mass.: Belknap Press of Harvard University Press, 1959, and Aileen S. Kraditor, *The Ideas of the Woman Suffrage Movement, 1890–1920* (New York: Columbia University Press, 1965).

3. Ahlstrom, 870.

4. Frances E. Willard, *Glimpses of Fifty Years: The Autobiography of an American Woman* (Chicago: Woman's Temperance Publication Association, 1889), 469–70.

5. Willard, 437.

6. Mary Earhart, *Frances Willard: From Prayers to Politics* (Chicago: University of Chicago Press, 1954), 246. By permission of the University of Chicago Press.

7. Earhart, 247–48.

8. Ahlstrom, 870.

9. Earhart, 382.

IV

Resources and Strategies for
Social Salvation

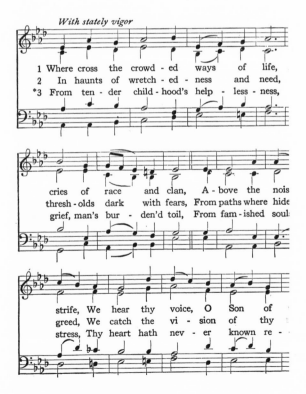

With stately vigor

1 Where cross the crowd - ed ways of life,
2 In haunts of wretch - ed - ness and need,
*3 From ten - der child - hood's help - less - ness,

cries of race and clan, A - bove the nois
thresh - olds dark with fears, From paths where hide
grief, man's bur - den'd toil, From fam - ished soul

strife, We hear thy voice, O Son of
greed, We catch the vi - sion of thy
stress, Thy heart hath nev - er known re -

Introduction

The new social sciences and the social gospel marched hand in hand through the final decades of the nineteenth century and the first of the twentieth. In this chapter these trends will be described and the reader introduced to some pioneer sociologists, teachers, politicians, and other proponents of social religion.

Professor Richard T. Ely, the leading spirit in the organization of the American Economic Association in 1885, was a prominent advocate of the social gospel;[1] the first meeting of the Association appealed to the church, "the chief of the social forces of this country," to join in "the revolt against the laissez faire theory," the investigation of the problems of social science, and the solution of "vast numbers of social problems" that lay "in the direction of practical Christianity."[2] A first handbook of *Practical Christian Sociology* appeared in 1895 and two years later the Reverend W. D. P. Bliss, whom the reader met in Chapter 3, brought out a monumental *Encyclopedia of Social Reform* that, revised and reprinted on 1,300 pages in 1908, became the forerunner of the great *Encyclopedia of the Social Sciences* of two decades later.

The importance of an adequate understanding of social science to the reformer or minister was pointed out in 1902 by the United States Commissioner for Labor, the distinguished Carroll D. Wright, Ph.D., when he told an audience of clergymen that he would not presume to speak on "the necessity of knowledge in the science of sociology."

[But] it may be intimated that the pulpit is not a lyceum, is not a platform for the especial discussion of sociological questions, but that it is and should be a medium of instruction on those deep, practical, religious principles which, applied to ordinary, everyday human affairs, will lead to a better understanding, to a truer reform than we have seen, and to the enlightenment of men. The attempt to apply religion to sociological conditions, without a knowledge of all that the science of society can disclose in any particular direction, comes very near to being an intellectual, if not a moral, crime. The pulpit is the place for the deepest religious instruction; but, as the deepest religious instruction means the welfare of the human race in its social relations, the pulpit has a power for good or evil in this direction which cannot be estimated. Let the teaching of the pulpit be in the light of actual sociological science, and then the broadest and the most satisfactory results will be reached. Whoever undertakes to study science in any department, . . . without understanding the religious interpretation of the facts which these sciences disclose, falls short of his duty, falls short in his comprehension of the real, living Christ that pervades all elements of all society and all revelations of science.[3]

The social gospel also utilized the techniques of the newly developed social survey to obtain a realistic picture of the actual social and religious needs of specific neighborhoods. It asked the sociologists for help in revising the curricula of Protestant theological schools, and some seminary professors themselves became students of social science, introducing field work and providing clinical opportunities for their students to experience social problems at first hand in the settlement houses, many of which were the agencies of theological schools, churches, or religious associations.

The ideas and hopes thus generated were portrayed in fiction; at least one such tract in which religiously-motivated reform was depicted, borne on a slender plot with a sentimental romance, rivaled the Bible itself in popularity. Dozens of magazines, Sunday School lessons, home missionary courses, and Christian socialist papers all sought to reach the church-going public. Denominational presses published their own materials while church federations emphasized the values of cooperation. The more sensitive religious leaders realized that the social gospel would lack emotional drive until it became an accepted part of the Christian cultus, so men like Walter Rauschenbusch and Frank Mason North wrote prayers and composed new hymns often set to old tunes.

All critics of the social gospel have pointed scornfully to its lack of political realism, but it must be remembered that in the Progressive era it was part and parcel of the political creed of hundreds of reformers and politicians, of whom Theodore Roosevelt and Woodrow Wilson were the most outstanding. One leading historian has gone so far as to declare that "in a real sense, Progressivism was the social gospel in practice."[4] From the perspective of the 1970's the various forms of Christian socialism appear naive, but most of their programs were adopted, sooner or later. And finally, in this chapter we shall observe, as an example of ten or a dozen such, how one leading denomination integrated the social gospel into its permanent organizational structure.

Notes

1. His *Social Aspects of Christianity* (New York: Crowell, 1889) was widely read; see also R. T. Handy, *The Social Gospel in America* (New York: Oxford University Press, 1966), 171–250, for an excellent sketch of Ely and a representative selection of his writings. In *Social Aspects,* Ely summarized the aim of the American Economic Association as "to advocate no opinions, but simply to strive to find out the underlying principles of industrial society, and to diffuse information among the working classes and all classes. Briefly stated, its purpose is to study seriously the second of the two great commandments on which hang all the law and the prophets, in all its ramifications, and thus to bring science to the aid of Christianity" (24–25).

2. Ely, "Report of the Organization of the American Economic Association," in its *Publications,* (1886), nos. 1, 9, 18.

3. Carroll D. Wright, *Some Ethical Phases of the Labor Question* (Boston: American Unitarian Association, 1902), 22.

4. Carl N. Degler, *Out of Our Past* (New York: Harper & Row, 1959), 371.

13   The Rise of the Social Sciences

In the early days of American sociology, many of its pioneers approached their subject from a religious or ethical point of view. Professor Scott Nearing of the Wharton School of the University of Pennsylvania began a book on *Social Religion* in 1913 with this challenge:

> While misery remains in the land; while men are condemned to underpay and overwork; while women are forced into prostitution, and children are compelled to labor, there will be need for a Social Religion.[1]

Two years earlier, Nearing's colleague of the political science department at Penn, Simon N. Patten, attempted to place a scientific foundation beneath religion by transferring its doctrines "from the traditional basis to the realm of social science." Here are the opening and closing paragraphs of *The Social Basis of Religion*:

This book is not an apology for religion, but a constructive defense. It identifies religion, not with morality, but with the social reaction against degeneration and vice. Were all men moral and normal, religion would have less vitality; it grows in power as the pressure of external conditions forces men into degradation and misery. Religion and morality are the reverse sides of a larger scheme of purifying and elevating humanity.

A generation ago the defense of religion was a subject of popular discourse. Thoughtful men wrote books on Christian Evidence that were widely read and made the basis of popular discussion. Many books are still written about religion, but they are mainly occupied with an exposition of its moral doctrines. It is regarded sufficient if it is shown that personal morality is advantageous and beyond the assaults of adverse critics. It seems to be taken for granted that the beliefs of earlier generations have been overthrown and that religion must utilize its waning forces to uphold morality and social stability. The Christian plan of salvation, however, is as important as ever and as capable of defense. It has fallen into disrepute, not because it lacks proof, but because its historical setting has been lost through the increase of knowledge and through better methods of investigation. If we make religion social instead of historical, proof can be found for its essential doctrines. I do not mean that all modern thought is in harmony with the Christian scheme of salvation, but that an energetic defense of it has fair chance of success. This is made clear by a restatement of the plan of salvation so as to emphasize its modern aspects. The following are its essential doctrines expressed in social instead of theological terms:—

1. The doctrine of one supreme God.

2. The doctrine of the fall of man, or of social degeneration.

3. The doctrine of regeneration, or the reincorporation of social outcasts into society, in contrast with the doctrine of elimination.

4. The doctrine of a personal uplift through contact, influence and suggestion, in contrast with the doctrine of evolution through biologic variation.

5. The doctrine of progress through peace and love, in contrast with progress through conflict.

6. The doctrine of the Messiah, or of lofty inspiring leadership, in contrast with the material concept of civilization.

7. The doctrine of service, in contrast with self-centered aggression.

8. The doctrine of social responsibility, in contrast with individual rights.

9. The doctrine of personal responsibility in contrast with fatalism or external domination.

10. The doctrine that the wages of sin are death.

Each of these doctrines is capable of a vigorous defense, and if stated in social terms the opposition to them does not come from science, but from a mistaken concept of history. Science is a method of proof, not a dogma. Any problem becomes scientific when it is so formulated that evidence may be collected, sifted and directed to a decision. It is true that every proposition about religion is subject to dispute; but it is equally true that none is without many verifying facts and principles. . . .

In religion these anticipations become the doctrine of a Messiah, a looked-for leader who will displace despair and defeat with courage and accomplishments. The origin of this anticipation is obscured by the claim that the predictions about Christ did not arise out of a natural inclination to seek for help and an equally natural belief that it would come. Yet nothing is plainer than that the depressed, hopeless condition of the Jewish nation must lead to such anticipations. Human hopefulness revolts against failure; it sets up goals to strive for. National ideals are anticipatory, and from them come some of the strongest motives that elevate humanity and give stability to political institutions. It is equally clear why after the death of Jesus, the Christ ideal should become prominent. Christ was to return immediately and in great glory. All the failures of the past were to be wiped out in the reconstruction and redemption He was to bring. The Christ of the future thus displaced the Jesus of history in the thought of the early Christians; with the change came hope in the place of despair. All this was a natural movement which elevated and strengthened the church until it changed its basis from anticipation to tradition. It thus became an authority that depressed, instead of a hope that strengthened. The old spirit and enthusiasm would come again if this process were reversed. We can have an upbuilding religion only when it looks to the future and arouses faith in human betterment.

The crust of religious tradition and the doctrine of total depravity have kept the social anticipations of modern races from assuming a religious form. Religion separated from national aspirations has remained static. The tendency towards social anticipation has been active in forming utopias and in creating ideals about the natural man and the brotherhood of men. The democratic spirit has done much to arouse anticipations of social reconstructions which blend and elevate humanity into a harmonious whole. The growth and stability of modern nations has also helped to turn men's attention to the future. Each nation has bright hopes of what is to come and expects an increase in power and influence that will transform and elevate the whole world. To-day anticipation is largely centered about socialistic schemes and gives them reality. Socialism is a combination of an economic program of reform and of an ideal reconstruction of society that is to follow. With its present emphasis on class struggle it is antagonistic to religion; but when class struggle has disappeared and the material obstacles to social progress are surmounted, social anticipation will be more prominent. Religious and social aspirations will then harmonize. Socialism will go the road of previous reforms. As the economic program for which it stands is worked out or displaced by a better one, the social background will blend with other movements of a similar nature and lead to a religious upbuilding. All progress starts with a definite scheme of economic reform coupled with new hope of social reconstruction. The economic part of the program depends for its success on definite changes. When these are made, there is a residue of social anticipation which unites with earlier anticipations to create higher social ideals. The same anticipation which shows itself in national life, in political reform and in socialism is also beginning to show itself in city life. This new unit about which social interests grow unites a program of improvement with anticipations of a higher social life. City planning, health and prosperity give a new direction to social ideals which in the end will be transformed into a religious movement to reconstruct what is within man as well as what is about him. The new City of God will not only be well planned, healthy and prosperous, but will also be the center of spiritual aspiration.

More powerful than any of these hopes and a complement to them is the thought of bodily and mental evolution as voiced by the eugenic movement and the disciples of a superman. Like other reforms, they start with a program that makes them antagonistic to religion. This especially is true of the superman concept, which has been made the base of a self-centered morality. There will be a direct clash between social morality and the unsocial morality at present associated with the concept of a superman. The conflict, however, is with the two types of morality and when social morality shows its superiority, the thought of a superman will survive the defeat of its morality. The Christ ideal is the superman viewed socially. Christ is one type of leader for the human race in its ascent, physical, mental and religious. The other type is the self-centered egoist who moves up through the elimination he creates. The contrast between progress by redemption and progress by elimination will be amply illustrated in the struggle between these two views. Both, however, contain social anticipation in a clearer and more vivid form than any antecedent social movement. Out of this transformation a movement in thought is coming that will force religion to discard traditions and dogmas that separate it from other social ideals. The blending of all social aspirations is but a matter of time. When it comes, social religion will have its full growth and be the expression of the forces that upbuild men and make social thought dominant.[2]

The social gospel also appropriated the techniques of the social survey. The most significant early socioreligious survey was that of Hartford,

taken by the Connecticut Bible Society in 1889 under the direction of
Professor Graham Taylor and largely carried out by his students in the
Hartford Theological Seminary. This compilation analyzed the population by nationalities and denominations, with a count of families,
domestics, and boarders, according to denominational preference and
church membership. The relative numbers of Protestants and Catholics, as well as Sunday School statistics, were tabulated in a 40-page report containing many graphic presentations. "Destructive forces" such
as saloons were enumerated; some mention was made of prostitution;
jail and "town farm" populations were studied; considerable space was
devoted to description of preventive, relief, industrial, and social
agencies—churches, young people's societies, missions, temperance
groups, boys' clubs, the Young Men's and Young Women's Christian
Associations, and a number of charitable institutions. An associated
charities organization was declared to be Hartford's greatest public
need. In concluding the report, Taylor wrote:

> This is an age when the study of social science is in its inception.
> It should be the science of Christian society. Its field is the world,
> including all classes and conditions of men from all nationalities.
> Its work is to investigate the conditions of social and personal
> life, discover the causes of suffering and the sources of inharmo-
> nious relations. When Christian sociology has done all this, it will
> be more possible to adjust differences, and harmonize the varying
> elements by applying the principles of Christianity.

The most famous religious survey, which did much to stimulate
church federation, was that carried on by the "Federation of Churches
and Christian Workers in New York City," an organization founded in
1895 largely through the instrumentality of the Reverend J. Winthrop
Hegeman, Ph.D. The census of Manhattan was begun about 1897 in
the Fifteenth Assembly District, between Forty-third and Fifty-third
Streets and Eighth Avenue and the Hudson River. Ten churches and
two religious organizations cooperated in this first survey. It was
found that in an area containing some 40,000 people, approximately
one half were neither church members nor attendants; 10 Protestant churches had a total membership of only 1,798, with but 7
pastors and 2 church visitors.

The Federation soon improved its technique and asserted a posi-
tion of genuine leadership under the direction of the Reverend Walter
Laidlaw, Ph.D., who had been trained in Germany and at New York
University. The census next took in a district contiguous to that first

surveyed. Concerning its work here the Federation reported in 1899 that two churches had been founded, public baths opened, libraries and a new park established, and "one of the most active and successful industrial settlements in the city" located; the religious life of the neighborhood had been "notably benefited," with pastors and workers meeting monthly to confer on the problems of the district. One minister declared that the survey had "secured a more thorough knowledge of the religious and irreligious condition of the neighborhood" than he had been able to obtain in twenty-five years. Publicity had brought in money and workers; kindergartens, clubs, cooking schools, and libraries had been started.

These were among the first fruits of the Federation's plans for bringing "the organized intelligence and love of our churches to bear upon the material, social, economic, civic, and spiritual interests of the family life of our city, and through interdenominational conference and cooperation to meet its every religious and moral need." The method whereby this was to be accomplished comprised the survey, cooperation of the Federation with existing agencies to meet the needs disclosed, and aid in the creation of new agencies as needed.

In taking the district census workers called upon every family, entering their findings upon carefully prepared cards. In addition to religious facts, information was secured concerning living quarters, length of residence, church affiliation, number and ages of children, occupations of all members of the family, boarders, and domestics, and many other items. The tabulation of this material gave the Federation a tremendously valuable and significant fund of authoritative sociological data concerning many phases of metropolitan life. In time it became a clearing house for information on races, nationalities, housing, and similar matters of great concern to welfare agencies and like organizations. It published studies of various aspects of the areas canvassed, dealing with tenements, saloons, parks, playgrounds, baths, kindergartens, and economic conditions. The Federation furnished churches with information about their parishes, distributed handbooks of the churches and social agencies, interpreted the United States Census, listed and rated various denominational enterprises, provided an exchange for the registry of church-extension schemes, and issued reports of religious and sociological conferences and their findings. Valuable data were published in the quarterly *Federation,* of which a remarkable edition was, for example, that for June, 1902, entitled *Handbook of Population and Religion in New York City*.

The religious purpose of these manifold activities was kept clearly in sight. The philosophy of the organization was once phrased as "devotion to the life which is more than meat . . . more than the largest wealth" and "devotion to men, in the midst of commercial processes, rather than to things." Christ's demands upon the church were declared to be "the removal of all traces of the commercial spirit from religion" and "the production of a society which will exhibit and demonstrate to the world the Fatherhood of God." The originating ideal of the Federation had been to utilize all agencies "fitted to bring Christ into the homes of the city." Its attempt to correlate all efforts to improve "the spiritual, physical, educational, economic and social interests" of the families of the nation's greatest metropolis marked this organization as the leader of the forces that were working for church coöperation, and that were utilizing the techniques of social science in the application of the social gospel.

As a result of the development of such techniques as these, and of the ministrations of the institutional church and the religious social settlement, the churches were recognized as significant social-service agencies. In 1907 an entire issue of the *Annals* of the American Academy of Political and Social Science was devoted to *The Social Work of the Church*. Social-gospel theory and descriptions of institutional church work, religious settlements, and social work, and discussions of difficult problems such as the church and the workingman, all written by experts, filled this 128-page volume. In 1911 the National Conference of Charities and Corrections discussed whether the church ought to inspire, interpret, guide, or administer social work. Viewpoints were presented by Washington Gladden and seven other Protestant and Catholic speakers.[3]

One of the most far-reaching actions in the social gospel period was the introduction of ethics, social science, and field work into the curricula of the Protestant schools for the training of ministers. Such changes were first discussed in the 1870's, were pioneered at Andover and Harvard in the next decade, and became fairly widespread in the 1890's. At Harvard, Francis Greenwood Peabody used the case-study method as an inductive approach to ethics but did not explore problem situations or delve into sociology.[4] At Andover, William Jewett Tucker, whom the reader met in Chapter 4, did exactly the opposite, exposing his students to field work and visitations to factories, prisons, tenements, labor unions, and correctional institutions.

All these developments were exemplified in the extraordinary career of Graham Taylor, who left his Hartford pastorate in 1892 to establish the first professorship of "Christian Sociology" at Chicago Theological Seminary. By 1894 he had opened "Chicago Commons," a settlement house in a working-class district peopled by German, Scandinavian, and Irish immigrants. When he began teaching he found that there were no textbooks, so he wrote them; his *Syllabus*, described below, was a fresh invention that marked him as an educational innovator as well as a "pioneer on social frontiers," if we may paraphrase the title of his autobiography, which is one of the great books of its kind.[5]   Involved not only in the training of ministers but also with social work in the slums, Taylor became a leader of reform in Chicago and ultimately a national social gospel figure. Nearly forgotten by the 1970's, Taylor's career was well recognized during his lifetime by such friends as Jane Addams, the founder and head of Hull House, another Chicago settlement.

Dr. Taylor [she wrote] was among the first men to introduce a systematic study of sociology into a theological institution, at Chicago Theological Seminary. Therefore, from the standpoint of a student of social history, familiar with the development of organised religions, he knows that the religious synthesis, or rather the competing religious syntheses, are constantly changing and differentiating themselves in response to special needs; that such adaptations in organised religion are evolved not only because new needs confront the Church from without, but also because there is a vigorous minority within the Church whom the existing forms of expression no longer satisfy.

It was as "a member of this inner group" that Dr. Taylor had written the book to which her remarks were an introduction, continued Miss Addams. In it, he "directly and fearlessly points out the adaptation going on in the Church at the present moment and the need for further changes":

Because the desire for just human relationships has seized upon the imaginations of a multitude of our contemporaries, it is possible that a group within the Church is now demanding that a new form of social action shall express their yearning sense of justice and compassion, quite as the schoolmen once insisted that creeds and dogmas should embody their philosophy, or the artists that their absorbing desire for beauty should be built into cathedrals and painted upon the walls of shrines. This thirst for beauty and order in human relationships may seize upon the religious spirits of our time as the desire for personal holiness and for unbroken communion with God, in another period of history, drove thousands of men to spend their lives in hermitage or monastery.

Certainly a distress of spirit for social wrongs, "the burden of souls," as Dr. Taylor calls it, expresses itself in many ways, as the most casual observer may see. Many a young person whose attention is fixed and whose emotions are absorbed by the vast and stupid atrocities of contemporary life—its aimless waste, its meaningless labour, its needless suffering—finds his only relief from the abiding horror over the existence of such things in the heated conviction that they are not inevitable. He expresses himself in such well-worn phrases as "there must be some way out," "such a state of things was never intended," "human nature can no longer tolerate it." . . .

As a sympathetic student of social movements, understanding the larger hopes of men, in the early years at Chicago Commons Dr. Taylor every week presided over a "free-floor" discussion where men of all social faiths were made welcome. Chicago was at that time characterised by a challenging discussion of the existing social order. Each school of social philosophy preached not so much its own remedies as the necessity of clearing away much of the present industrial organisation before any remedies could be applied, or rather before social reconstruction could begin. Even among the socialists there were many radicals of more zeal than learning, who felt that the end of the competitive system was approaching and urged a morality such as could be applied only to a world on the brink of destruction. These ardent speakers, therefore, distrusted all tendencies towards social improvements and denounced any compromise on the part of socialists with the existing state. They looked askance at any accommodating spirit evinced by a capitalistic society, and at the growing humanitarianism of an enfeebled bourgeoisie. Above all they disliked the theory of the common interest of labour and capital for which the social settlement stood, as well as the gradual interpenetration of the two classes.

In spite of these radical differences, Dr. Taylor held the respect of these men of various social beliefs, shall we say, because of his religious faith in the unity and solidarity of mankind. He judged them righteously and generously, not as disturbers of the peace, but as men who like himself were concerned that the knowledge of economic forces should be intelligently applied to the progress of society. He did not despise half-baked theories, because as a student of economic history, he was familiar with the fact that each distinct historical epoch begins with striking economic changes which society joyfully hails as indubitable signs of progress, but that soon after the more sensitive men of the epoch begin a long struggle to make the social readjustments, and that at last the epoch ends with more or less reorganisation.

Miss Addams then went on to describe the various contributions that Taylor had made to the improvement of Chicago—his membership on the Vice Commission and on Illinois state commissions that obtained "effective legislation to protect the workers from dangerous machinery and insanitary conditions, and to safeguard life and property from loss in the mines," his active identification with the Municipal Voters' League of Chicago, his twenty years' residence at Chicago Commons, his instrumentality in founding the Chicago School of Civics and Philanthropy [which ultimately became the Graduate School of Social Service Administration of the University of Chicago], and finally his well-deserved recognition through the presidency of the National Conference of Charities and Correction.[6]

We conclude this chapter with a backward look at Taylor's struggle to prepare materials for his students:

The pioneer character of this teaching was well illustrated in Graham Taylor's efforts to develop a Biblical Sociology. Hampered both at Hartford and later at Chicago by the absence of materials, he nevertheless developed his course into a well-rounded survey of Christian sociology. Printed in 1900, his *Syllabus of Biblical Sociology* outlined its data in five divisions. Subject and method were defined as ". . . the attempt to collate and classify the social phenomena and relationships referred to in, or inferable from, Scriptural data and teachings, and to apply the inductions from the same to the development of life, individual and social, in accordance with the Divine ideal . . ." Such a methodology would be based upon the life and words of Christ, particularly in his conception of the kingdom of God. The second part of the course traced the origins of the kingdom idea in the Old Testament, and the third outlined a Christian social order as disclosed by Christ, taking up his social ideals. Next the social life and teachings of the early church were studied, and lastly the fundamental social concepts of the Bible synthesized. Taylor pointed out to his students that the important spheres of social life there delineated were the family, the neighborhood, and the areas of economic, political, and religious activity. Of these "the source and norm of society" and "the primary unit of state and church" were the family. Field work was carried on at Chicago Commons, which Taylor had founded partially to provide a clinic for his students.[7]

Notes

1. Scott Nearing, *Social Religion, An Interpretation of Christianity in Terms of Modern Life* (New York: Macmillan, 1913), vii.

2. Simon N. Patten, *The Social Basis of Religion* (New York: Macmillan, 1911), 3–5, 244–47.

3. C. H. Hopkins, *Rise of the Social Gospel* (New Haven: Yale, 1940), 275–78.

4. F. G. Peabody, *Jesus Christ and the Social Question* (New York: Macmillan, 1903).

5. Graham Taylor, *Pioneering on Social Frontiers* (Chicago: University of Chicago Press, 1930); see also Louise C. Wade, *Graham Taylor, Pioneer for Social Justice, 1851–1938* (Chicago: University of Chicago Press, 1964).

6. Jane Addams, "Introduction," to Graham Taylor, *Religion in Social Action* (New York: Dodd, Mead, 1913), xi-xxxv.

7. Hopkins, 168–69; Taylor, *Pioneering*, 390–99.

14 Popular Culture and Social Religion

Leaders of the social gospel early realized that the new ideology could accomplish little unless it reached the people in the pews. In this chapter we shall look at representative examples of the many expressions of social gospel ideas in popular forms—fiction, Sunday-School lessons, magazines, prayers, hymns, and lyceum and Chautauqua lectures and courses of study.

Although most Protestant church members of the decades around the turn of the century would have disdained to pick up a dime novel at the corner newsstand, they did consume millions of copies of fictionalized propaganda for the social gospel. These stories usually rode on overly sentimental romances and were normally laid in the puzzling new urban context about which thoughtful Americans were concerned. British Christian Socialism had been stimulated a generation earlier by two lesser novels—*Yeast* and *Alton Locke*—by Charles Kingsley (mentioned in Chapter 3), better known for *Hypatia* and *Westward, Ho!* Millions of Americans of that generation had been profoundly affected by *Uncle Tom's Cabin.* As the social gospel began to emerge it appeared in fictional form in dozens of paperbacks, but only one reached mass market circulation that is impressive even in the twentieth century: *In His Steps,* by Charles M. Sheldon, a Congregational minister of Topeka, Kansas. In 1933 Sheldon estimated, perhaps too generously, that the book had sold 23,000,000 copies and had then been translated into twenty-one foreign languages.

The story was written to draw young people to Sheldon's Sunday evening services, each episode being read from the pulpit, something like the early movies that ended with "continued next week." The book opened with a "dusty, worn, shabby-looking young man" confronting the fashionable congregation of the "First Church of Raymond" after a smooth sermon on "following Jesus." A short excerpt reveals the genre:

"I'm not an ordinary tramp, though I don't know of any teaching of Jesus that makes one kind of a tramp less worth saving than other. Do you?" He put the question as naturally as if the whole congregation had been a small Bible class. He paused just a moment and coughed painfully. Then he went on.

"I lost my job ten months ago. I am a printer by trade. The new linotype machines are beautiful specimens of invention, but I know six men who have killed themselves inside of the year just on account of those machines. Of course I don't blame the newspapers for getting the machines. Meanwhile, what can a man do? I know I never learned but the one trade, and that's all I can do. I've tramped all over the country trying to find something. There are a good many others like me. I'm not complaining, am I? Just stating facts. But I was wondering as I sat there under the gallery, if what you call following Jesus is the same thing as what He taught. What did He mean when He said: 'Follow me!' The minister said," here the man turned about and looked up at the pulpit, "that it is necessary for the disciple of Jesus to follow His steps, and he said the steps are 'obedience, faith, love and imitation.' But I did not hear him tell you just what he meant that to mean, especially the last step. What do you Christians mean by following the steps of Jesus?

"I've tramped through this city for three days trying to find a job; and in all that time I've not had a word of sympathy or comfort except from your minister here, who said he was sorry for me and hoped I would find a job somewhere. I suppose it is because you get so imposed on by the professional tramp that you have lost your interest in any other sort. I'm not blaming anybody, am I? Just stating facts. Of course I understand you can't all go out of your way to hunt up jobs for other people like me. I'm not asking you to; but what I feel puzzled about is, what is meant by following Jesus. What do you mean when you sing "I'll go with Him, with Him, all the way?' Do you mean that you are suffering and denying yourselves and trying to save lost, suffering humanity just as I understand Jesus did? What do you mean by it? I see the ragged edge of things a good deal. I understand there are more than five hundred men in this city in my case. Most of them have families. My wife died four months ago. I'm glad she is out of trouble. My little girl is staying with a printer's family until I find a job. Somehow I get puzzled when I see so many Christians living in luxury and singing 'Jesus, I my cross have taken, all to leave and follow Thee,' and remember how my wife died in a tenement in New York City, gasping for air and asking God to take the little girl too. Of course I don't expect you people can prevent every one from dying of starvation, lack of proper nourishment and tenement air, but what does following Jesus mean? I understand that Christian people own a good many of the tenements. A member of a church was the owner of the one where my wife died, and I have wondered if following Jesus all the way was true in his case. I heard some people singing at a church prayer meeting the other night,

> *'All for Jesus, all for Jesus,*
> *All my being's ransomed powers,*
> *All my thoughts, and all my doings,*
> *All my days, and all my hours.'*

and I kept wondering as I sat on the steps outside just what they meant by it. It seems to me there's an awful lot of trouble in the world that somehow wouldn't exist if all the people who sing such songs went and lived them out. I suppose I don't understand. But what would Jesus do? Is that what you mean by following His steps? It seems to me sometimes as if the people in the big churches had good clothes and nice houses to live in, and money to spend for luxuries, and could go away on summer vacations and all that, while the people outside the churches, thousands of them, I mean, die in tenements, and walk the streets for jobs, and never have a piano or a picture in the house, and grow up in misery and drunkenness and sin."[1]

And the questioner collapsed in the center aisle of the church. Cared for in the pastor's home, he died the next Sunday morning. Shortly after, the deeply stirred minister challenged an unusually large congregation with the implications of the previous Sunday's question. Interpreting the stranger's query as "a challenge to Christianity as it is seen and felt in our churches," the pastor asked his hearers to join him in a pledge "not to do anything without first asking 'What would Jesus do?' " and then "to follow Jesus as exactly as [they] knew how, no matter what the results. . ." Among the fifty volunteers were an heiress, a gifted soprano, the president of the local college, a railroad superintendent, a newspaper editor, and a leading merchant. The efforts of these characters to live out the pledge comprised the narrative of *In His Steps*—with the embellishment of several romances.

The singer refused an alluring offer to go on tour, giving her voice
to rescue mission work. The editor dedicated his newspaper to the kingdom of God instead of to profit and drew up a code of ethics for a
"Christian daily" that would lack sensational features and questionable
advertising, while providing "news of the Christian world" and "the
news that people ought to know." This policy so reduced the paper's
income that an endowment became necessary. It was conveniently
provided by the heiress and her converted brother, who further in-
vested their now-consecrated wealth in rebuilding the tenement district
of the town. The railroad superintendent resigned his position after
finding the company engaged in illicit practices, for which it was in-
dicted on his evidence. He found reemployment in his old occupation
as a telegraph operator. The college president forsook his aloofness to
run for mayor on a prohibition platform; his failure revealed to the
reformers the power and unscrupulousness of the liquor interests. The
merchant reorganized his business according to a paternalistic policy
of "intelligent unselfishness" that provided profit sharing for his employees. These and other effects of the pledge upon the life of the First
Church and of "Raymond" gradually crept into the newspapers and
spread to other churches with the result that a national revival of social
religion seemed imminent.

In the final scene, the pastor himself was faced with the question;
he decided to live the simple life in order to serve better. In a vision,
Sheldon had his pastor reject the current materialistic solutions to social ills; to another sad young man he replied that when the kingdom of
God shall have been realized on earth no man will lack for work. As
Ralph H. Gabriel put it in *The Course of American Democratic
Thought,* "Sheldon repudiated the Christian Socialism of Bliss" and
added to Gladden's concept of the socialized individual "the
[George D.] Herron doctrine [which we shall examine shortly] of social redemption through individual sacrifice."[2] In a trance the minister
saw a great victory in which "the Christendom of this age" decided to
follow Jesus "all the way!"

He rose at last with the awe of one who has looked at heavenly things.
He felt the human forces and the human sins of the world as never before. And with a hope that walks hand in hand with faith and love,
Henry Maxwell, disciple of Jesus, laid him down to sleep and dreamed
of the regeneration of Christendom, and saw in his dream a church of

Jesus without spot or wrinkle or any such thing, following him all the way, walking obediently in His steps.[3]

We can examine only briefly a few of the more than twenty periodicals that were published to spread the social gospel. Some of them were single-minded almost to the point of fanaticism. Some were concerned with the whole range of social reform. A few were dedicated specifically to socialism. A very few reached large audiences and could be said to have had a national influence.[4]

EQUITY, A Journal of Christian Labor Reform, had a brief life from April, 1874, to December, 1875. The first social gospel paper, it was dedicated to discussion of the labor question "from the stand-point of the Bible"; its masthead carried a verse from Proverbs 1: "To receive the instruction of wisdom, justice, judgment, and equity." An early editorial declared that "Jesus Christ was the Supreme Reformer of all history, as well as the Savior from sin" and that the reorganization of society into the kingdom of heaven is "essential to curing men of sin." The paper reflected the concerns of its editor, Edward H. Rogers, and a brilliant but quixotic Congregational minister named Jesse Henry Jones, both members of the miniscule "Christian Labor Union," whose roll also listed George E. McNeill, "father of the American Federation of Labor." The final issue of *Equity* announced that "the wage class" of Rogers' district arose spontaneously in a day and nominated and subsequently elected him to the Massachusetts legislature. Two years later, Jones and Rogers tried another publishing venture which they called *The Labor-Balance,* but its life was shorter than that of *Equity;* nevertheless, later reformers were to regard these men as the pioneers of all social gospel agitation in the labor field.[5]

At the opposite social, intellectual, and economic scale was *The Andover Review,* begun in January, 1884, by faculty members of Andover Theological Seminary, primarily to disseminate the New Theology which we met in Chapter 4. The *Review* regularly featured articles on reform by recognized authorities. In its first year there were discussions of American government, competition and combination, literacy and crime, Russian socialism, labor and capital, and the new psychology, by John Dewey. Editorials generally took a liberal stance on issues such as the discussion of social problems by the pulpit, the separation of classes in America, the failure of Protestantism in industrial centers.

A highly respectable and popular magazine was *Our Day,* begun in 1888 by the famous "Boston Monday Lecturer," Joseph Cook; its aim was to unite evangelical Christianity with "practical reform." It featured Cook's addresses on current themes together with articles on many reform subjects. A voice in the urban wilderness was a little eight-page monthly called *For the Right,* edited by Walter Rauschenbush, J. E. Raymond, Elizabeth Post, and Leighton Williams, and naively dedicated to "the interests of the working people of New York City." It proposed "to discuss, from the standpoint of Christian-socialism, such questions as engage their attention and affect their life."

Nor has it any new theories to propound. Its aim is to reflect in its pages the needs, the aspirations, the longings of the tens of thousands of wage-earners who are sighing for better things: and to point out, if possible, not only the wrongs that men suffer, but the methods by which these wrongs may be removed. The editors freely give their time and labor to this undertaking, animated solely by the hope that their efforts may aid the advancement of that kingdom in which wrong shall have no place, but Right shall reign for ever more.

The friends of social reform are invited to write for the columns of this paper and wage earners are especially requested to do so.

Unusual for the time, *For the Right* commented in November, 1889, on the Indian problem, quoting one who had "lived among the Indians for fifteen years":

I have become convinced that the following truths contain the key to the Indian problem.

1. The Indians are men and cannot be saved without recognizing the rights of manhood.

2. What they need is not special legislation in their behalf, but the protecting laws securing equal justice to all men.

3. A homestead should be given to every Indian and the rest of the reservation should be open to other settlers.

4. All distinctions of race should be abolished and the laws administered impartially.

How will these principles solve the Indian problem? Apply them and the Indians will solve it themselves. They are made of human nature as well as we and all they want is a fair chance, equally with ourselves.[6]

A few months later the paper announced the organization of a Society of Christian Socialists in New York City, and soon afterward printed its "Declaration of Principles."

The first of several papers propounding Christian Socialism had been started in Boston in 1889 by W. D. P. Bliss for the Boston Society of Christian Socialists and the "Church of the Carpenter,"[7] a small group of Bliss's friends and supporters which included Edward Bellamy, author of *Looking Backward. The Dawn* took its name from the Society's conviction that society was "awakening to new light upon Social Problems." It occasionally reprinted statements by earlier reformers, such as Wendell Phillips' 1872 address on the labor question, and looked upon Edward H. Rogers, Jesse H. Jones, and *Equity* as Christian Socialist pioneers. Its hard-working editor became an authority on reform, his paper containing much solid material. The paper appears to have prospered for a time; it continued until 1900.

At the same time that Bliss was urging his friends and fellow Episcopalians to become Christian Socialists, the Christian Social Union, a Church-related society, under the prestigious editorship of Professor Richard T. Ely of the University of Wisconsin, began a long-lived *Bulletin* that was both the organ of that very effective society and a vehicle for reprinting study materials used by its many branches throughout the United States and Canada. In 1897 Bliss became the traveling secretary of the C.S.U., which voluntarily disbanded in 1910 after successfully pressuring the Episcopal General Convention to recognize the claims of social Christianity by establishing a permanent official commission on what was called "Social Service."[8]

The growing popularity of reform in the 1890's was demonstrated by the addition of social gospel topics to the ever-widening network of lectures and entertainment that emanated from the summer institute at Lake Chautauqua in western New York.[9] Although such topics had been discussed occasionally at Chautauqua earlier, the social gospel appeared on this platform prominently in 1889 with lectures by Ely, Gladden, Lyman Abbott, and others. In the next decade Ely appeared many times, and the roster of well-known advocates of reform came to include Jacob Riis, Graham Taylor, Theodore Roosevelt, John R.

Commons, Charles R. Henderson, Josiah Strong, Francis G. Peabody, Jane Addams, and a score of others, several of whom wrote textbooks for Chautauqua study courses.

As the Chautauqua idea spread across the country, local forums reflected the widespread concern generated by the Bryan-McKinley campaign of 1896. Graham Taylor, who lectured widely that summer, reported as "simply astonishing" the attendance and attention given to classes in the social teachings of the Bible and his talks on labor and related problems. He was scheduled for eighteen lectures at Ottawa, Kansas, but spoke thirty times to audiences containing as many as fifty pastors concerned with "the social aspects of their own and the Church's ministry." Everywhere he was aware of a "tremendous moral earnestness" as people discussed the main issue of the presidential race.[10]

For exactly five years between 1894 and 1899 there was published in Minneapolis the most popular and the most radical journal of the social gospel period. *The Kingdom,* intended as the weekly mouthpiece of the prophetic George D. Herron, whom we will meet in the next chapter, was also a vehicle for expressing the vast midwestern discontent of late Populism stirred into a peculiar mix of social gospel radicalism. The chief of a distinguished board of editors was George A. Gates, then president of Iowa [Grinnell] College. Its first issue proclaimed the right of Christ to rule supreme "in all the affairs of life—intellectual, social, commercial, political and ecclesiastical." The field to which the paper addressed itself was "that of 'applied Christianity'—the application to social conditions everywhere of the plain teachings of the Founder of Christianity and Humanity's Savior." Later it declared its allegience to Christian Socialism:

Fearless and uncompromising with wrong in every sphere, it will yet be tolerant of differing intellectual opinions. It will seek . . . to illustrate the spirit of Jesus rather than to discuss questions regarding his personality. It will aim to cultivate in its readers a proper temper of mind regarding all questions of social reform rather than to insist upon a particular method as being the only and infallible course to be taken. In Politics it will remain absolutely independent, upholding the principles of true democracy.[11]

Contributors dealt with the burning issues of the times, and they pulled
no punches. During the Pullman strike of 1894, John R. Commons
wrote that Pullman, Carnegie, and corporations and proprietors generally were like Charles I or Louis XIV: employees have a right to an interest in a business, and the public is another partner. Existing laws, he
continued, had been made by capitalists and politicians in their own interests; the only solution is for workingmen to enter politics and secure
legislation in their own behalf. Commons edited a column on "Christian
Sociology," and during its five-year span the magazine printed something by almost every social gospel leader. It reached a circulation between 10,000 and 20,000. Its demise was dramatic: Gates wrote a carefully documented booklet attacking the American Book Company as a
trust. The company sued. Unfortunately the tract had been printed by
The Kingdom, which won the first round. Libel suits followed; again
the paper won, but legal technicalities forced it to cease publication.
The treasurer of the defense fund had been Henry Demarest Lloyd and
Clarence Darrow one of the lawyers.

A curious by-product of *The Kingdom* was a communal colony in
Georgia (which we shall describe in the next chapter) that printed a
magazine called *The Social Gospel* which gave the movement its name.
The first issue declared that the magazine was being published "in the
faith that the wrongs of society can be realized."

It is a journal of the practice of Christianity. It will be its purpose to inspire faith in the economic teachings of Jesus, and courage to put them
into life. While gladly and gratefully alive to the good that has been and
is, its editors shall study to see and to clearly present the reform that
needs in our day to be accomplished in order that humanity may be
made at one with God.

The social gospel is the brotherhood of man and the fatherhood of
God. It is the old gospel of peace on earth among men of good will. It is
the proclamation of the kingdom of heaven, a divinely ordered society,
to be realized on earth. It is the application of Christ's Golden Rule and
Law of Love to all the business and affairs of life. It is the glad tidings
of peace and purity and plenty.

We believe that our vision is clear and our message true. We beseech
our readers to test them by the highest teachings of the New Testament, or any book, or by their best knowledge of social needs and social possibilities.

That The Social Gospel has its distinctive mission and message we are confident our careful readers will not dispute.[12]

During its life of a little more than three years, *The Social Gospel* circulated widely enough throughout the liberal and reform segments of American magazine subscribers to make a modest profit for the Colony and to fix its name on the movement.[13]

An important group of periodicals represented the church federations and urban church movements around the turn of the century, but the most significant publication of this kind was *Social Service,* the organ of Josiah Strong's nondenominational League for Social Service, which he established upon leaving the Evangelical Alliance (see Chapter 18). *Social Service* was a clearing house for information on a wide variety of reform and social betterment projects, appealing to the popular preconception that if the public were fully aware of social problems and fully informed about them, improvement would follow. For a time, Strong also published *Social Progress,* yearbooks and encyclopedias "of economic, industrial, social and religious statistics," but these were superseded by *The Encyclopedia of Social Reform,* which appeared in a revised edition in 1908. For a time the League published a small paper called *Social Engineering,* its title reflecting a popular concept.

In 1903 the League became the "American Institute of Social Service," with an impressive board of sponsors that included Mrs. Andrew Carnegie, Grover Cleveland, and Woodrow Wilson. Its major contribution to the social gospel was the issuance of monthly study outlines covering all the reforms of the period, including the race problem, from 1908 to Strong's death in 1916. Prepared by W. D. P. Bliss under the title *The Gospel of the Kingdom,* they were used in churches, "Y's," schools, even colleges, and reached some forty thousand readers. The subjects ranged from child labor to women in industry. Of the writing and publishing of such social study courses by the denominational presses there was no end—to this day. Those we have described were the pioneers. Not described was the secular press, which also carried a large social gospel burden.

The first two "aims" of the Brotherhood of the Kingdom had been to see "the Kingdom of God once more the great object of Christian preaching" and "the inspiration of Christian hymnology." Although the social gospel was to be criticized for its early lack of new hymns, prayers, and other liturgical materials, it did produce them. Gladden,

Herron, and Rauschenbusch, all of whom were aware of the need to integrate the new message into worship, wrote on the social implications of the Lord's Prayer. Francis G. Peabody emphasized the social aspects of prayer in his writings and during his twenty years as University Preacher at Harvard. The Brotherhood of the Kingdom introduced new hymns and prayers into its conference worship and one of the brothers, Mornay Williams, compiled a booklet of forty-four hyms embodying the new ideology, some of which later found their way into denominational hymn books. Here are a few examples:

Stay, Master, stay upon this heavenly hill:
A little longer, let us linger still;
With all the mighty ones of old beside,
Near to the Awful Presence still abide;
Before the throne of light we trembling stand,
And catch a glimpse into the spirit land.

Stay, Master, stay! we breathe a purer air;
This life is not the life that waits us there:
Thoughts, feelings, flashes, glimpses come and go;
We cannot speak them—nay, we do not know;
Wrapt in this cloud of light we seem to be
The thing we fain would grow—eternally.

"No!" saith the Lord, "the hour is past,—we go;
Our home, our life, our duties lie below,
While here we kneel upon the mount of prayer,
The plough lies waiting in the furrow there!
Here we sought God that we might know his will;
There we must do it,—serve Him,—seek him still!"

If man aspires to reach the throne of God,
O'er the dull plains of earth must lie the road.
He who best does his lowly duty here,
Shall mount the highest in a nobler sphere:
At God's own feet our spirits seek their rest,
And he is nearest Him who serves him best.

Two stanzas by Gerald Massey reflected Brotherhood ideology:

Creeds, Empires, Systems rot with age,
    But the great People's ever youthful!
And it shall write the Future's page,
    To our Humanity more truthful;

The gnarliest heart hath tender chords,
   To waken at the name of "Brother!"
'Tis coming when these scorpion-words;
   We shall not speak to sting each other.
      'Tis Coming! yes, 'tis Coming!

Aye, it must come! The Tyrant's throne
   Is crumbling, with our hot tears rusted;
The Sword earth's mighty men have leant on
   Is cankered, with our best blood crusted.
Room for the men of Mind! Make way
   You Robber Rulers!—pause no longer!
You cannot stay the opening day!
   The world rolls on, the light grows stronger,
      The People's Advent's coming!

Williams included Ebenezer Elliott's well-known "When wilt thou save
the people?" and Gladden's "O Master, let me walk with thee." This
stanza is by R. M. Offord:

Not in some cloistered cell
Dost Thou, Lord, bid me dwell,
   My love to show:
But mid the busy marts
Where men with burdened hearts
   Do come and go.

And these by T. Hughes:

O God of truth, whose living Word
   Upholds whate'er hath breath,
Look down on Thy creation, Lord,
   Enslaved by sin and death.

We fight for Truth, *we* fight for God,
   Poor slaves of lies and sin!
He who would fight for Thee on earth,
   Must first be true within.[14]

In *The Christian City,* of which Frank Mason North was founder
and editor, he printed in 1903 this poem which became the best-known
social gospel hymn:

Where cross the crowded ways of life,
Where sound the cries of race and clan,

Above the noise of selfish strife,
We hear thy voice, O Son of Man.

In haunts of wretchedness and need,
On shadowed thresholds dark with fears,
From paths where hide the lures of greed,
We catch the vision of thy tears.

From tender childhood's helplessness,
From woman's grief, man's burdened toil,
From famished souls, from sorrow's stress,
Thy heart has never known recoil.

The cup of water given for thee
Still holds the freshness of thy grace;
Yet long these multitudes to see
The sweet compassion of thy face.

O Master, from the mountain side,
Make haste to heal these hearts of pain;
Among these restless throngs abide,
O tread the city's streets again.

Till sons of men shall learn thy love,
And follow where thy feet have trod;
Till glorious from thy heaven above,
Shall come the City of our God.[15]

In 1914, *The Survey,* a magazine of social work, published a collection of one hundred "Social Hymns of Brotherhood and Aspiration," many of which found their way into later hymnals. A study of Methodist hymn books over a century found that when the social gospel first appeared in the edition of 1905, there were four or five such hymns, but that by 1935 there were sixty-eight hymns listed under "Kingdom of God."[16] The Brotherhood had planted well! A comparable shift could readily be found in the hymnals of other denominations.

In 1963 Professor Horton Davies reached some interesting conclusions concerning "The Expression of the Social Gospel in Worship":

[The first, he wrote,] is that, however critical the exponents of the social gospel were of the other-wordly individualism of evangelical piety in the Protestant churches, and however unguardedly they sometimes expressed such criticisms, they wished to broaden piety, not to abolish it.

The second conclusion is that, . . . far from the social gospel having failed because it did not create suitable expressions for its prophetic concerns in worship, it tried valiantly both in its intercessory prayers and its stirring social hymns to awaken the social conscience of Protestantism. Thus it is wholly inaccurate to affirm that prophetic sermons were preached in a conservative cultus. The cultus itself was significantly changed.

The third conclusion is that the social gospel succeeded better in finding worship expressions in the flexible Puritan-Pietist tradition of prayer than in the churches with a relatively unchanging liturgy. But even here, as in the case of the Protestant Episcopal Church, the social gospel hymns found their way and many of the great city churches provided special ministries for immigrants and unemployed. There is evidence that in the essential tension between fidelity to the historically-given nature of Christian revelation and the concern to be able to communicate relevantly to the age, a liturgical church chooses fidelity and non-liturgical churches select relevance. The social gospel found greatest acceptance and opportunity for the reconstruction of worship in the Free churches. But it should be added, as a necessary qualification, that Biblically conservative sections of denominations resisted liberal theology and therefore also the social gospel which was its ethical and radical consequence.

The final conclusion is that the weakest feature of the social gospel in its expression in worship was a serious undervaluation of the nature of the Sacraments. Here it may be suggested that the inadequate understanding of the nature of the Church and of the Sacraments could have been rectified if the doctrine of the Incarnation, rather than the doctrine of the Kingdom of God, had been made the foundation of the social awakening, as it had been the foundation of Christian Socialism in F. D. Maurice.[17]

We conclude this chapter with another of Walter Rauschenbusch's contributions to the social gospel, a small book of "prayers of the social awakening" entitled *For God and the People,* first published in 1910. In the introduction he wrote enthusiastically of how "the new social purpose" was "enlarging and transforming our whole conception of the meaning of Christianity," and uttered his hope that the "new religious emotions ought to find conscious and social expression." Because the ordinary hymnal "rarely contained more than two or three hymns in which the triumphant chords of the social hope" were struck, and the liturgies and devotional manuals offered little that was "fit to enrich and purify the social thoughts and feelings," he humbly presented this effort to help meet the need "to blaze new paths to God for the feet of modern men."

The opening essay on the "social meaning of the Lord's Prayer" is a classic:

The Lord's Prayer is part of the heritage of social Christianity which has been appropriated by men who have had little sympathy with its social spirit. It belongs to the equipment of the soldiers of the kingdom of God. I wish to claim it here as the great charter of all social prayers.

When he bade us say, "Our Father," Jesus spoke from that consciousness of human solidarity which was a matter of course in all his thinking. He compels us to clasp hands in spirit with all our brothers and thus to approach the Father together. This rules out all selfish isolation in religion. Before God no man stands alone. Before the All-seeing he is surrounded by the spiritual throng of all to whom he stands related near and far, all whom he loves or hates, whom he serves or oppresses, whom he wrongs or saves. We are one with our fellow-men in all our needs. We are one in our sin and our salvation. To recognize that oneness is the first step toward praying the Lord's Prayer aright. That recognition is also the foundation of social Christianity.

The three petitions with which the prayer begins express the great desire which was fundamental in the heart and mind of Jesus: "Hallowed be thy name. Thy kingdom come. Thy will be done, as in heaven, so on earth." Together they express his yearning faith in the possibility of a reign of God on earth in which his name shall be hallowed and his will be done. They look forward to the ultimate perfection of the common life of humanity on this earth, and pray for the divine revolution which is to bring that about.

There is no request here that we be saved from earthliness and go to heaven which has been the great object of churchly religion. We pray here that heaven may be duplicated on earth through the moral and spiritual transformation of humanity, both in its personal units and its corporate life. No form of religion has ever interpreted this prayer aright which did not have a loving understanding for the plain daily relations of men, and a living faith in their possible spiritual nobility.

And no man has outgrown the crude selfishness of religious imma-

turity who has not followed Jesus in setting this desire for the social salvation of mankind ahead of all personal desires. The desire for the
Kingdom of God precedes and outranks everything else in religion, and
forms the tacit presupposition of all our wishes for ourselves. In fact,
no one has a clear right to ask for bread for his body or strength for his
soul, unless he has identified his will with this all-embracing purpose of
God, and intends to use the vitality of body and soul in the attainment
of that end.

With that understanding we can say that the remaining petitions
deal with personal needs.

Among these the prayer for the daily bread takes first place. Jesus
was never as "spiritual" as some of his later followers. He never forgot
or belittled the elemental need of men for bread. The fundamental
place which he gives to this petition is a recognition of the economic
basis of life.

But he lets us pray only for the bread that is needful, and for that
only when it becomes needful. The conception of what is needful will
expand as human life develops. But this prayer can never be used to
cover luxuries that debilitate, nor accumulations of property that can
never be used but are sure to curse the soul of the holder with the
diverse diseases of mammonism.

In this petition, too, Jesus compels us to stand together. We have
to ask in common for our daily bread. We sit at the common table in
God's great house, and the supply of each depends on the security of
all. The more society is socialized, the clearer does that fact become,
and the more just and humane its organization becomes, the more will
that recognition be at the bottom of all our institutions. As we stand
thus in common, looking up to God for our bread, every one of us
ought to feel the sin and shame of it if he habitually takes more than
his fair share and leaves others hungry that he may surfeit. It is inhuman, irreligious, and indecent.

The remaining petitions deal with the spiritual needs. Looking
backward, we see that our lives have been full of sin and failure, and we
realize the need of forgiveness. Looking forward, we tremble at the
temptations that await us and pray for deliverance from evil.

In these prayers for the inner life, where the soul seems to confront God alone, we should expect to find only individualistic religion.
But even here the social note sounds clearly.

This prayer will not permit us to ask for God's forgiveness without
making us affirm that we have forgiven our brothers and are on a basis
of brotherly love with all men: "Forgive us our debts, as we also have

forgiven our debtors." We shall have to be socially right if we want to
be religiously right. Jesus will not suffer us to be pious toward God and
merciless toward men.

In the prayer, "Lead us not into temptation," we feel the human
trembling of fear. Experience has taught us our frailty. Every man can
see certain contingencies just a step ahead of him and knows that his
moral capacity for resistance would collapse hopelessly if he were
placed in these situations. Therefore Jesus gives voice to our inarticulate
plea to God not to bring us into such situations.

But such situations are created largely by the social life about us. If
the society in which we move is rank with sexual looseness, or full of
the suggestiveness and solicitations of alcoholism; if our business life is
such that we have to lie and cheat and be cruel in order to live and prosper; if our political organization offers an ambitious man the alternative
of betraying the public good or of being thwarted and crippled in all his
efforts, then the temptations are created in which men go under, and
society frustrates the prayer we utter to God. No church can interpret
this petition intelligently which closes its mind to the debasing or invig-
orating influence of the spiritual environment furnished by society. No
man can utter this petition without conscious or unconscious hypocrisy
who is helping to create the temptations in which others are sure to fall.

The words "Deliver us from the evil one" have in them the ring of
battle. They bring to mind the incessant grapple between God and the
permanent and malignant powers of evil in humanity. To the men of
the first century that meant Satan and his host of evil spirits who ruled
in the oppressive, extortionate, and idolatrous powers of Rome. Today
the original spirit of that prayer will probably be best understood by
those who are pitted against the terrible powers of organized covetousness and institutionalized oppression.

Thus the Lord's Prayer is the great prayer of social Christianity. It
is charged with what we call "social consciousness." It assumes the social solidarity of men as a matter of course. It recognizes the social basis
of all moral and religious life even in the most intimate personal relations to God.

It is not the property of those whose chief religious aim is to pass
through an evil world in safety, leaving the world's evil unshaken. Its
dominating thought is the moral and religious transformation of mankind in all its social relations. It was left us by Jesus, the great initiator
of the Christian revolution; and it is the rightful property of those who
follow his banner in the conquest of the world.[18]

There followed various prayers. This one is "For This World"; it should please twentieth-century ecologists:

O God, we thank thee for this universe, our great home; for its vastness and its riches, and for the manifoldness of the life which teems upon it and of which we are part. We praise thee for the arching sky and the blessed winds, for the driving clouds and the constellations on high. We praise thee for the salt sea and the running water, for the everlasting hills, for the trees, and for the grass under our feet. We thank thee for our senses by which we can see the splendor of the morning, and hear the jubilant songs of love, and smell the breath of the springtime. Grant us, we pray thee, a heart wide open to all this joy and beauty, and save our souls from being so steeped in care or so darkened by passion that we pass heedless and unseeing when even the thornbush by the wayside is aflame with the glory of God.

Enlarge within us the sense of fellowship with all the living things, our little brothers, to whom thou hast given this earth as their home in common with us. We remember with shame that in the past we have exercised the high dominion of man with ruthless cruelty, so that the voice of the Earth, which should have gone up to thee in song, has been a groan of travail. May we realize that they live, not for us alone, but for themselves and for thee, and that they love the sweetness of life even as we, and serve thee in their place better than we in ours.

When our use of this world is over and we make room for others, may we not leave anything ravished by our greed or spoiled by our ignorance, but may we hand in our common heritage fairer and sweeter through our use of it, undiminished in fertility and joy, that so our bodies may return in peace to the great mother who nourished them and our spirits may round the circle of a perfect life in thee.

These were "for social groups and classes":

For Children Who Work

O thou great Father of the weak, lay thy hand tenderly on all the little children on earth and bless them. Bless our own children, who are life of our life, and who have become the heart of our heart. Bless every little child-friend that has leaned against our knee and refreshed our soul by its smiling trustfulness. Be good to all children who long in vain for human love, or for flowers and water, and the sweet breast of Nature. But bless with a sevenfold blessing the young lives whose slender shoulders are already bowed beneath the yoke of toil, and whose glad growth is being stunted forever. Suffer not their little bodies to be utterly sapped, and their minds to be given over to stupidity and the vices of an empty soul. We have all jointly deserved the millstone of thy wrath for making these little ones to stumble and fall. Grant all employers of labor stout hearts to refuse enrichment at such a price. Grant to all the citizens and officers of states which now permit this wrong the grace of holy anger. Help us to realize that every child of our nation is in very truth our child, a member of our great family. By the Holy Child that nestled in Mary's bosom; by the memories of our own childhood joys and sorrows; by the sacred possibilities that slumber in every child, we beseech thee to save us from killing the sweetness of young life by the greed of gain.

This plea was contributed by Mornay Williams, president of a large boys' school:

For the Children of the Street

O Heavenly Father, whose unveiled face the angels of little children do always behold, look with love and pity, we beseech thee, upon the children of the streets. Where men, in their busy and careless lives, have made a highway, these children of thine have made a home and a school, and are learning the bad lessons of our selfishness and our folly. Save them, and save us, O Lord. Save them from ignorance and brutality, from the shamelessness of lust, the hardness of greed, and the besotting of drink; and save us from the greater guilt of those that offend thy little ones, and from the hypocrisy of those that say they see and see not, whose sin remaineth.

Make clear to those of older years the inalienable right of childhood to play, and give to those who govern our cities the will and ability to provide the places for play; make clear to those who minister to the appetite for recreation the guilt of them that lead astray thy chil-

dren; and make clear to us all that the great school of life is not encom-
passed by walls and that its teachers are all who influence their younger
brethren by companionship and example, whether for good or evil, and
that in that school all we are teachers and as we teach are judged. For
all false teaching, for all hindering of thy children, pardon us, O Lord,
and suffer the little children to come unto thee, for Jesus' sake.

For Women Who Toil

O God, we pray thee for our sisters who are leaving the ancient shelter
of the home to earn their wage in the factory and the store amid the
press of modern life. Save them from the strain of unremitting toil that
would unfit them for the holy duties of home and motherhood which
the future may lay upon them. Give them grace to cherish under the
new surroundings the old sweetness and gentleness of womanhood, and
in the rough mingling of life to keep their hearts pure and their lives un-
tarnished. Save them from the terrors of utter want. Teach them to
stand loyally by their sisters, that by united action they may better
their common lot.

   If it must be so that our women toil like men, help us still to reverence in them the mothers of the future. But make us determined to
shield them from unequal burdens, that the women of our nation be
not drained of strength and hope for the enrichment of a few, lest our
homes grow poor in the wifely sweetness and motherly love which have
been the saving strength and glory of our country. To such as yearn for
the love and sovereign freedom of their own home, grant in due time
the fulfilment of their sweet desires. By Mary, the beloved, who bore
the world's redemption in her bosom; by the memory of our own dear
mothers who kissed our souls awake; by the little daughters who must
soon go out into that world which we are now fashioning for others,
we beseech thee that we may deal aright by all women.

For Workingmen

O God, thou mightiest worker of the universe, source of all strength
and author of all unity, we pray thee for our brothers, the industrial
workers of the nation. As their work binds them together in common
toil and danger, may their hearts be knit together in a strong sense of
their common interests and destiny. Help them to realize that the in-

jury of one is the concern of all, and that the welfare of all must be the aim of every one. If any of them is tempted to sell the birthright of his class for a mess of pottage for himself, give him a wider outlook and a nobler sympathy with his fellows. Teach them to keep step in a steady onward march, and in their own way to fulfil the law of Christ by bearing the common burdens.

Grant the organizations of labor quiet patience and prudence in all disputes, and fairness to see the other side. Save them from malice and bitterness. Save them from the headlong folly which ruins a fair cause, and give them wisdom resolutely to put aside the two-edged sword of violence that turns on those who seize it. Raise up for them still more leaders of able mind and large heart, and give them grace to follow the wiser counsel.

When they strive for leisure and health and a better wage, do thou grant their cause success, but teach them not to waste their gain on fleeting passions, but to use it in building fairer homes and a nobler manhood. Grant all classes of our nation a larger comprehension for the aspirations of labor and for the courage and worth of these our brothers, that we may cheer them in their struggles and understand them even in their sins. And may the upward climb of Labor, its defeats and its victories, in the farther reaches bless all classes of our nation, and build up for the republic of the future a great body of workers, strong of limb, clear of mind, fair in temper, glad to labor, conscious of their worth, and striving together for the final brother-hood of all men.

For Immigrants

O thou great Champion of the outcast and the weak, we remember before thee the people of other nations who are coming to our land, seeking bread, a home, and a future. May we look with thy compassion upon those who have been drained and stunted by the poverty and oppression of centuries, and whose minds have been warped by super-stition or seared by the dumb agony of revolt. We bless thee for all that America has meant to the alien folk that have crossed the sea in the past, and for all the patient strength and God-fearing courage with which they have enriched our nation. We rejoice in the millions whose life has expanded in the wealth and liberty of our country, and whose children have grown to fairer stature and larger thoughts; for we, too, are the children of immigrants, who came with anxious hearts and halting feet on the westward path of hope.

We beseech thee that our republic may no longer fail their trust. We mourn for the dark sins of past and present, wherein men who are held in honor among us made spoil of the ignorance and helplessness of the strangers and sent them to an early death. In a nation dedicated to liberty may they not find the old oppression and a fiercer greed. May they never find that the arm of the law is but the arm of the strong. Help our whole people henceforth to keep in leash the cunning that would devour the simple. May they feel here the pure air of freedom and face the morning radiance of a joyous hope.

For all the oppressed afar off who sigh for liberty; for all lovers of the people who strive to break their shackles; for all who dare to believe in democracy and the Kingdom of God, make thou our great commonwealth once more a sure beacon-light of hope and a guide on the path which leads to the perfect union of law and liberty.

For Writers and Newspaper Men

O thou great source of truth and knowledge, we remember before thee all whose calling it is to gather and winnow the facts for informing the people. Inspire them with a determined love for honest work and a stanch hatred for the making of lies, lest the judgments of our nation be perverted and we be taught to call light darkness and darkness light. Since the sanity and wisdom of a nation are in their charge, may they count it shame to set the baser passions of men on fire for the sake of gain. May they never suffer themselves to be used in drugging the mind of the people with falsehood and prejudice.

Grant them boldness to turn the unwelcome light on those who love the darkness because their deeds are evil. Put into their hands the shining sword of truth, and make them worthy successors of the great champions of the people who held truth to be a holy thing by which nations live and for which men should die. Cause them to realize that they have a public function in the commonwealth, and that their country may be saved by their courage or undone by their cowardice and silence. Grant them the heart of manhood to cast their mighty influence with the forces that make the people strong and free, and if they suffer loss, may they rejoice in that as proof to their own souls that they have fought a good fight and have been servants of the higher law.

Rauschenbusch allowed himself several "prayers of wrath":

Against War

O Lord, since first the blood of Abel cried to thee from the ground that drank it, this earth of thine has been defiled with the blood of man shed by his brother's hand, and the centuries sob with the ceaseless horror of war. Ever the pride of kings and the covetousness of the strong has driven peaceful nations to slaughter. Ever the songs of the past and the pomp of armies have been used to inflame the passions of the people. Our spirit cries out to thee in revolt against it, and we know that our righteous anger is answered by thy holy wrath.

Break thou the spell of the enchantments that make the nations drunk with the lust of battle and draw them on as willing tools of death. Grant us a quiet and steadfast mind when our own nation clamors for vengeance or aggression. Strengthen our sense of justice and our regard for the equal worth of other peoples and races. Grant to the rulers of nations faith in the possibility of peace through justice, and grant to the common people a new and stern enthusiasm for the cause of peace. Bless our soldiers and sailors for their swift obedience and their willingness to answer to the call of duty, but inspire them none the less with a hatred of war, and may they never for love of private glory or advancement provoke its coming. May our young men still rejoice to die for their country with the valor of their fathers, but teach our age nobler methods of matching our strength and more effective ways of giving our life for the flag.

O thou strong Father of all nations, draw all thy great family together with an increasing sense of our common blood and destiny, that peace may come on earth at last, and thy sun may shed its light rejoicing on a holy brotherhood of peoples.

The last section of the little book was titled "The Progress of Humanity." This prayer embodies the theme of Rauschenbusch's life:

For the Kingdom of God

O Christ, thou hast bidden us to pray for the coming of thy Father's kingdom, in which his righteous will shall be done on earth. We have treasured thy words, but we have forgotten their meaning, and thy great hope has grown dim in thy Church. We bless thee for the inspired souls of all ages who saw afar the shining city of God, and by faith left the profit of the present to follow their vision. We rejoice that to-day the hope of these lonely hearts is becoming the clear faith of millions. Help us, O Lord, in the courage of faith to seize what has now come so near, that the glad day of God may dawn at last. As we have mastered Nature that we might gain wealth, help us now to master the social relations of mankind that we may gain justice and a world of brothers. For what shall it profit our nation if it gain numbers and riches, and lose the sense of the living God and the joy of human brotherhood?

Make us determined to live by truth and not by lies, to found our common life on the eternal foundations of righteousness and love, and no longer to prop the tottering house of wrong by legalized cruelty and force. Help us to make the welfare of all the supreme law of our land, that so our commonwealth may be built strong and secure on the love of all its citizens. Cast down the throne of Mammon who ever grinds the life of men, and set up thy throne, O Christ, for thou didst die that men might live. Show thy erring children at last the way from the City of Destruction to the City of Love, and fulfil the longings of the prophets of humanity. Our Master, once more we make thy faith our prayer: "Thy kingdom come! Thy will be done on earth!"[19]

The book ended with petitions for the Church, "for our city," "for the cooperative commonwealth," and a modest "author's prayer." Had all evangelists for the social gospel kept the religious note uppermost, as did Rauschenbusch, it might not have suffered decline in the next generation.

Notes

1. Charles M. Sheldon, *In His Steps* (New York: Grossett and Dunlap, n.d. [c. 1935], 8–9.

2. R. H. Gabriel, *The Course of American Democratic Thought* (New York: Ronald Press, 1940), 322.

3. Sheldon, 242. For a stimulating analysis of Sheldon, see James H. Smylie, "Sheldon's *In His Steps:* Conscience and Discipleship," *Theology Today*, 32 (Apr., 1975), 32–45.

4. Some of these periodicals are rare; most can be found through the *Union List of Serials.*

5. Hopkins, *Rise of the Social Gospel,* 42–49.

6. *For the Right* (New York), 1, no. 1 (Nov., 1889), 1.

7. W. D. P. Bliss, "The Church of the Carpenter and Thirty Years After," *Social Preparation for the Kingdom of God,* 9, no. 1 (Jan., 1922), 12–15. Vida D. Scudder, *On Journey* (New York: Dutton, 1937), 165.

8. Hopkins, 165–167.

9. For Chautauqua, see J. L. Hurlbut, *The Story of Chautauqua* (New York: Putnam, 1921); J. E. Gould, *The Chautauqua Movement* (New York: State University of New York, 1961); Gay MacLaren, *Morally We Roll Along,* (Boston: Little, Brown, 1938).

10. Hopkins, 163–165. Much research needs to be done on the relation of the social gospel to Populism.

11. *The Kingdom,* unsigned editorial, 9 (April 30, 1897), 877.

12. Hopkins, 196–197; *The Social Gospel,* 1, no. 1 (Feb., 1898), 1.

13. About fifteen years passed between the first casual use of the term "social gospel" and its general acceptance. The phrase was first used in the spring of 1886 by the Rev. Charles O. Brown, pastor of a Congregational church in Dubuque, Iowa. In the first of a series of *Talks on Labor Troubles* (Chicago: Revell, 1886), page 9, given "prior to the Anarchist outbreak in Chicago," he described *Progress and Poverty* as "a new social gospel." B. F. Westcott, Canon of Westminster, used the phrase twice later that year in sermons in the Abbey *(Social Aspects of Christianity* [London and New York: Macmillan, 1887], v and 96); similarly, W. D. P. Bliss used it on the front page of the first issue of *The Dawn* in 1889, and there were others on both sides of the Atlantic. A leading magazine conducted a poll in 1895 but found no consensus; "Christian Socialism," the British term, was not congenial to most Americans, some preferring "Christian Sociology" or the "Gospel of the Kingdom." "Social Gospel" gradually took over upon the publication of the colony's magazine; within a few years after its demise, its title was generally accepted—the distant influence of midwestern Populism via Herron and Georgia. For a detailed account of the origins of the term, see C. H. Hopkins, *The Rise of Social Christianity in American Protestantism, 1865-1912* (Ph. D. diss. Yale University, 1937) II, 753–55; Xerox–University Microfilm #76-11, 786.

14. Mornay Williams, *Hymns of the Kingdom of God* (pam.; New York?: n.d.) 9, 23, 27, 41.

15. The date of this hymn is usually given as 1905, when it was published in *The Methodist Hymnal,* but it appeared in *The Christian City* (New York) for June, 1903.

16. B. F. Crawford, *Religious Trends in a Century of Hymns* (Carnegie, Pa.: Carnegie Church Press, 1938), 122–126; Henry W. Foote, *Three Centuries of American Hymnody* (Cambridge: Harvard University Press, 1940), ch. 9.

17. Horton Davies, "The Expression of the Social Gospel in Worship," *Studia Liturgica,* 2 (1963), 191–92. Courtesy of Dr. Davies.

18. Walter Rauschenbusch, *For God and the People: Prayers for the Social Awakening* (Boston–New York–Chicago: Pilgrim, 1910), 17–23.

19. Rauschenbusch, 47–48, 51–52, 53–54, 55–60, 79–80, 97–98, 107–8.

15   Socialism
as Christian Strategy

Until the three great strikes of 1877, 1886, and 1894, American Christianity was only barely aware of the existence of socialism; those "three earthquakes" not only opened the eyes of thoughtful Americans to industrial and urban maladjustment, but forced a new awareness of the remedies proposed by socialism. We have previously glimpsed several individuals and groups that prescribed remedies they called "Christian Socialism." When one of them, W. D. P. Bliss, revised his *Encyclopedia of Social Reform* in 1908, he summarized the views held by American Christian Socialists as follows; the reader will note the almost complete absence of Marxism.

Christian Socialism is the application to society of the way of Christ. Christ has a social way, and only in this way are there healing and wholeness for the nations. Christian Socialists do not deny the necessity of individual Christianity. Christian Socialism is no salvation by the wholesale, by machinery, by power of environment; it is no new gospel. It is, rather, the carrying out of the old full gospel, which is to all people. It holds that Christian Socialism follows from and is involved in personal obedience to Christ. It is Christian. Its starting-point is the Incarnation.

But this being so, it quickly adds, that while Christian Socialism follows from personal obedience to Christ, *it is not enough to-day to say that all that is needed is for the individual to follow Christ.* This, *while true,* begs the question. *We need to be told what it means to follow Christ.* Those sentimental Christians who say that all that is necessary is for individuals to obey Christ are in danger of saying, "Lord, Lord," without showing what the Lord would have us do. Christian Socialism tries to voice the social law that it has learned from Christ.

First, it declares that all men are the children of God. It follows that men are not *merely* individuals; they are born united. The world *is* one. Society makes the individual, more than the individual makes society. Society begins in God. The first social necessity is to recognize this. We are to develop the social unity we derive from God. *Second,* the *law* for the social life is revealed in part in the Old Testament. The Mosaic revelation founded a theocracy on earth. God was the Universal Father; every man of the theocracy a brother. Property in land was not absolute; the land was conceived as belonging to God. No individual could own it in fee simple. He could only use it. In its use he was inalienably protected. It came to him through the family as an inalienable inheritance. If, through poverty or misfortune, he temporarily parted with it, it returned to him in the year of jubilee. No landless, homeless class could, therefore, be *permanently* developed among the Hebrews.

The law went farther. It cared especially for the poor, the opprest, the children, the fatherless, the widow. Usury (or interest: all scholars agree that the two words originally meant the same thing) was forbidden between members of the theocracy. The law provided for every one's independence. It not only provided land for the worker, but defended him in the ownership of clothes, tools, etc. (capital), which could not *permanently* be taken from him. If taken as a pledge, they must be returned before night. No permanent mortgage indebtedness was, therefore, possible on either land or capital; that is, the law was truly socialistic in providing in the name of organized society for both land and capital for every family. And this was *not,* be it remembered, a law of mere individual righteousness. *In order to reap its benefits, the family had to belong to the theocracy.* The Jew could take interest from a foreigner; the foreigner could be enslaved, even killed. The law was essentially national and institutional.

Third, this law is to be fulfilled in *Jesus Christ.* The Hebrew law did not work; no law can work; *man must work the law;* hence the Christ, conversion, the sacraments, the means of grace. Jesus Christ came to enable us to fulfil the law. What the law could not do, in that it was weak through the flesh, that Jesus Christ came to fulfil. Individualism forgets law; institutionalism forgets grace. A true Christian Socialism fulfils the social law through grace. The Old Testament gives the world its social track; Jesus Christ gives the locomotive power. To preach as Tolstoy and most Protestants do, the latter without social organization, is to try and run a locomotive without a track. Protestantism has run the world into a quagmire. Jesus Christ is the locomotive power drawing the world along the social track.

Fourth, a social law must be fulfilled *socially.* Protestantism has here made a grievous mistake. But to make a mistake here is to misconceive the whole Incarnation. In Christ, God became man on earth. He took all humanity into Himself. Christ was not only a man, but MAN; man in all that is in man or possible to man; man in art, in science, in letters, in politics, in society, in commerce, in industry. In the Incarnation God entered into all life. God's laws are practical. What is impractical is not divine. Individualism has been found impractical. Men have tried to carry out the Golden Rule on individual lines, and they have failed. We do not say they have wholly failed. No earnest effort, even tho mistaken, wholly fails. But, generally speaking, they have failed. Large numbers of business men say to-day that the Golden Rule cannot be applied to business. They are right on the present system of business, because the system is wrong. You "cannot serve God and Mammon." Pathetic, noble but impractical are the desperate efforts of Christian men and women to do good and be Christ-like in modern business. It is a hopeless task. God's way demands a social basis.

Fifth, Christian Socialism would fulfill the social law by striving to build up a socialism based on Christ.

It would aid the eight-hour movement. It would reduce the hours of labor in factory and in shop, that men may have longer hours of labor in the home, the library, and the church. Christian Socialism would favor *direct legislation,* through the initiative, the referendum, and proportional representation, purging our politics of corruption, breaking down the machine, and teaching the people self-government. It would emancipate woman as well as man. It does not believe in a democracy of half the people. It would develop a true municipalism, as is being done in Birmingham, Glasgow, London, Berlin, and other cities. Glasgow, by spending $7,000,000 in tearing down and rebuilding the worst tenements, and by municipally clearing courts and passages; by providing municipal baths, wash-houses, etc. has reduced her death-rate from 54 to 29 per 1,000. This Christian Socialism considers practical Christianity. It would have the city employ the unemployed, in ways not to compete with present labor. Says Turgot, whom Matthew Arnold calls "the wisest statesman France ever had": "God when he made man with wants and rendered labor an indispensable resource, made the right of work the property of every individual; and this property is the first, the most sacred, and the most imprescriptible of all kinds of property." It would have cities obtain the funds for doing this by conducting gas works, surface railroads, etc. for a profit for the city, instead of having them owned by rich capitalists favored by city franchises.

Christian Socialists would have the nations own and manage railroads, the telegraph, expressage, etc. In every way it would replace competition by fraternal combination, and it would press toward reform in all these ways. It is not one reform. It is many reforms on one *principle.* Perhaps most important of all is land reform. Christian Socialism would revert to the Bible principle, that God is the owner of all the earth, and men only entitled to its use. It would, therefore, favor the reclaiming of the land for the use of all the people, by taxing land values on a graduated scale, and increasingly every few years, till finally the whole value of the natural resources of the earth be taken for the people, and not for the favored few. Christian Socialism would not go out of the world to save the world. It would be in it, tho not of it. Gradually it would influence cities and states and nations.[1]

But this was evolutionary progress rather than revolutionary radicalism. As H. Richard Niebuhr said: "Evolution, growth, development, the culture of the religious life, the nurture of the kindly sentiments, the extension of humanitarian ideals and the progress of civilization took the place of the Christian revolution."[2]

There was one social gospel radical of the 1890's who admitted that the Christian revolution might need to use coercion to accomplish necessary reforms. This was George D. Herron, whose meteoric flash across the social gospel sky was the most dramatic career of the movement. Embodying many of the qualities of the prophet, Herron was an enigmatic mixture of zeal, insight, sensitivity to wrong, and martyrdom. From his post as professor of "applied Christianity" at Grinnell College he soon after 1893 became a flaming evangelist calling on the Church to reconstruct society. The very incarnation of the midwestern populist–social gospel radicalism of the decade, Herron lectured across the country, wrote furiously, and was greeted as prophet or heretic. As his distrust of human institutions deepened, he questioned the permanence of marriage. After being sued for divorce, he married an heiress in 1901, and soon joined the Socialist Party. His career shattered and the movement compromised, Herron spent the remainder of his life in Europe, where he labored to promote the popularity of President Wilson and performed some special diplomatic services for the President at Versailles.[3]

A prophet born out of season, Herron phrased the Populist discontent of the 1890's in terms that could be congenial to the late twentieth century. His "system" was in brief, a challenge to the church not to reform but to reconstruct society in accordance with the standards of Jesus. This essentially socialistic proposal involved criticism of the existing order and of the church, and demanded social justice. The goal was outlined as a "Christian state" to be based upon the principle of social sacrifice. Herron's strictures against capitalism were neither gentle nor tactful. Rooted in traditional Protestant and democratic ideology, his critique traced the widespread poverty and discontent of the times to the centralization of wealth and control of business by an irresponsible industrial despotism created by a false science of society. The unwarranted and unethical assumption that natural law must be allowed to run its course has produced "the unspeakably corrupt world of 'business,' now the chief danger to the nation and the greatest enemy of human life." Competition is not law, but anarchy; this magnification of selfishness into a universal principle is resulting in social disintegration. It is social imbecility, economic waste, the atheism of civilization, and hell on earth. Monopoly is its natural fruit and the whole social issue is rapidly resolving itself into a question of whether or not capital can be controlled by law. Our industrial order is wicked and doomed; the social traits we once lauded have become vices and tyrannies.

To approve of such a civilization is to reject Christ and all that he stood for, said Herron. Any man who believes that a Christian life can be lived in the present order is either profound in ethical ignorance or he deliberately lies. "The worst charge that can be made against a Christian is that he attempts to justify the existing social order." The church, whose duty it is to proclaim righteousness, is subservient to wealth; its efforts to reconcile the business morality of modern industrialism with the ethics of Christ is treason to the kingdom of God. The prevailing forms of conservative Christianity are a gigantic moral heresy; as an institution the church is not Christian. A caste religion, Protestantism misrepresents Jesus Christ, does not know what he taught, and believes his teachings impractical.

Loyalty to Christ means rejection of the prevailing economic morality by individual, church, and society. If we believe that Jesus' doctrines are true we must take fundamental issue with those who assume that man's first duty is to gain a living. To be a Christian is to make righteousness the chief pursuit of life: the application of Christianity is the church's opportunity. No infidelity is so terrible as that of the so-called Christian who fails to exert himself toward the regeneration of social conditions, and no atheism is so frightful as the belief that society must remain as it is. The church is a means to an end—the kingdom of God, a just social order. Its work is the salvation of society. It was sent to be a sacrificial and redemptive life in the world. Not the cross, but the church that bears and offers no cross is turning men from Christ.

The central theme of Herron's evangel was the principle of sacrifice, which . . . was related but subordinate to the doctrine of stewardship. . . . The notion of social self-denial gradually assumed more importance in his thought and led him finally to socialism. What is needed, said Herron, is not successful men, but a generation great enough to fail according to worldly standards. The imperative of the hour is the assertion of the cross as the eternal principle of all divine and human action. The driving forces of the universe are sacrificial and redemptive. "Christianity is the realization of the universal sacrifice, of the philanthropy of God, of the redemptive righteousness of Christ, in society. . . . The fulfillment of Christianity will be the mutual sacrifice of God and his world in the society of a common need. . . . " This is not merely the old Hebrew principle of loving one's neighbor as much as oneself: the true Christian is he who makes his life an offering to human need. Likewise a society that partakes of this sacrificial and redemptive quality will thus become Christian.

Such a society would be a socialistic one. The connecting link between socialism and the principle of sacrifice was provided in Herron's belief that "every religious and political question is fundamentally economic." Economic relations concern the social prophet because they are the root of spiritual life, which can flourish only in soil enriched by the equal opportunity provided by social justice. The growth of monopoly and governmental corruption is turning the economic question into a moral one, because conscience demands the right to organize material things as the foundation of spiritual freedom. Unemployment, scarcity, and poverty, due to monopoly and organized selfishness, will be wiped out only by a changed economic system. Herron stated this view in a commencement oration in 1898:

> Some of us believe that the public ownership of the resources and means of production is the sole answer to the social question. In order that each may have according to his needs, and be secure in the private property wherewith to express his individuality, the resources upon which the people in common depend must by the people in common be owned and administered. The common ownership of the earth, with industrial democracy in production, is the only ground upon which personal property and liberty can be built, the only soil in which individuality may take root.

Such an arrangement would be the political appearing of Christ, "manifest in the increasing social functions of the state, and the socialization of law"; paralleling this development Herron observed around him an increasing appreciation of Christ's law of sacrifice as "the fundamental law of society."

Although privately a supporter of the Socialistic Labor party throughout this period, Herron did not advocate political socialism as a religious creed, for he distrusted it as he did other panaceas such as the single tax because at best they could incarnate the teachings of Jesus only in part. Herron was, however, ready to follow any man or program that would take even the blindest first steps toward the organization of "the peace of goodwill among men." Thus he could assert that "a pure socialism becomes the only form through which religion can express itself in life and progress," once the fundamental character of sacrifice is acknowledged. Human justice and peace, order and harmony are but a dream save through apprehension of sacrifice as the law of social and universal coherence. Religion becomes supersition and tyranny unless translated into social values and manifested in social justice. The demand for social justice and industrial democracy was often repeated by Herron. The revival we need today is "the restitution of stolen goods, of wealth gained through oppression, extortion, and economic atheism." There is no justice as long as capital is allowed to do as it pleases without regard for the welfare of society as a whole. Democracy, good for the state, is also good for industry. George III's taxation of Americans without representation was no more unjust than the practice of claiming advantages from society on the part of corporations that refuse society a voice in their affairs. "An industrial democracy would be the actualization of Christianity. It is the logic of the Sermon on the Mount, which consists of the natural laws by which industrial justice and social peace can be obtained and established."

Herron's "Christian state," based upon "a clear line of Christian teaching" begun by Jesus Christ, was his answer to the problem of how to effect an economic organization that would express in material form the highest spiritual forces. It was to represent society organized for the good of all its members, and serving no selfish ends of its own. If the state is thus to fulfill the present longings of the masses, it must become Christian, wrote Herron:

> Except the state be born again, except it be delivered from pagan doctrines of law and government, from commercial and police conceptions of its functions, from merely individual theories of freedom, it cannot see the divine social kingdom. . . . If the state

would be saved from the wrath of the rising social passion, it must believe in Christ as its Lord, and translate his sacrifice into its laws. Our institutions must become the organized expression of Christ's law of love, if the state is to obey the coming social conscience that is to command great moral revolutions in political thought and action. For society is the organized sacrifice of the people.

To Herron this was not merely mystical or utopian. The state would not need to legislate in religious terminology in order to become "the social organ of the Christian life of the people." It would simply embody "the common faith and will of men to fuse their differences, justify their inequalities, universalize their interests, communize their aims and efforts" by translating Christ's principles into "political association and collective action." It would provide "a new social machinery in order that love and conscience (might) organize the world for the common good of all." In such a society Christianity would supply "the forces that can procure social justice," which forces can be actualized only through the agency of the state.

In the social stirrings of his day Herron saw "the beginnings of a great political movement, inspired for the purpose of translating the righteousness of Christ into the legislation of the nation, and the making of his mind the national political sense." Spurred by his feeling of crisis Herron's preaching bore the prophetic note of urgency: the assertion of the cross as "the eternal principle of all divine and human action" was the imperative of the hour. Herron felt that near at hand there was a religious movement unlike anything in the past—the beginnings of a new spiritual development, churchless, the bringer of liberty, springing from "the seed of Christ" in the soil of common humanity. The social revolt likewise portended the retribution of the Lord: "The kingdom of the Christ is coming among men as a divine judgment, deep and swift, sudden and unobserved, straightening out the crooked things of the earth. It hurls upon us vast problems, travailing with the destinies of nations and civilizations."[4]

Americans who demonstrated in the streets three generations later might have heard Herron gladly, though it had then been decades since radicalism had flourished in the Midwest. James Dombrowski, a Marxist historian, believes that while Herron held that religion should appeal to good will and renunciation, it must be willing to use coercion if necessary in the struggle for economic power. Herron accepted the class struggle as a fact of history, believing that the workers must organize to obtain justice; as his thought matured he became more radical and would have approved the use of force to bring in the revolution.[5] "It will not do to say that revolution is not coming, or pronounce it of the devil," wrote Herron, declaring that it had required the Spanish Inquisition "to usher in religious freedom," and the French Revolution "to translate this into political freedom; God knows what it may yet cost to translate both into the freedom of economic equality."[6] Even in their wildest forms, revolutions are "the impulses of God moving in tides of fire through the life of man."[7]

Through the pages of *The Kingdom,* the magazine provided as a mouthpiece for Herron by his friends, as we have seen, a diverse group of "come-outers" assembled to establish a "Christian Commonwealth Colony" on a thousand acres in Georgia—a unique experiment in the checkered history of American communitarian enterprises. Superficially unified by the inspiration derived from Herron, these cooperators were also influenced by disparate and in the long run centrifugal ideas from Marx, St. Francis, Jesus, and Tolstoi, whose doctrine of nonresistance was in vogue. Their goal was to organize "an educational and religious society whose purpose [was] to obey the teachings of Jesus Christ in all matters of life, and labor, and in the use of property." Everything was owned in common and everyone who came was equally welcomed, from college professor to one-legged man with nine children. In the first issue of *The Social Gospel* the ideology of the Colony was set forth:

The Christian Commonwealth is organized [the editor wrote] to extend the sphere of the dominion of Christ that it may cover all the days, all the dollars, and all of life; to enable men and women who have been filled with a divine inspiration for salvation and righteousness to make that inspiration an abiding, perpetual, permanent force in their lives. It is organized to enable all who will to love and labor for one another and for all who need. Its men and women are so moved by a burning zeal for the Kingdom of God and His righteousness, for the altruistic principles and life of the Christ whose they are and whom they serve, that no selfish considerations, nor life itself, can turn them from their service of love.

Our constitution is the law of love. "Thou shalt love the Lord thy God with all thy heart, and thy neighbor as thyself." Our love is a pouring out of all labor and all property that can be used to make others happy, and our neighbors extend to even the "least" of Christ's brethren who need. The selfish love of property has gone with the selfish uses of property. The question of individual property-holding rights and personal privileges vanishes like mist before the rising sun in the presence of the Holy Spirit of Love who inspires an all-consuming passion for the good and welfare and salvation and happiness of all men. The property question, the transfers from me to thee and from thee to me, and the dividing lines between "thine and mine," are no more a problem or a source of anxiety to us than they were to the Pentecostal Church which was full of the Holy Ghost. Our main problems are as to how we may house more homeless, and feed more hungry, and provide industry for more labor, and bind up more broken-hearted, and inspire more faith and courage, and minister to more need, and contribute more happiness. In the presence of these causes every selfish strife and every selfish love goes down. And the Kingdom of Heaven, the most practical, sensible, and livable system of human life ever proposed to men, is at hand for you and for me, and for all who will receive it.[8]

As with most colonies, matters went well for a time—the experiment lasted about three years—but nonresistance proved powerless against slander, frost, and typhoid fever. It was, however, this group of idealists who unwittingly named the social gospel movement through the title of the magazine, *The Social Gospel,* as we saw in Chapter 14.

History repeated itself in the first decade of the twentieth century when another generation of socially minded agitators banded themselves into the "Christian Socialist Fellowship" after reading an obscure Iowa paper called *The Christian Socialist.* This group flourished for a while, as did numerous miniscule church-related bodies dedicated to persuading the church that social redemption was to be obtained by adopting the platform of the Socialist Party of America. "The essential points" of our crusade, they said, are the fatherhood of God, the brotherhood of man, the earth for all, "and loyalty to the International Socialist Movement as the means of realizing the social ideal of Jesus." Undoubtedly this propaganda helped to swell the record-breaking vote cast for Eugene Debs in the presidential campaign of 1912, but socialism was then as far from capturing the church as it had been when Edward H. Rogers and Jesse H. Jones had challenged the status quo in the 1870's. It was a major ingredient in the social gospel of Walter Rauschenbusch and it raised up leaders like Herron and Norman Thomas. Its influence upon the socializing of American Protestantism

was incalculable, but the true political vehicle of the social gospel was
to be Progressivism.

Notes

1. *The New Encyclopedia of Social Reform* (New York and London: Funk
and Wagnalls, 1908), 204.

2. H. Richard Niebuhr, *The Kingdom of God in America* (Chicago–New
York: Willett, Clark, 1937), 192–93.

3. Hopkins, *Rise of the Social Gospel,* ch. 11; Dombrowski, *The Early
Days of Christian Socialism in America* (New York: Columbia University Press,
1936), ch. 12. Some of Herron's books were: *The Larger Christ* (1891), *The New
Redemption* (1893), *The Christian Society* (1894), *The Christian State* (1895),
Social Meanings of Religious Experiences (1896).

4. Hopkins, 189–94.

5. Dombrowski, 190.

6. Herron, *Social Meanings,* 14. Dombrowski, 192.

7. Herron, *The New Redemption,* 15. Dombrowski, 193.

8. *The Social Gospel* (Commonwealth, Ga.) 1, no. 1 (Feb., 1898), 15–16.
A great deal of research remains to be done on the relationship between midwestern populism and the social gospel.

16   Progressivism
        as Christian Strategy

The first two decades of the twentieth century are known as the Progressive era, a period during which the country was swept by a reforming wave such as it had not felt since the 1840's. The middle class awoke to the mockery that the factories and the cities were making of the American dream, and, as had the Populists in the 1890's, turned to reform with enthusiasm. The problems discussed in this book, plus the corruption of government at all levels, and the mushrooming of giant corporations produced reform legislation that ranged from the strengthening of the Interstate Commerce Commission to the inspection of food and drugs. Perhaps the income tax, authorized by constitutional amendment a few weeks before Wilson's inauguration in 1913, symbolized as nothing else could the arrival of the industrial age.

A leading historian calls Progressivism "a phase in the history of the Protestant conscience, a latter-day Protestant revival."[1] Another writer points out that the characters in *In His Steps* "sound and act like the Progressives of a later day": they engage in politics, demand regulation of the railroads, volunteer to serve in settlement houses, and organize home mission projects instead of foreign.[2] Both Theodore Roosevelt and Woodrow Wilson, the greatest of the Progressives, consulted with Walter Rauschenbusch on their social programs.

Rauschenbusch's biographer, D. R. Sharpe, recounts a conversation in which Rauschenbusch professed his belief that socialism was the wave of the future for the United States. Roosevelt replied: "Not so long as I am President . . . ." But he admitted his intention to adopt socialistic ideas "so far as those theories are wise and practicable."[3] The virtual chaplain of Roosevelt's Progressivism was Lyman Abbott, editor of the *Outlook*, the country's leading magazine of news comment; he was also pastor of Plymouth (Congregational) Church of Brooklyn, one of the nation's most prestigious pulpits. Abbott once attended a news conference in the White

House at which Roosevelt was reading a forthcoming message.
Suddenly the President stopped, swung his swivel chair around, and
declared: "My critics will call this preaching. But I have got such a
bully pulpit." Abbott commented that in his judgment none of the
many services Roosevelt rendered to his country could transcend in
importance his having awakened the nation's civic conscience.[4]

Abbott invited Roosevelt to publish his speeches on "Big
Corporations Commonly Called Trusts" in the *Outlook*, because
"here was a voice to which the whole nation would listen, urging
on the people that policy of government regulation of great organized
industries which "The Outlook" had been urging for years."[5]   When
Roosevelt retired from the presidency in 1909, Abbott invited him to
join the *Outlook's* staff of contributing editors. Here was another
"bully pulpit"; Roosevelt accepted because he believed the magazine
to be preaching "the things that are most necessary to the salvation
of this people."[6] He worked at a desk like any other writer and
contributed comments on the whole gamut of reforms over several
years.

Roosevelt would mount any pulpit offered. An avid reader of
the new sociological literature, he admired men like Professor Edward
A. Ross of the University of Wisconsin who were opening up new ter-
ritories. After reading advance copy of Ross's *Sin and Society* in 1907,
Roosevelt wrote the sociologist this letter, which was included in the
published book, the thesis of which anticipated both Rauschenbusch's
and Reinhold Niebuhr's definitions of social sin:

You define "sin" as conduct that harms another in contradistinction to
"vice," by which we mean practices that harm one's self; and you
attack as they should be attacked the men who at the present day do
more harm to the body politic by their sinning than all others. With
almost all that you write I am in full and hearty sympathy. As you well
say, if a ring is to be put in the snout of the greedy strong, only
organized society can do it. You war against the vast iniquities in
modern business, finance, politics, journalism, due to the ineffective-
ness of public opinion in coping with the dominant types of wrong-
doing in a huge, rich, highly complex industrial civilization like ours.
You show that the worst evils we have to combat have inevitably
evolved along with the evolution of society itself, and that the perspective of conduct must change from age to age, so that our moral judg-

ment may be recast in order more effectively to hold to account the really dangerous foes of our present civilization. You do not confine yourself to mere destructive criticism. Your plea is for courage, for uprightness, for far-seeing sanity, for active constructive work. There is no reason why we should feel despondent over the outlook of modern civilization, but there is every reason why we should be fully alert to the dangers ahead. Modern society has developed to a point where there is real cause for alarm lest we shall go the way of so many ancient communities, where the state was brought to ruin because politics became the mere struggle of class against class. Your book is emphatically an appeal to the general sense of right as opposed to mere class interest. As you put it, the danger is as great if the law is twisted to be an instrument of the greed of one class as if it is twisted to be an instrument of the vengefulness of another. You reject that most mischievous of socialist theses, viz.: that progress is to be secured by the strife of classes. You insist, as all healthy-minded patriots should insist, that public opinion, if only sufficiently enlightened and aroused, is equal to the necessary regenerative tasks and can yet dominate the future. Your book is wholesome and sane and I trust that its influence will be widespread.[7]

Roosevelt told the Progressive Convention in 1912 that they "stood at Armageddon" and battled for the Lord. Woodrow Wilson fought on a different plain. In an almost forgotten speech to an assemblage of Episcopal clergymen in 1910, the then president of Princeton University formulated the ethical basis of Progressivism in terms of their particular vocation:

It is evident to us all that within the past few years there has been an extraordinary awakening in civic consciousness, and, beyond this, an extraordinary awakening of the public mind with relation to the moral values involved in our national life. We are now witnessing the dawn of a day when there will be a universal re-valuation of men and of affairs. There is no mistaking the present dissolution of political parties; no mistaking the fact that you cannot restore the enthusiasm of our existing parties by turning backward in any respect and merely recalling the formulas, or shouting the slogans, of past campaigns and past transactions. The Nation is not looking over its shoulder, nor acting in retrospect; it has its eyes on the future.

And because of this, the Nation has to grapple, on an extraordinary scale, with the newness of the day in which we live. The elements of our modern life are so new that we are bewildered when we try to form moral judgments regarding them. For example, how difficult it is now to assess an individual, in view of the fact that he does not now act as an integer, but as merely a fraction of modern society, inextricably associated with others in the conduct of business, and dominated by corporate responsibility. It is impossible that he should exercise, except within a very narrow circle, independent judgment. And therefore the old forms of moral responsibility we find it very difficult to apply. For, in order that we should be morally responsible, there must be freedom of individual choice, and that is so much circumscribed, narrowed, and confined by the divisions of modern life that we are groping to find a new basis, a new standard, and a new guide of responsibility, by which we shall walk, and to which we may hold our consciences square.

Every man that I meet, who comes from any large city, tells me the same thing: that the city he is in is suddenly acquiring a civic consciousness that it never had before, bestowing minute and critical attention upon its own affairs. We have, it seems, come again to an era like that in which our Federal Government was formed. De Tocqueville in his admirable book, "Democracy in America," calls attention to the self-possession with which the American people examined their own affairs in the time of the re-formation of their Government, and changed the whole of their Government without, as he says, having "drawn a tear or a drop of blood from mankind." We are again turning our eyes upon ourselves, re-examining, as it were, the very foundations of our institutions, and determining that, come what may, we will rectify what is wrong. Let us cherish the hope that we may again draw the attention of the world by bringing in the dawn of a day of veritable liberty and self-government.

Every pulse ought to be quickened by such an age; and it is in the guidance of such a day that the clergyman's obligations lie. Every age has had its own misgivings about the Church. The prevailing temptation, the persistent temptation of the Church, is to ally itself with certain social interests. The temptation has been not to be democratic in its organization, in its sympathies, in its judgments.

In looking back through the history of political society, I have often been struck by the circumstance that the polities of the middle ages would certainly have broken down for lack of administrative capacity if it had not been for the Roman Catholic Church. It supplied administrative ability to all the chancelleries of Europe during that long period when Europe was aristocratic, and not democratic. For the Church in that period was democratic in that it had its rootage in the common people. No peasant was so humble that he could not become a priest; no priest so obscure that he might not rise to be the Pope of Christendom. All sources of power were supplied in the organization of the Church. The political capacity of Europe renewed itself constantly by drawing upon that all-inclusive institution. While aristocracy was decaying, the people were feeding fresh blood into the great Church.

So long as the Church—any Church—retains this conception, keeps the sources of its strength open, it will not only serve itself, but will serve society as perhaps no other organization could conceive of serving. It will then keep true to its fundamental conception, the fundamental conception of Christianity: that there is no difference between man and man in respect to his relationship to his God. We do not arrange the pews of our churches on this principle. We do not arrange the worship of our churches on this principle; and in proportion as we do not, we lose, and deserve to lose, the confidence of the great mass of the people, who are led by our practices to believe that Christianity is not for the obscure, but for the rich and prosperous and contented.

It seems to me perfectly clear that an extraordinary opportunity is afforded by the present day to the Church; to the whole Church, whether Protestant or Catholic—an opportunity to supply what society is looking for; that is, a clear standard of moral measurement, a standard of revaluation, a standard of re-assessment, of men and affairs.

When I ask myself how the Church is going to do this, the first thing that is apparent is that the Church must do it through the example of her ministers. They must devote themselves to those ideals which have no necessary connection with any form or convention of society whatever, but which take each human soul and make it over and weigh it in the scales of revelation. I have known a good many ministers in my day who were very careful of the social connections they formed. I have known a great many who did not afford to society an example of that general, universal sympathy and contact with all sorts and conditions of men which was afforded by our Lord and Master Himself, who did not make any social distinctions in His choice of associates. I have not seen the ministers of our churches, as a rule, follow His example in that respect.

I have, it is true, seen them do, under a sudden and temporary impulse, things which they supposed were equivalent to this. For instance, I have known ministers to frequent places where they ought not to go, and where no self-respecting man ought to go, under the impression, apparently, that what Christ allied Himself with was places, not human souls. What He sought out was the individual spirit, not its environment. It is not necessary to go to saloons in order to make one's self the friend of a man who drinks. The best way to serve such a man is not to find him in such surroundings, but to lead him into better; not to find him there, but to draw him thence, by counsel and sympathy.

The singularity of the ministerial profession, it seems to me, is in this. In any other profession it is sufficient that the man who follows it should *do* something well, or *know* something well. But it is expected of a minister that he should *be* something. It is not necessary that a lawyer should be separated from the world about him in point of character; it is not necessary that a physician should be separate from the world in habit of life. If he has knowledge, skill of hand, and sympathetic touch, he may treat the human being under treatment or operation as he would treat a laboratory substance or a cadaver. Indeed, a too-sympathetic physician would be a peril to the patient. But the minister must *be* something as well as *do* something. He must consistently make an impression upon everybody he approaches that he is in something unlike the ordinary run of men. I do not mean that he should be sanctimonious, for that repels; it must be something in his own consciousness. My own dear father was a clergyman. One of the most impressive incidents of my youth occurs to me. He was in a party of gentlemen, when one of them used a profane word, unthinkingly. With a start he turned to my father, and said, "I beg your pardon, Dr. Wilson." My father said, very simply and gently, "Oh, sir, you have not offended *me.*" The emphasis he laid upon that word "me" brought with it a tremendous impression. All present felt that my father regarded himself as an ambassador of Someone higher; their realization of it showed in their faces.

If ministers would acquire this—would move among men like the standard-bearers of God, they would do the first thing necessary to establish this new guide and standard for which the world is looking.

The Church can in its definite teaching contribute to the enlightenment and guidance of our, for the time being, bewildered society. The Church ought to expound the difference between individual responsibility and corporate responsibility. The Church ought to discover the individual in modern society. The great temptation to every man in business affairs in our day is that he can so easily run to covert in some organization. That is the great difficulty also, with our political organizations. We have so divided up responsibility that we cannot put our finger on the man who ought to be held responsible. Tom Nast, the famous cartoonist, drew a picture, you remember, of the Tweed Ring as a circle of men, each pointing his thumb to his neighbor and saying, " 'Twan't me." The imperative necessity of politics is to obtain a " 'Tis you!" form of government. The Church ought to assist society to pick out individuals. It ought to show, in its administration and discipline, that it will not tolerate for a moment men who have been responsible for demoralizing our corporate life.

I dare say every man who has aided to demoralize society finds refuge and harborage in some Church; and so long as the Church harbors these men, it cannot afford society the standard for which society longs. I mean that in the case of all such individuals the Church should make them realize that absolute reformation is the price of their continuing to consort with the members of the Church. Full opportunity to repent, but the absolute obligation of reformation must be the programme of regeneration—an absolute, unhesitating, uncompromising analysis of what it is that they have done, and what they have imperilled and then absolute insistence that they square their conduct with the standards of the Church. They should be dealt with with sympathy and tenderness, but given no absolution. If the Church with any degree of unanimity should undertake this, the dockets of our courts would not be so full. It would not be necessary to set the majesty of the law in operation, if the majesty of opinion were first set in operation. Men are not afraid of the penalties of the law; but men are afraid of the look into the accusing eyes of their friends and acquaintances. The most terrible punishments are spiritual punishments; the heart-breaking thing is that the people who trusted you have ceased to trust you, and that you are not free of their company on any terms except those which show utter repentance. What rules the heart is what moulds society; and the standards of opinion are the standards of private conduct.

Then it seems to me that the Church could, in the administration of all its affairs, in handling its congregations, in the conduct of its charitable work, in all those things in which it reaches out to touch and raise society, show to society that it is acting upon unworldly standards, and not upon worldly ones; that it does not matter to it whether it have properly appointed churches and parish houses or not; that the work will go on through its love of men whether the proper instrumentalities be afforded it or not; and that it will be conducted upon an absolutely democratic principle which distinguishes man from man by his spiritual, and not by his social position.

The Church ought to make itself in every respect a society of mutual self-sacrifice and self-abnegation; and then it will have afforded society that standard of which it is in search. I know, to my cost, that society is in search of standards; because what society now wants more than anything else is disinterested advice. It is resorting to the colleges for this sort of advice. It takes it for granted that a college teacher is not a self-seeking person, or he would not have been foolish enough to go into an underpaid profession. It believes that he is likely to know what he is talking about, and can be counted upon to speak it, because presumably free from those obstacles to candor which so embarrass the lips of other men. So college professors are appealed to, here, there and everywhere; not because they are specially able, but because they at least are supposed to be disinterested. It is as if society were now calling upon the colleges to do what it ought to call upon the Church to do. It ought to be a matter of course that the priest, the minister, has devoted himself to unworldly objects, and that he can be counted on to speak his mind without fear except to transgress the law of God.

The attitude of ministers to the State, if what I have been saying is even in part true, is a matter susceptible of the most rigid analysis. The minister ought to be an instrument of judgment, with motives not secular but religious; who conceives in his mind those reforms which are based upon the statutes of morality; who tries to draw society together by a new motive which is not the motive of the economist or of the politician, but the motive of the profoundly religious man.

"Christian Socialism" I believe to be a contradiction in terms. The motives of the pure Socialist are clearly Christian motives; but the moment you translate Socialism into a definite programme, into which you are going to force men by a universal social compulsion, it ceases to be a spiritual programme. Socialism as a programme of organization is the negation of Socialism as a body of motives. I can understand Christian anarchism; for Christian anarchism means a state of society where no government will be needed, because each man will live within the law of an enlightened and purified conscience. But "Christian Socialists" are contending that a certain political, material and economic programme will be the best for all spiritual interests. If true, it would be the millennium. I understand all descriptions of the millennium to be descriptions of that Christian *anarchism* in which every man will be a law unto himself, but every man's will will be purified and rectified by being centred not upon himself, but upon Christ; anarchism not meaning disorder, but that broadest of all order which is based on self-sacrifice, charity and friendship. The programme of the minister, therefore, is a programme of devotion to things always outside of himself, never centred upon himself.

The old casuists used to reduce all sin to egotism. So soon, they said, as a man got moral values, or any other values, centred in himself, he had skewed the whole moral universe, since the centre is not man, but God; and such a man became saturated with selfishness. Sin is, in almost all its forms, selfishness. It is not always enlightened selfishness, but it is always selfishness. A man may be doing, when sinning, what will yield him nothing but sorrow, bring him anything but satisfaction. But it is satisfaction that he is seeking, and not the right. Therefore the whole morality of the world depends upon those who exert upon men that influence which will turn their eyes from themselves; upon those who devote themselves to the things in which there is no calculation whatever of the effect to be wrought upon themselves or their own fortunes. For when a man most forgets himself he finds himself—his true relation to all the rest of the spiritual universe. A man astray in a desert or a forest has not lost himself; he has lost everything else. Self is the only thing he has not lost. If he can discover in which direction, north, or east, or south, or west, lies any one thing by which he can establish his relation to the world at large, then, and then only, has he truly found himself. A man finds himself only when he finds his relation to the world.

It is the minister's first vocation so to find himself, and to devote himself to a common interest, which may or may not be his own private or selfish interest. It is the duty of every priest to do what it is the duty of the whole Church to do—to judge other men, with love but without compromise of moral standards; uncompromisingly to assess what they have done, without ceasing to love them for having done it; so as to let no man escape from full reckoning of his conduct. That is a task too great for the courage of most ministers. I am not criticising. It is the hardest thing in the world to do. I am not saying for a moment that I would have the grace to do it. But that is one reason why I have kept out of the ministry.

There are ways and ways of performing such a duty. You can deal justly without insult, with gentleness and kindness. I have had men tell me things of that sort in a way that made me love them, because I knew they were willing to take risks for my sake; and there is no finer proof of friendship and love than that. But whether it is hard or easy, that is the moral obligation of the ministry.

To pass further than that; the minister ought to make those with whom he is dealing realize that he holds the integrity of souls higher than any other kind of prosperity; higher than fortune, wealth, social position—than any other kind of success. I believe, as the profoundest philosophy in the world, that only integrity can bring salvation or satisfaction; can bring happiness; that no amount of fortune can, in a man's own consciousness, atone for a lost integrity of the soul. Beyond question, a minister lets down all the levels of morality in the world by compromising with his own or any other man's conscience. The moral levels of the world are to be maintained by him, or they will collapse with a general subsidence of all that is steadfast in the universe. If you are going to admit fear into your calculations, then the world is infinitely imperilled. The Church is the mentor of righteousness, and the minister must be the exemplar of righteousness.

The central force that makes for righteousness is the fountain of it all. The Church, when it uncovers those waters which alone can quench the thirst of mankind, will prove to have been the source of all the life-giving influences that kept weary men alive. For she is the guardian of that sure belief that there are things beyond this life, when we shall see face to face, shall know as we are known.[8]

Notes

1. Richard Hofstatder, *The Age of Reform* (New York: Knopf, 1955), 152; see also H. F. May, *Protestant Churches and Industrial America* (New York: Harper, 1949), 170–81.

2. Carl N. Degler, *Out of Our Past* (New York: Harper & Row, 1959), 371–72.

3. D. R. Sharpe, *Walter Rauschenbusch* (New York: Macmillan, 1942), 413–14.

4. Lyman Abbott, *The Roosevelt Pilgrimage of 1922* (n.p., 1922), 15.

5. Abbott, *Reminiscences,* (Boston–New York: Houghton, 1915), 442–43.

6. *The Outlook,* March 5, 1909, 511.

7. E. A. Ross, *Sin and Society: An Analysis of Latter-Day Iniquity, with a Letter from President Roosevelt* (Boston–New York: Houghton, 1907), ix–xi.

8. Woodrow Wilson, "The Clergyman and the State," an address at the General Theological Seminary in New York, April 6, 1910, originally printed in the New York *Churchman,* 101 (April 23, 1910), 577–79; reprinted in Arthur S. Link, ed., *The Papers of Woodrow Wilson,* 20 (Princeton: Princeton University Press, 1975), 328–35.

17 Church Agencies for Social Action

The maturity of the social gospel movement was proved when, during the first fifteen years of the twentieth century, it was recognized by most major Protestant denominations.[1] This was done by official commissions that were added to the national organizations and staffed by paid secretaries. The first denominations to establish such programs were the (Northern) Presbyterians and the Episcopalians, both of which acted in 1901. They were soon followed by the Congregationalists; the Methodists came on in 1907, and the next year when the Northern (now American) Baptist Convention was organized it authorized such a move. Let us follow these developments in the Congregational denomination.

Congregationalists had been reticent about establishing a national organization, but when they met in Boston in 1865 to do so, they adopted a statement that reflected their historic stance and looked confidently ahead:

> It was the grand peculiarity of our Puritan Fathers, that they held this gospel, not merely as the ground of their personal salvation, but as declaring the worth of man by the incarnation and sacrifice of the Son of God; and therefore applied its principles to elevate society, to regulate education, to civilize humanity, to purify law, to reform the church and the State, to assert, to defend, and to die for liberty: in short, to mold and redeem by its all-transforming energy everything that belongs to man in his individual and social relations.[2]

Needled in the 1880's by Josiah Strong, Washington Gladden, and William Jewett Tucker, and in the 1890's by Graham Taylor, David Starr Jordan, David N. Beach, and others, the denomination first set up a commission on labor at its national meeting in 1901. When it next met in 1904, this commission presented a program outlining the functions of labor committees in local churches and suggesting that sympathetic relations be established with both organized and unorganized labor, and that workers' efforts for physical, social, and moral betterment be aided. The committee was agreed that the industrial question had "come to stay," that "justice to capital and labor alike" was necessary, and that "only by the principles of the Gospel" could viable solutions be reached.

The 1904 meeting of the National Council at Des Moines held a joint session with the local labor council, hearing addresses by Graham Taylor and E. E. Clark, the Grand Chief Conductor of the Order of Railway Conductors. Not until 1910 was the commission given a paid secretary, but he, the Reverend Henry A. Atkinson, soon produced a three-year correspondence course in "social service studies," traveled widely, investigated strike conditions in Michigan and Colorado, studied plants using profit-sharing plans, and aided in several urban religious surveys. In 1913 the denomination created a supervisory "Commission on Social Service" that acted as guide, irritant, and overseer until 1934. In 1915 it had set forth these objectives:

To make known the social principles of Christianity.

To arouse the spirit of social service in our churches.

To secure the cooperation of the churches with all other agencies doing social service work.

To outline programs for churches in their work for community betterment.

To interpret the gospel of Jesus Christ and the new purpose of the church to industrial workers.

To represent the denomination in official capacity at meetings where labor and social service subjects are discussed.

To study and give leadership within the denomination for service in bettering the rural conditions and making more effective the ministry of our country churches.

To study the social waste caused by vice, crime and bad economic conditions, and to develop programs for meeting these needs.

To organize, develop, unify, and inspire the masculine forces of the denomination.[3]

When this statement became outdated, the National Council adopted a fresh, if lengthy, new description of its social ideals in 1925:

We believe in making the social and spiritual ideals of Jesus our test for community as well as for individual life; in strengthening and deepening the inner personal relationship of the individual with God, and recognizing his obligation and duty to society. This is crystallized in the two commandments of Jesus: "Love Thy God and Love Thy Neighbor." We believe this pattern ideal for a Christian social order involves the recognition of the sacredness of life, the supreme worth of each single personality and our common membership in one another—the brotherhood of all. In short, it means creative activity in cooperation with our fellow human beings, and with God, in the everyday life of society and in the development of a new and better world social order. Translating this ideal:

I. Into Education Means:

1. The building of a social order in which every child has the best opportunity for development.

2. Adequate and equal educational opportunity for all, with the possibility of extended training for those competent.

3. A thorough and scientific program of religious and secular education designed to Christianize everyday life and conduct.

4. Conservation of health, including careful instruction in sex hygiene and home building, abundant and wholesome recreation facilities, and education for leisure, including a nation-wide system of adult education.

5. Insistence on constitutional rights and duties, including freedom of speech, of the press, and of peaceable assemblage.

6. Constructive education and Christian care of dependents, defectives, and delinquents, in order to restore them to normal life whenever possible, with kindly segregation for those who are hopelessly feeble-minded. (This means that such institutions as the jails, prisons, and orphan asylums should be so conducted as to be genuine centers for education and health.)

7. A scientifically planned program of international education

promoting peace and goodwill and exposing the evils of war, intoxicants, illiteracy, and other social sins.

II. Into Industrial and Economic Relationship Means:

1. A reciprocity of service—that group interests, whether of labor or capital, must always be integrated with the welfare of society as a whole, and that society in its turn must insure justice to each group.

2. A frank abandonment of all efforts to secure something for nothing, and recognition that all ownership is a social trust involving Christian administration for the good of all and that the unlimited exercise of the right of private ownership is undesirable.

3. Abolishing child labor and establishing standards for employment of minors which will insure maximum physical, intellectual and moral development.

4. Freedom from employment one day in seven, the eight-hour day as the present maximum for all industrial workers.

5. Providing safe and sanitary industrial conditions especially protecting women; adequate accident, sickness, and unemployment insurance, together with suitable provision for old age.

6. An effective national system of public employment bureaus to make possible the proper distribution of the labor forces of America.

7. That the first charge upon industry should be a minimum comfort wage and that all labor should give an honest day's work for an honest day's pay.

8. Adequate provision for impartial investigation and publicity, conciliation and arbitration in industrial disputes.

9. The right of labor to organize with representatives of its own choosing and, where able, to share in the management of industrial relations.

10. Encouragement of the organization of consumers' cooperatives for the more equitable distribution of the essentials of life.

11. The supremacy of the service rather than the profit motive in the acquisition and use of property on the part of both labor and capital, and the most equitable division of the product of industry that can be devised.

Part III concerned agriculture, share-cropping, and rural destitution.

IV. Into Racial Relations Means:

1. The practice of the American principle of the same protection and rights for all races who share our common life.

2. The elimination of racial discrimination, and substitution of full brotherly treatment for all races in America.

3. The fullest cooperation between the churches of various races even though of different denominations.

4. Educational and social equipment for the special needs of immigrants, with government information bureaus.

V. Into International Relations Means:

1. The removal of every unjust barrier of trade, color, creed, and race, and the practice of equal justice for all nations.

2. The administration of the property and privileges within each country so that they will be of the greatest benefit not only to that nation but to all the world.

3. Discouragement of all propaganda tending to mislead peoples in their international relations or to create prejudice.

4. The replacement of selfish imperialism by such disinterested treatment of backward nations as to contribute the maximum to the welfare of each nation and of all the world.

5. The abolition of military armaments by all nations except for an internal police force.

6. That the church of Christ as an institution should not be used as an instrument or an agency in the support of war.

7. A permanent association of the nations for world peace and goodwill, the outlawry of war, and the settling of differences between nations by conference, arbitration, or by an international court.

We believe it is the duty of every church to investigate local moral and economic conditions as well as to know world needs. We believe that it is only as our churches themselves follow the example and spirit of Jesus in the fullest sense—translating these social ideals into the daily life of the church and the community—that we can ever hope to build the Kingdom of God on earth.

These affirmations we make as Christians and loyal citizens of our beloved country. We present them as an expression of our faith and patriotism. We urge upon all our citizens the support of our cherished institutions, faithfulness at the ballot, respect for law, and loyal support of its administrators. We believe that our country can and will make a great contribution to the realization of Christian ideals throughout the world.[4]

By 1942 this statement came under revision, to meet the needs of a new era. At the bottom of the Depression, the National Council had reorganized the commission as the Council for Social Action. For several decades its monthly magazine *Social Action* led the field of denominational expressions of social concern. The many issues that this one church confronted during the Depression and World War II belie the allegation that the social gospel was dead.

In the late 1950's the denomination merged with the Evangelical and Reformed churches to form the "United Church of Christ," partly in the hope that the name would induce other denominations to join in what might become a major body. Social action continued to be a priority in the new church, the national synod of 1975 replacing the Council for Christian Social Action with a new Office for Church in Society. The moderator saw this action as "strong affirmation of the UCC's commitment to social action."

Notes

1. Hopkins, *Rise of the Social Gospel* (New Haven: Yale University Press, 1940), ch. 17 reviews these developments.

2. C. Howard Hopkins, "A History of Congregational Social Action," *Social Action,* 8, no. 5 (May 15, 1942), 6; from the report of the National Council, Boston, 1866, 347.

3. Hopkins, "Congregational Social Action," 20.

4. Hopkins, "Congregational Social Action," 41–43.

V

An Ecumenical Movement

Introduction

In 1897 a discerning historian wrote that in contrast to the markedly solid political unity of the country, the American churches presented an appearance of diversity—an ecclesiastical miscellany with no coordination, common leadership, or "system of mutual counsel and concert."[1] The most significant development in American religion in the twentieth century has been the effort to overcome this separatism by conscious effort toward cooperation among individuals and churches, and toward the union or reunion of separated churches, all in the hope of an ultimate full restoration of the unity of Christendom. The social gospel was a major factor, if not the major factor, in all this.

Before the Civil War the Y.M.C.A. was introducing Christians of various faiths to one another. During that war a nondenominational agency called the United States Christian Commission rendered social and religious services to the men of the Union armies; after the war it continued as the American Christian Commission to minister to the urban poor. In 1867, the Evangelical Alliance was organized in the United States; it brought together persons of all denominations, as we shall see. Under the dynamic leadership of Josiah Strong, it attempted to unite American Protestants in social action, as Professor Jordan shows in Chapter 18.

During the last quarter of the nineteenth century the nationwide evangelism of Dwight L. Moody was an exercise in denominational cooperation. Moody refused to stage a revival unless the local arrangements were made by a broadly interdenominational committee; often this function was performed by the Y.M.C.A.[2] John R. Mott, Robert E. Speer, and Sherwood Eddy, all protégés of Moody, promoted the nondenominational student Y.M.C.A., in partnership with the student Y.W.C.A., on the college and university campuses of the nation.[3] The social gospel was an early program interest. The missionary branch of the student Associations, known as the Student Volunteer Movement, recruited youthful missionaries for all churches. An outgrowth of these was the World's Student Christian Federation, which Mott promoted

around the world; it proved to be the chief ecumenical training ground
for generations of men and women who worked toward unity in their
own countries and finally brought their churches into the World Council of Churches after World War II.[4]

By the turn of the century there were numerous local federations
of churches and their social service agencies throughout the United
States, the strongest and most influential of which were those in New
York City. In 1900 a great "ecumenical missionary conference" was
held in Carnegie Hall in New York City, which popularized the idea of
missionary cooperation. Five years later another group representing
twenty-nine denominations convened in that same hall. It expressed its
disapproval of the persecution of Jews in Russia and the cruelties being
perpetrated in the Belgian Congo, but its real purpose was to plan for a
national federation of churches. The thrust of the social gospel is apparent in its objectives:

I. To express the fellowship and catholic unity of the Christian Church.[5]
II. To bring the Christian bodies of America into united service for Christ and the world.
III. To encourage devotional fellowship and mutual counsel
concerning the spiritual life and religious activites of the
churches.
IV. To secure a larger combined influence for the churches
of Christ in all matters affecting the moral and social condition of
the people, so as to promote the application of the law of Christ
in every relation of human life.[6]

Delegates to such meetings were still chuckling over President
Roosevelt's earlier remark at a similar gathering: "There are plenty of
targets we need to hit without firing into each other." In 1908 the Federal Council of the Churches of Christ came into being, voted into existence by thirty denominations. It began an aggressive program of social
action at once.[7]

All through the period we have been describing, the Roman Catholic Church in the United States was almost entirely engrossed in the suf-
focating problems forced upon it by the waves of Catholic immigrants
that inundated America's shores. Nevertheless, as we shall see in Chapter 19, a few prophetic spokesmen appeared, and some foundations for
acceptance of the social gospel were laid before World War I.[8] A similar
comment may be made concerning the Jewish community, whose liberal leaders leaned toward reform, but much of their message was alien to

the thousands of their coreligionists who also flocked to the promised land during these years, when the melting-pot ran over. We shall examine their stance in Chapter 20.[9]

Notes

1. Samuel McCrea Cavert, *The American Churches in the Ecumenical Movement, 1900–1968* (New York: Association, 1968), 15, quoting Leonard W. Bacon, *A History of American Christianity* (New York, 1897), 398ff.

2. C. Howard Hopkins, *History of the Y.M.C.A. in North America* (New York: Association, 1951), 370. J. F. Findlay, Jr., *Dwight L. Moody, American Evangelist, 1837–1899* (Chicago–London: University of Chicago Press, 1969), 197–206.

3. Hopkins, ch. 7.

4. Ruth Rouse, *The World's Student Christian Federation* (London: S.C.M., 1948); Ruth Rouse and S. C. Neill, *A History of the Ecumenical Movement* (London: S.P.C.K., 1954), 330ff, 599–612.

5. The word "catholic" as used in this context meant universal or ecumenical.

6. Cavert, pp. 48–49. There was a fifth objective, to foster local and/or state branches of the Federal Council, but this was not done.

7. C. H. Hopkins, *Rise of the Social Gospel* (New Haven: Yale University Press, 1940), 312–17.

8. For a broad introduction to Catholic social action in the United States, see A. I. Abell, *American Catholicism and Social Action* (Notre Dame: University of Notre Dame Press, 1960).

9. For a short history of Judaism in America, see Nathan Glazer, *American Judaism* (Chicago: University of Chicago Press, 1957), or Will Herberg, *Protestant, Catholic, Jew* (New York: Doubleday, 1955), especially ch. 8.

18   Cooperation among Protestants

From its inception in 1847–50 and its rebirth in 1866, the Evangelical Alliance for the United States of America was the vehicle of nineteenth-century attempts to articulate a Christian self-definition conducive to unity. The Alliance embodied those features of nineteenth-century Protestantism that have come to be regarded as its essential characteristics—human sin and responsibility, individual need for redemption, and God's loving kindness. Its members were leaders of the mainline evangelical denominations and of evangelical parties within the other churches. Quite often in advance of its time, the Alliance centered in the cities where it aided its middle- and upper-class constituency in coping with contemporary religious and secular problems.[1]

The post–Civil War Alliance was far more energetic and successful than its predecessor in its attempts to increase evangelical comity worldwide through defense of religious and civil liberty and exportation of American democratic standards. During the 1880's, however, Alliance spokesmen began to realize their program was ill-equipped to solve the urban unrest, poverty, and mass alienation from the churches becoming evident at home. By October 22, 1886, the Alliance's executive structure affirmed plans for a national evangelical conference designed to assess the many perils facing the land. According to the report approved on this date, immigration swelled the population and contributed a dangerous heterogeneity to culture and religion. The geometric growth of Roman Catholicism and the expansion of Mormonism into states neighboring Utah threatened the political fabric of the Republic—evangelicals assumed both religions so controlled their members that they voted according to Church dictates, thereby threatening that independence of mind requisite to democracy. Evangelicals also held Mormonism repugnant for its polygamy and assumed crimes of violence. To cap it all, the report cited that a high level of illiteracy and intemper-

Note: The first part of Chapter 18, on the Evangelical Alliance, is by Philip D. Jordan, who is Associate Professor and Coordinator of History at Western State College of Colorado, Gunnison.

ance provided the means for socialism and secularism to attack the moral base of America at the very time when a "tendency to class distinctions" both "within and without the Church" hindered the one agency capable of defending the nation. These developments were "evil" because they threatened the reality upon which American evangelical identity rested. Introduction of conflicting moralities, cultural attachments, and religious allegiances augured ill for the national mission. How could evangelical America transmit its democratic culture, morality, and proper religious perspective to the world if America ceased to be evangelical? The dangers appeared to be real. The American mission was at stake.[2]

Convinced that transformation of the social environment was essential to save urban man, and turning from international to national ecumenism, the Alliance reorganized its structure, rewrote its program, hired Josiah Strong as General Secretary, and launched into its most energetic and successful period of activity. Secretary Strong's first major work was to reformulate Alliance goals into the timely and popular October, 1887, "Call for the Washington Conference" and then to direct Alliance efforts toward convening that first of a series of successful national evangelical conferences. From 1886 to 1898, the Alliance was one of the foremost popularizers of the social gospel. It encouraged pragmatic denominational cooperation as well, both to solve national and Protestant problems and to foster a spirit conducive to federation of the churches. Indeed, Alliance activities throughout the nineteenth century laid the basis for the twentieth-century Federal Council and subsequent National Council of the Churches of Christ in America.

Call for the Washington Conference:
To the Christian Public

Thoughtful men are convinced that the closing years of the nineteenth century constitute a momentous crisis in the history of the nation. There is a march of events which will not tarry. The necessity of planting Christian institutions in the formative West, and of strengthening them in older states, the duty of overtaking the rapid growth of our cities with adequate church provision, the importance of closing the widening chasm between the church and the multitude, and of bringing the regenerative power of the gospel to bear upon every character and life, demand the instant attention of the Christian church and the full exercise of all its energies.

Popular education has multiplied wants and created tastes which wealth has not been sufficiently distributed to gratify; hence a growing discontent among workingmen, which in prosperous times is an ill omen, suggesting grave questions concerning the next financial panic and the consequent industrial depression. The conflict with the saloon drawing to a crisis, and the manifest determination of the liquor power to accomplish its ends by fraud, corruption or violence; a wide-spread spirit of lawlessness; the apathy of the popular conscience; the alienation of the masses from the churches, and increasing immigration—all these point to growing complications in the near future.

Under monarchical governments, men have thought that if power could be popularized the ills of life would mostly disappear. In this country, until recently, by reason of abundant public lands, a sparse and substantially homogeneous population, and an almost limitless demand for labor, we have been exempt from many of the evils suffered by European peoples. But we are now beginning to approximate European conditions of society. The existence of great cities, severe competition, an unemployed class, increasing pauperism and crime, are the occasion and evidence of a wide-spread discontent, for which the ballot affords no remedy. Has not the time come for us to make demonstration of the truth that the gospel can do what popular suffrage cannot do? Is not this the nation, and is not this the generation, providentially called to make such application of the gospel to the life of the people as has never yet been made? Will not those who have enjoyed "government of the people, by the people, and for the people," be the first to learn that the essential evils of society are caused not by misrule, but by sin, and that the gospel, therefore, must furnish the solution of the great social problems?

The Christian church has not yet fully recognized its relations to the entire life of the community and the nation. Even Christian men, preoccupied with private concerns and overburdened by the demands of their time, are prone to neglect the public welfare, and are loath to accept any responsibility for existing evils.

Denominations and local churches, each intent on its own good work, have fallen into a harmful competition instead of engaging in an intelligent and comprehensive co-operation.

Our marvelous material growth and the progress of invention have produced new conditions, to which business has been quick to adapt its methods. Do not important changes in population and in the habits and temper of the people require some changes in the methods of Christian work?

The undersigned, therefore, unite in calling a GENERAL CONFER-
ENCE of all Evangelical Christians in the United States, to be held under
the auspices and direction of the Evangelical Alliance for the United
States, in the city of Washington, December the 7th, 8th and 9th, 1887,
to study in effect the following questions:

1st. What are the present perils and opportunities of the Christian
church and of the country?

2d. Can any of them be met best by a hearty co-operation of all
Evangelical Christians, which, without detriment to any denominational
interests, will serve the welfare of the whole church?

3d. What are the best means to secure such co-operation, and to
waken the whole church to its responsibility?[3]

When the Federal Council of Churches was organized in 1908, it
adopted a lengthy statement comprising both the ethical and religious
bases of social action and an outline of the critical areas of need, most
of which were depicted as clustering around the thorny issues of labor—
in fact, the report was called "The Church and Modern Industry."
Based on a thoroughgoing analysis that had recently been made for the
Methodist Church (North), the heart of this statement became known
as "The Social Creed of the Churches." It was at once both a challenge
and a program for action.[4] Modified by the Council in 1912, it stood
until 1932 as a guide for social action programs for the member
churches of the Council as well as a directive to its own staff:

The Social Creed of the Churches: Adopted December 9, 1912

For equal rights and complete justice for all men in all stations of
life.

For the protection of the family, by the single standard of purity,
uniform divorce laws, proper regulation of marriage, and proper housing.

For the fullest possible development for every child, especially by
the provision of proper education and recreation.

For the abolition of child-labor.

For such regulation of the conditions of toil for women as shall
safeguard the physical and moral health of the community.

For the abatement and prevention of poverty.

For the protection of the individual and society from the social, economic, and moral waste of the liquor traffic.

For the conservation of health.

For the protection of the worker from dangerous machinery, occupational disease, injuries, and mortality.

For the right of all men to the opportunity for self-maintenance, for safeguarding this right against encroachments of every kind, and for the protection of workers from the hardships of enforced unemployment.

For suitable provision for the old age of the workers, and for those incapacitated by injury.

For the right of employees and employers alike to organize and for adequate means of conciliation and arbitration in industrial disputes.

For a release from employment one day in seven.

For the gradual and reasonable reduction of the hours of labor to the lowest practicable point, and for that degree of leisure for all which is a condition of the highest human life.

For a living wage as a minimum in every industry, and for the highest wage that each industry can afford.

For a new emphasis on the application of Christian principles to the acquisition and use of property, and for the most equitable division of the product of industry that can ultimately be devised.[5]

In conclusion the report declared: "The final message is redemption, the redemption of the individual in the world, and through him of the world itself, and there is no redemption of either without the redemption of the other":

The Gospel is outgrown, the Christian pulpit is superfluous, the Church of the living Christ goes out of existence when the truths of the gospel, the vocabulary of the preacher, and the constitution of the Church no longer contain the words, God, Sin, Judgment, and Redemption, and they are gigantic and capacious words, belonging to a vocabulary that can interpret the whole universe of right and wrong, both individual and social. They are applicable to every problem in God's world.[6]

Although the Federal Council was not a strong body in its early years, it struck an effective blow for economic justice by investigating the Bethlehem steel strike of 1910, at a time when the steel industry was still on the twelve-hour day and the seven-day week. Its committee, consisting of Charles Stelzle, Josiah Strong, and Paul U. Kellogg, made two sets of recommendations. Those to the Federal Council and to the public declared the twelve-hour day and the seven-day week "alike a disgrace to civilization" and listed the industries operating on this schedule, declaring that there ought to be laws requiring three shifts in all industries operating twenty-four hours a day and that the churches should work for such laws. The churches should inaugurate a movement to place in the hands of the courts or other authoritative agencies the determination of when industrial operations are continuous. The federal government should purchase only materials made on a six-day basis, with three shifts instead of two for twenty-four-hour work. The churches and the Federal Council were urged to set aside a day at their conferences and conventions for the discussion of industrial conditions and the relation of the churches to them. The attention of the churches in all parts of the country should be called to the existence of the continuous processes in such industries as iron and steel, paper, railroads, street railways, telephones, mines, smelters, and glass, and ministers should be urged to visit such works in their localities in order to learn to what extent employees were obliged to work seven days a week. Federal and private studies on wages and hours of labor were recommended, as was their investigation by government bureaus. Some method should be provided whereby employee grievances could be aired. In summary, attention was called to the basic tenets of the "Social Creed" as the principles on which the Federal Council had previously asserted that the churches must stand.

To the ministers in Bethlehem the committee proposed that they collectively take a stand against the seven-day week in order that the people might know their position. In view of the contention that workers abuse their Sunday, a committee should be appointed to investigate "what opportunities for clean recreation are open to the working people of the Bethlehems; what opportunities a six-day, twelve-hour man has for enjoying any outdoor amusement except on Sunday; what opportunities the seven-day, twelve-hour man has at any time for enjoying them; what the mechanics and others who have Saturday half holiday do with it," and other specific points. A forum for fearless discussion might be organized; the churches could give over at least four meetings a year to social problems; the company might be asked for a report of the number of men working Sundays; and a committee could be appointed to investigate industrial accidents and other conditions having a bearing on the situation.[7]

The Council also inquired into conditions and reported to the churches and the general public on the industrial situation in Muscatine, Iowa, in 1912, and in Colorado in 1914, but it confronted many obstacles before it became an effective force.[8]

By 1932 the Great Depression had created a plethora of new problems and issues demanding the attention of the American people. The revision of the Social Creed in 1932 indicates not only how the economic and social situation had changed but also the new directions of progressive thought twenty years after 1912. In actuality, the Depression evoked a fresh expression of the social gospel. The 1932 Creed reveals the same religious motivation and commitment to the basic principles of social justice as had the statement of 1912, but it bespeaks for a new liberalism that called for social planning and control. The farmer gains recognition, and pacifism is emphasized, but the Council is not yet ready to endorse birth control. A historian of the Federal Council considers the creed of 1932 to be "a body of social thought which in scope and in the strength of its affirmations approaches the status of a significant social philosophy." Differing widely from historic Christian social philosophies, this viewpoint "continues to gain both in critical perception and religious insight."[9]

The Social Creed of the Churches, 1932

The Churches should stand for:

I. Practical application of the Christian principle of social well-being to the acquisition and use of wealth; subordination of speculation and the profit motive to the creative and cooperative spirit.

II. Social planning and control of the credit and monetary systems and economic processes for the common good.

III. The right of all to the opportunity for a self-maintenance; a wider and fairer distribution of wealth; a living wage, as a minimum, and above this a just share for the worker in the product of industry and agriculture.

IV. Safeguarding of all workers, urban and rural, against harmful conditions of labor and occupational injury and disease.

V. Social insurance against sickness, accident, want in old age and unemployment.

VI. Reduction of hours of labor as the general productivity of industry increases; release from employment at least one day in seven, with a shorter working week in prospect.

VII. Such special regulation of the conditions of work of women as shall safeguard their welfare and that of the family and the community.

VIII. The right of employees alike to organize for collective bargaining and social action; protection of both in the exercise of this right; the obligation of both to work for the public good; encouragement of cooperatives and other organizations among farmers and other groups.

IX. Abolition of child labor; adequate provision for the protection, education, spiritual nurture and wholesome recreation of every child.

X. Protection of the family by the single standard of purity; educational preparation for marriage, home-making and parenthood.

XI. Economic justice for the farmer in legislation, financing of agriculture, transportation and the price of farm products as compared with the cost of machinery and other commodities which he must buy.

XII. Extension of the primary cultural opportunities and social services now enjoyed by urban populations to the farm family.

XIII. Protection of the individual and society from the social, economic and moral waste of any traffic in intoxicants and habit-forming drugs.

XIV. Application of the Christian principle of redemption to the treatment of offenders; reform of penal and correctional methods and institutions, and of criminal court procedure.

XV. Justice, opportunity and equal rights for all; mutual good-will and cooperation among racial, economic and religious groups.

XVI. Repudiation of war, drastic reduction of armaments, participation in international agencies for the peaceable settlement of all controversies; the building of a cooperative world order.

XVII. Recognition and maintenance of the rights and responsibilities of free speech, free assembly, and a free press; the encouragement of free communication of mind with mind as essential to the discovery of truth.[10]

Thus was the Federal Council the pioneer of all types of interchurch cooperation in the United States; the pattern was widely adopted abroad. The social gospel played a significant role in the worldwide ecumenical movement. Many national councils of churches promulgated statements comparable to the Social Creed and established programs of social action, as did the World Council of Churches from its organization in 1948.[11]

From 1894 when intercollegiate Y.M.C.A. secretary John R. Mott proposed that college and university Associations try to "interest their members in the burning present-day problems in the realm of Christian sociology, and to lead them to find and take their true place in the Kingdom of God," the Student Christian Movement became increasingly concerned with the social gospel. Leaders such as Stelzle and Rauschenbusch often lectured in the colleges, campus Bible-study groups were reading books with titles like *The Political and Social Significance of the Life and Teachings of Jesus,* and various forms of social service were becoming popular with students, so that by 1912 three secretaries were devoting their energies to this phase of the program, and social Christianity could be regarded as "a major part" of the philosophy and program of the movement.[12]

In 1914 Mott called a conference at Garden City, New York, to plan the future strategy of the Associations. Among the guest experts were twenty social gospel leaders, half of whom have been mentioned in this book. During the conference a committee was directed to summarize the findings of the meeting. It came to "the conviction that this conference has brought into clearer light such facts and principles as these":

Responsibility. While we clearly recognize the splendid spirit of sacrifice, the democratic ideals, and fine leadership in many departments of national life, of men of toil, we also insist that, in view of their privileges, students of our educational institutions should be, in the main, the chief intellectual guides, instructors and inspirers of the nation, and they should be the principal agents for forming public opinion which underlies legislation and administration and which establishes ruling sentiments and customs wherever trained intellect is required.

It follows that students will be *responsible* in very large measure, for the action or negligence of the Church, of municipalities, states, provinces, and federal authorities.

Christian students, in considerable numbers, ought to be taught and trained to render *volunteer personal service* in the philanthropic, educational and public activities of the communities in which they live.

Many Christian students should be prepared for professional careers in connection with voluntary associations and public institutions, civic and humanitarian.

Christian men and women should be prepared in institutions of higher education to understand the aims and methods of the principal agencies for protecting the feeble, righting wrongs, and promoting progress in art, science, fellowship, personal morality and public righteousness. Thus the associations of specialists should have with them a vast body of enlightened citizens, alert, instructed, consecrated, whose influence would be promptly and wisely brought to bear on the electorate and their representatives in the local and general legislatures.

We should believe in the power of truth and reason, and show this faith by encouraging the study and discussion of social needs and methods of improvement in connection with religious associations and churches. Frequently a tolerant, friendly and intelligent discussion will bring representatives of conflicting interests to agreement on practical measures and teach them to respect each other even where there is difference of opinion. We need many Christian scholars in all the liberal professions to stimulate and direct these discussions and class work.

Among the Christian students will be found a certain number of persons, men and women, who should be encouraged and aided to devote their lives to some special investigations where they may become experts, with that higher authority which goes with the mastering of a particular field. This suggestion applies to men and women who in secondary schools and colleges have demonstrated their special aptitudes in social science and have thorough training, independence of intellectual life, and power to carry forward scientific research.

Such study should be given to the vital problems that have led to the woman's movement, that Christian leaders, both men and women, shall unite their efforts for the uplift of humanity. In all directions we recognize the absolute necessity of the co-operation of men and women in a spirit of Christian comradeship. We believe that all the ability of all Christians should find free expression in study, in discussion and in practical activity,—that there should be a contribution from each person according to the divine gift and calling.

The supreme influence in ameliorating the outward conditions and the inner life of mankind is found in the presence among us of the living Christ.

The social problems of our age are more complex than those of any former time and call for the exercise of the highest qualities of mind and heart. Those who are to contribute most to the correction of evils, conservation of order and security, and the positive progress of the peoples, must have adequate knowledge as well as the Christian spirit.

In the application of the "mind of Christ" to these problems of character, order, peace and progress, Christian leaders must have not only a consecrated will but an instructed mind; and all who are eager to see the Church perform its full duty to mankind must be deeply concerned for the adequate preparation of leaders for this sublime and difficult enterprise.

The program of the Federal Council of the Churches, which has already been considered by your Council, demands for its realization the cooperation of a multitude of persons trained in economics, statistics, sociology, law and other branches of science.

Christian students, if thus properly equipped and trained, can contribute to this enterprise. In their life calling, in which they become specialists, they may so live and act as to further the welfare of those with whom they come in contact. While they are preparing for their professional careers they should all be taught how they can make their special knowledge and skill contribute to the well-being of the community in every direction.

We must sincerely and steadily hold fast the truth that all useful ministrations to human well-being, all honorable work, when performed in His name, is part of one sacred ministry; that consecration of personality to our Lord places all Christian labor on one ethical plane of highest dignity and holiness.[13]

The committee went on to outline a program of action, study, and education in socially responsible vocations, convinced that the discontent of the times should be spiritualized; in the colleges, the conference was convinced, lay "the most critical battlefield" of the time, rather than in "the actual areas of social injustice and neglect." The conference marked an epoch in the social thinking of the student community, but most of those to whom its message was directed would soon find themselves either in the armed forces or expressing their social service in prisoner of war camps, in "Y" huts behind the lines, or driving ambulances in World War I.

Notes

1. This short selection is based on a book-length manuscript by Philip D. Jordan, entitled "Evangelical Identity and Ecumenism: The Evangelical Alliance for the United States of America, 1847–1900."

2. These citations are from Evangelical Alliance documents for October 23, 1886, in the Alliance Collection, Union Theological Seminary, New York City.

3. Evangelical Alliance, *National Perils and Opportunities: The Discussions of the General Christian Conference, Held in Washington, D.C., December 7th, 8th, and 9th, 1887* (New York, 1887), v–vii.

4. C. H. Hopkins, *Rise of the Social Gospel* (New Haven: Yale, 1940). 306–17; S. M. Cavert, *Church Cooperation and Unity in America, 1900–1970* (New York: Association Press, 1970), 120–22.

5. Harry F. Ward, *The Social Creed of the Churches* (New York–Cincinnati: Eaton and Mains, 1914), 8: Cavert, 126–28.

6. Hopkins, 317.

7. Hopkins, 314–15; Cavert, 122–25, 128–29.

8. C. S. Macfarland, *Across the Years* (New York: Macmillan, 1936), chs. 12–13.

9. John A. Hutchison, *We Are Not Divided* (New York: Round Table, 1941), 106.

10. Hutchison, 104–5; Cavert, 126–28; both are from the Federal Council annual *Report* for 1932, p. 57. The F.C.C. was enlarged into the National Council of Churches in 1951.

11. For the World Council, see Edward Duff, *The Social Thought of the World Council of Churches* (New York: Association, 1956), and Paul Bock, *In Search of a Responsible World Society: The Social Teachings of the World Council of Churches* (Philadelphia: Westminster, 1974).

12. Hopkins, 298–300; Hopkins, *History of the Y.M.C.A. in North America* (New York: Association, 1951), 635–36; W. H. Morgan, *Student Religion during Fifty Years* (New York: Association, 1935), 87; C. P. Shedd, *Two Centuries of Student Christian Movements* (New York: Association, 1934), 100–2.

13. "Report of the Committee of Ten, . . . Garden City, . . . 1914," mimeo., Historical Library of the Y.M.C.A., New York.

19 Catholicism and Social Questions

The full story of Catholic involvement in the social gospel, which can be touched upon only briefly in this book, has been well told in Aaron I. Abell's *American Catholicism and Social Action.*[1] As early as Henry George's campaign for the mayoralty of New York City in 1886, the attention of Church and public to the interrelated problems of labor and socialism was aroused by a priestly supporter of George, Dr. Edward McGlynn, pastor of St. Stephen's Church. Burdened, as was Walter Rauschenbusch, "by the never-ending procession of men, women and little children" begging at his door "not so much for alms as employment," McGlynn had several years earlier been given a copy of *Progress and Poverty,* which, except for Marx and Engels' *Capital,* was the most widely read tract ever written on an economic theme. A consummate orator with a large following, McGlynn once described his reaction to the book:

I found an excellent exposition of the industrial and social condition of man in Henry George's book, a poem of philosophy, a prophecy and prayer. In language rare and unequalled the author presents a picture of perishing lives, and in glowing poetic language tells of God's bounties to His children, but that somehow with the increase of the use of wealth there is an increase of poverty, and where there is the congregation of the greatest wealth, by its side is the greatest poverty and misery.

I had never found so clear an exposition of the cause of the trouble, involuntary poverty, and its remedy, as I found in that monumental work.

I became all aglow with a new and clearer light that had come to my mind in such full consonance with all my thoughts and aspirations from my earliest childhood, and I did, as best I could, what I could to justify the teachings of that great work based upon the essence of all religion—the Fatherhood of God and the Brotherhood of Man.

214

The concluding chapter of *Progress and Poverty* is more like the utterance of an inspired seer of Israel, or of some ecstatic contemplating the great processes of eternity, than the utterance of a mere political economist.[2]

Forbidden to speak on the controversial subject, McGlynn defied his superiors to deprive him of his rights to free speech, and was excommunicated. The issue, precipitated by the recent outlawing of the Knights of Labor by the Canadian hierarchy, was compounded by the problems of socialism and secret orders; only the heroic efforts of Cardinal Gibbons averted the American Knights being banned.[3] While he was under exclusion, McGlynn addressed a sympathetic audience in the Brooklyn Academy of Music, defending without rancor his right to advocate the single tax because it was compatible with "the highest Christian truth and the best Christian justice" and had not actually been condemned "by Christ or the highest tribunal of his Church." Called "The Cross of a New Crusade," a reference not unfamiliar to politically minded Americans at that time, the speech was both an explanation of the single tax and a defense of his own rights. We excerpt a few paragraphs:

The crusade that we have chosen to call a "new crusade" is for the enforcing of one of those great truths of which I have already spoken to you—the truth that, with diversity of natural gifts, God has given an equality of essential rights to all His children just because they are His children; that for every mouth He sends into the world to be fed, He sends with rare exceptions a pair of hands to feed it; that He has made us land animals, and not fishes or birds, and therefore that He has made us to live upon the land and not to fly in the air or swim in the water, and that because He has made us land animals, and because He has made us at all, He has given us the right, with these two hands somehow or other to dig for a living in order to feed these mouths; and that any man or set of men, who shall by law or in any other way deny, impair, diminish or restrain the equal right of every human being, to the possession of the general bounties of nature, the sunlight, the air, the water and the land, is guilty of blasphemy against the goodness of the universal Father. They are perverting under the name of law the right of men;

they are desecrating the holy name of law to sanction a monstrous injustice. Under the name of right they are doing a horrid wrong; under the pretense of guarding the best interests of society, they are opposing the very germinal principle of rightly ordained society. They are guilty of the monstrous crime of making hundreds of thousands, yea, millions of God's creatures feel that this life is a wretched mistake, or worse than that, the joke of some most hateful fiend, rather than the gift of an all-wise and all-loving Father.

It is not for nothing that He who came to save the souls of men did so much to minister to the relief of their bodily wants. He healed their diseases; He raised their dead; He cured their distempers; He bore their sorrows; He felt compassion for the multitude, lest they should faint by the wayside. He miraculously supplemented the laws of nature and fed them with miraculous loaves and fishes in the wilderness. He did all this, because doing it He knew full well that the bodies of men as well as their souls are the creatures of God, and that their bodies and the capacities of those bodies are but signs and symbols of the spiritual things within, even as all the vast universe of God is but His garment, is but the sign and symbol and the thin veil that surrounds Him, through the rifts in which we catch on every hand glimpses of God and of heaven.

The heavens are telling the glory of God. There is a greater heaven here, vaster and more wondrous than the physical universe, in the intelligent mind and the affectionate heart of the least of God's creatures. All the multitudinous and multifarious beauties and glories of the physical world are not equal to the dignity and the sanctity of the mind and the heart of the least of God's children; and therefore it is that Christ tells us that at the very peril of our souls we must look after the bodies of these little ones; we must feed the hungry; they shall afford them food, raiment, shelter, for the erection of works not merely of utility, but of ornament, that out of these materials the children of men shall have equal, indefeasible rights to pluck, to catch, to delve, in order not merely to satisfy the necessities of the animal body or to keep it from the inclemency of the blast, but to do more than this—to make the very shelter itself a thing of beauty, to make the home a kind of temple in which there may be a family altar, to erect great public works that shall serve not merely purposes of utility, but shall educate the eye and the fancy, and shall gladden the habitations of men during their brief temporal abode, to add something to the mere garments that shall clothe and preserve the body from the inclemency of the atmosphere, to make even the raiment of man a work of art, to give a charm and a grace and a dignity even to the mere feeding of the animal. All men then have this right; and it is a part of the gospel of this new crusade that while we may make much allowance for the ignorance in which these great cardinal truths are too often forgotten, the barbarism and the slavery in which because of might right went under and stayed under for centuries; while we may be very indulgent to the errors and even be willing to forgive in some measure the crimes of the past, we hold aloft the banner upon which is inscribed this truth, that ever and always in the past, the present, and the future, the earth and the fulness thereof were given by God, and therefore should belong to all the children of God. . . .

How are we going to give back to the poor man what belongs to him? How shall we have that beautiful state of things in which naught shall be ill and all shall be well? Simply by confiscating rent and allowing people nominally to own, if you choose, the whole of Manhattan Island, if it will do them any good to nominally own it; but while they have the distinguished satisfaction of seeming to own it we are going to scoop the meat out of the shell and allow them to have the shell. And how are we going to do that? By simply taxing all this land and all kindred bounties of nature to the full amount of their rental value. If there isn't any rental value then there won't be any tax. If there is any rental value then it will be precisely what that value is. If the rental value goes up, up goes the tax. If the rental value comes down, down comes the tax. If the rental value ceases, then the tax ceases. Don't you see? It is as clear as the nose on your face.

. . . . We would simply tax all these bounties of nature, where there is a scramble for them, to the full rental value. In a new community, where the people are few, land is comparatively limitless; there is no such thing as rent; the land is pretty equally distributed; there is no choice; it would be a senseless thing for men to quarrel about it; there is land enough for all. What is the law of rent? Where there is competition for a larger or choicer portion of the common bounties, for a portion of land that is nearer a river, that is next to the junction of two great rivers, that is near to a great city, for a corner lot, say at the corner of Broadway and Wall street, or at Broadway and Twenty-third street, there rent exists. And how is the competition for the use of such land to be decided? Simply by allowing it to go to the highest bidder. Thus would be provided, through the exercise of the taxing power, a fund for the common treasury, a munificent fund growing with the growth of population and civilization, supplied by a beautiful providential law, a simple, economic law that works with the same simplicity and the same regularity as the law of gravitation itself—a magnificent ever-increasing fund to supply the wants of increasing civilization and increasing population.[4]

A true social gospel pioneer, McGlynn remains an almost forgotten prophet, although he was restored to the priesthood, says one biographer, in italics, *"without having retracted one jot or tittle of the economic philosophy which his Archbishop had condemned."*[5]

In Chicago in 1893 there took place, as part of the great Columbian Exposition, a "World's Parliament of Religions," which brought to its platform spokesmen for virtually all religions. Among the ten Roman Catholic speakers was the Reverend James M. Cleary of Minneapolis, who gave a brief explanation of the recently promulgated papal encyclical *Rerum novarum,* which would be the magna carta of Catholic social policy:

The church having taught every child of Adam who earned his bread by laborious toil to assert his own dignity and to understand his own worth, and having led a hitherto hopeless multitude from the dismal gloom of slavery to the cheering brightness of the liberty of the children of God, bravely defended the rights and the privileges of her emancipated children. "The church has guarded with religious care the inheritance of the poor." None need the Divine Comforter more than the weary children of toil, and none need and have received the sympathy of the church as they do.

In his exhaustive encyclical on the condition of labor Leo XIII. lays down the principle that the workman's wages is not a problem to be solved by the pitiless arithmetic of avaricious greed. The wage-earner has rights which he cannot surrender, and which no man can take from him, for he is an intelligent, responsible being, owing homage to God and duties to human society. His recompense, then, for his daily toil cannot be measured by a heartless standard of supply and demand, or a cruel code of inhuman economics, for man is not a money-making machine, but a citizen of earth and an heir to the Kingdom of Heaven.

The definition of a minimum wage, given by Leo XIII., as "sufficient to enable a man to maintain himself, his wife and his children" in decent frugality, shows how clearly he understands the rights of individuals and the best interests of human society. "Homeless men are reckless." The homes of the people are the safeguards of national stability. Religion sanctifies domestic life by sustaining the inviolability of the marriage bond, and by constantly reminding fathers and mothers of their first and holiest duty to their offspring, the duty of leading them to learn the love of God and the love of the neighbor. Hence the duties of the wife and mother should retain her at her own hearthstone. Modern society can never justly boast of its enlightenment and progress while because of insufficient wages paid to labor, mothers and children are chained to the wheels of industrialism.

While the church shows such ceaseless concern for the welfare of labor, and has so bravely contended for the rights of the poor, she has not failed to remind them of the duties that they owe to capital and vested rights. Throughout all her contests with barbarism, feudalism and imperial tyranny, the church suffered her greatest persecutions in battling for the rights of the people against the encroachments of despotism. But "Thou shalt not steal," and "Thou shalt not covet they neighbor's goods," are divine injunctions which the church has faithfully taught to all classes of men. She has guarded the rights of ownership, saved from destruction and caused to be restored to the rightful proprietors much of the goods of this world.

Labor has a right to freedom; labor has also a right to protect its own independence and liberty. Hence labor unions are lawful and have enjoyed the sanction and protection of the church in all ages. But labor must use its power for its own protection, not for invading the rights of others. That form of strike by which labor unions use unlawful means to prevent willing men, who are anxious to earn a livelihood for their families, from engaging in honest work, can in no way be defended and must surely fall under the unqualified censure of religion.

Religion's. duty is to teach the rich the responsibilities of wealth and the poor respect for order and law. Hers is the only influence that has been able to subdue the pride and the passions of men, to refine the manners and guide the conduct of human society, so that rich and poor alike, mindful of their common destiny, respect each other's rights, their mutual dependence and the rights of their common Father in Heaven.[6]

During these years Catholics were as concerned as were Protestants about socialism. Although the Church was adamant in her rejection of

all such doctrines, a few loyal Catholics flirted with the Christian
Socialist Fellowship, and there were occasional brave souls who left
the Church rather than abjure their socialistic faith.[7] To explain the
official position on socialism, the scholarly Bishop William Stang of
Fall River wrote *Socialism and Christianity* in 1905. Admitting that a
few Catholics had joined the socialist ranks and that some misguided
workingmen had imbibed unorthodox ideas, Stang gave an excellent
commentary on *Rerum novarum* and the history of the Catholic social
movement, while pinning his hope on social reform as the best deter-
rent of socialism. Like a good Progressive, comments Professor Abell,
Stang blamed bad conditions on corrupt politics and inadequate labor
legislation, believing that a sound insurance system, limited public
ownership, and effective trade unionism would keep the laboring
classes from drifting into socialism.[8]

John A. Ryan, in 1906 a young teacher fresh from his doctoral
studies at the Catholic University of America, who was destined to become the outstanding social gospeler of American Catholicism, published *A Living Wage: Its Ethical and Economic Aspects.* The book
became, as one commentator put it, the *Uncle Tom's Cabin* (or he
might better have put it, the *In His Steps*) of the movement for
minimum wage laws.[9]

Untroubled by socialism, Ryan argued convincingly that "the
average family of that day . . . could not live decently on less than six
hundred dollars a year and that at least sixty per cent of adult male
wage earners received less than this sum." One is reminded of
Rauschenbusch's and McGlynn's experiences in their New York
pastorates. In his preface, Ryan explained his purpose:

This work does not profess to present a *complete* theory of justice
concerning wages. It lays down no minute rules to determine the *full*
measure of compensation that any class of laborers ought to receive.
The principles of ethics have not yet been applied to the conditions of
modern industry with sufficient intelligence, or confidence, or
thoroughness, to provide a safe basis for such an undertaking. The
conclusions to which it would lead would be either too general to be of
any practical value, or too uncertain to yield more than a misleading
approximation to ethical truth. At any rate, the doctrine advanced
would probably fail to convince any considerable section of those to
whom it was addressed. The great majority of fair-minded persons

believe, indeed, that labor does not get its full share of the wealth that it helps to create, but they are not agreed as to the precise measure of that ideal share.

Upon one principle of partial justice unprejudiced men are, however, in substantial agreement. They hold that wages should be sufficiently high to enable the laborer to live in a manner consistent with the dignity of a human being. To defend this general conviction by setting forth the basis of industrial, religious and moral fact upon which it rests, is the aim of the present volume. Several considerations have led the author to think that this task is well worth while. In the first place, the Living Wage doctrine points the way to a very considerable amelioration of the condition of millions of American workingmen; in the second place, a Living Wage would enable those raised to its level to improve their position still further; and, in the third place, this volume shows that religion, as represented by the oldest and largest of the Christian denominations, professes, nay, urges, a definite and considerable measure of industrial justice.

While insisting that every laborer has a right to at least a Living Wage, the author does not commit himself to the view that this quantity of remuneration is full and adequate justice in the case of any class of laborers. His concern is solely with the ethical minimum.[10]

Professor Richard T. Ely wrote a brief introduction to what was virtually the pioneer American Catholic social gospel book:

I am glad to have an opportunity to point out briefly the significance of Professor Ryan's book, as it impresses itself on my mind. We have had repeated efforts to stimulate the conscience of the Christian world to a keener appreciation of its duties to the men, women and children who toil for wages. Christian socialism, so-called, has been presented frequently by men of various religious denominations. A greater sensitiveness to right and wrong in economic affairs has undoubtedly been the result of this preaching of righteousness. Enlightenment has, however, not kept pace with good intention. On the contrary, nothing is more noticeable than the confusion of mind which very generally accompanies good intention. The "plain man" of whom we hear so much, has a feeling that our teachers and preachers are vague and indefinite. Is there after all such a thing as a Christian doctrine of wages? The writer of this book, a priest in the Roman Catholic Church and a teacher in St. Paul Seminary, a theological school of that Church, presents to us in the following pages, a clear-cut, well-defined theory of wages, based upon his understanding of the approved doctrines of his religious body. There have been attempts in other lands to deduce from the teachings of this Church, clear and precise directions for our industrial life. We recall the works of Bishop von Ketteler of Mainz and the more conservative writings of Professor Charles Périn of the University of Louvain in Belgium. While Cardinal Manning of England some years ago startled the English-speaking world by his enunciation of the right of man to a subsistence as prior to the rights of property as a doctrine of the Church, and while Cardinal Gibbons in the United States has on several occasions expressed himself firmly and positively in regard to the rights of labor, the present work is, so far as I am aware, the first attempt in the English language to elaborate what may be called a Roman Catholic system of political economy. When I say, a Roman Catholic system of political economy, I mean an attempt to show exactly what the received doctrines of the Church signify in the mind of a representative Catholic when they are applied to the economic life. It strikes me as a meritorious performance at the present juncture to endeavor to express as precisely as may be what Christianity has to say about wages.

    While members of other religious bodies, Christian and Jewish, cannot receive the doctrine of wages here set forth merely because it is assumed to rest on the approved teachings of the Roman Catholic Church, they are not precluded from an examination of this question: Does or does not this doctrine of wages rest upon broad Christian, religious and ethical foundations? It will be observed that Professor Ryan combines economic and ethical arguments with those derived from authority and that it is by no means impossible to receive arguments of the first class, while refusing adhesion to those of the second class. My own feeling then is that this book is to be welcomed as an attempt on the part of a religious teacher to get beyond vague and glittering generalities to precise doctrine, and to pass from appeals to sentiment to reasoned arguments.[11]

In his summary, Ryan proposed minimum-wage legislation:

The main argument of this volume may be summarized as follows: the laborer's right to a Living Wage is the specific form of his generic right to obtain on reasonable conditions sufficient of the earth's products to afford him a decent livelihood. The latter right is, like all other moral rights, based on his intrinsic worth as a person, and on the sacredness of those needs that are essential to the reasonable development of personality. Among the things to which these needs point there is included a certain amount of material goods. A man's right to this indispensable minimum of the bounty of nature is as valid as his right to life: the difference is merely in degree of importance. Now when the man whose social and economic function is that of a wage earner has expended all his working time and energy in the performance of some useful task, he has fulfilled the only condition that in his case can be regarded as a reasonable prerequisite to the actual enjoyment of his right to a decent livelihood. The *obligation* of providing him with the material means of living decently rests in a general way upon all his fellow men. That is to say, they are all under moral restraint not to do anything that would be an unreasonable interference with his access to these means. However, it is only those persons who are in control of the goods and opportunities of living that are practicably within his reach, who can effectively hinder or promote his enjoyment of the right in question. When they prevent him from peaceably getting possession of the requisite amount of goods, they are morally responsible for his failure to obtain a decent livelihood. Their action is as unjust as that of the majority of the first occupants of a No-man's Land who should force the minority to work for a bare subsistence.

This specific obligation of the class of persons that we are considering falls primarily upon the employer; for his economic position as direct beneficiary of the laborer's exertion and as payer of wages, renders this the only practicable outcome of any reasonable division of the community's opportunities of living and of the corresponding responsibilities. Nor can the employer escape this duty of paying a Living Wage by taking refuge behind the terms of a so-called free contract. The fact is that the underpaid laborer does not *willingly* sell his labor for less than the equivalent of a decent livelihood, any more than the wayfarer willingly gives up his purse to the highwayman. It is the superior *economic force* (which consists essentially in the ability to wait, while the laborer must go to work to-day or starve) possessed by the employer that enables him to hire labor for less than a Living Wage.

And the employer who can afford to pay a Living Wage is no more justified in using his superior economic strength in this way than he would be justified in using superior physical strength to prevent the laborer from taking possession of a sack of flour or a suit of clothes that the latter had bought and paid for. In both cases the laborer is deprived by superior strength of something to which he has a right. As a determinant of rights, economic force has no more validity or sacredness than physical force. The other economic classes in the community, the landowner, the loan-capitalist, the consumer, and the man of wealth, share the responsibility of providing the laborer with a decent livelihood in a secondary degree, and in accordance with the nature and possibilities of their several economic positions. Finally, the State is morally bound to compel employers to pay a Living Wage whenever and wherever it can, with a moderate degree of success, put into effect the appropriate legislation.

Ryan then reviewed certain economic aspects of his proposal and discussed how "the universal application of the Living Wage principle would cause an immense improvement in our industrial and social conditions." In conclusion, he turned to the oft-heard statement that "only religion will solve the labor question":

Most certainly it will not be permanently and adequately solved *without* religion, that is, without the aid of religious agencies and a larger infusion of the religious spirit into the minds and hearts of men; but neither will religion suffice in the absence of a detailed application of moral principles to the relations of employer and employee. Men may be religious in the ordinary meaning of the term, and yet remain so thoroughly dominated by the ethical code of unlimited competition that they are blind to the many forms of moral wrong which that code sanctions. There are thousands of employers in every church organization who wish to live up to the standards of their respective denominations, and believe that they are succeeding fairly well, who nevertheless feel no conscientious scruples when they pay their employees much less than a Living Wage. They see no wrong in this, for are they not paying the current rates? In other words, they conform to the standard of business ethics, instead of to the standard of Christian ethics. The moral suasion that will produce results implies earnest, continuous, and enlightened activity on the part of public teachers and moulders of public opinion. If clergymen would give as much attention to preaching and expounding the duty of paying a Living Wage as they do to the explanation of other duties that are no more important, and if they would use all the power of their ecclesiastical position to deprive recalcitrant employers of the church privileges that are ordinarily denied to persistently disobedient members; and if public speakers and writers who discuss questions of industrial justice would, *in concrete terms,* hold up to public denunciation those employers who can pay a Living Wage and will not,—the results would constitute an ample refutation of the libelous assertion that employers cannot be got to act justly by moral suasion. They have never been made to feel a fraction of its power. The term, social effort, is here used to describe the activity both of private associations, such as Labor Unions, and of the State. It is true that the efficiency of social effort is limited by the character of the individuals through whom the effort is made. If individuals have not an intelligent grasp of the ethical principles involved in the Living Wage question, and the will to apply these principles in practice, their achievements as an organization will be seriously diminished. But it is also true that organized effort will add very materially to the results that can be accomplished through moral suasion addressed to individuals. This very obvious general truth is superlatively true in our time, when man's social relations have become so numerous and so complex. Both methods are necessary. There must be an appeal to the minds and hearts of individuals, and the fullest utilization of the latent power of organization and social institutions. A reasonable and sustained endeavor to employ the two methods in extending the Living Wage principle will accomplish more for the laboring class, especially for its poorest-paid members, than a like amount of effort expended in any other way. Speaking comparatively, the remedy is efficacious, and the means of putting it into effect practicable.[12]

Ryan's book was followed by an increasing flow of Catholic literature on social concerns, which included his own *Distributive Justice,* a "basic frame" for a plan for social justice. Shortly after World War I, the bishops established the National Catholic Welfare Council and Ryan was put in charge of its Washington office's social action department, from which vantage point he became an advisor to President

Franklin D. Roosevelt and was nicknamed *Right Reverend New Dealer*.[13]

An excerpt from an unpublished paper read by Professor Abell to a group of historians about 1949, in which he reviews the developments we have emphasized, seems an apt conclusion for this chapter:

As the welfare crusade gathered momentum, it won favor with many Protestants, especially those devoted to theological and social liberalism. These persons were now willing to defend the Catholic Church against persecution on condition that it hold fast to its moral and reformatory work. This proffered alliance was eagerly accepted by many of the new bishops—among them, Gibbons of Baltimore, Keane of Richmond, Spalding of Peoria and Ireland of St. Paul. These men with growing approval of clergy and laity insisted on the compatibility of the Catholic Church with modern civilization, with nineteenth-century social liberalism that is, especially in its American form.

Thus motivated, these Catholics were in a position to bring the Church into co-operative relations with all the significant social movements of the later nineteenth century. First of all, they reversed the Church's attitude on the salient aspects of the labor question, namely trade unionism and the right of the state to regulate private property in the public interest. The numerous Catholics who after 1880 seriously investigated economic conditions concluded that social injustice as well as evil men caused industrial upheaval and conflict. Rather than being "miserable associations," effective trade unions now seemed necessary and harmless organizations for "praiseworthy" ends. This view, as is well known, became official when in 1886 the American archbishops acquiesced in the successful attempt of Cardinal Gibbons to secure a suspension of Rome's decision upholding the Canadian hierarchy's condemnation of the Knights of Labor. His letter to the Holy Office was a magnificent defense of workingmen's associations as necessary and legitimate means to the attainment of a better economic order. Gone now were the old feelings of apprehension and distrust. The Knights of Labor, he insisted, was not a secret society in the sense condemned by the Church; in associating with non-Catholic workingmen, Catholics did not imperil their faith but helped to defeat the machinations of atheists, communists and anarchists; the bloodshed and violence were only incidental—in fact, the Knights of Labor prevented far more violence than it provoked.

Besides trade unionism, association to secure state intervention in the economic field was a requirement of justice, many Catholics came to believe. The bitter controversy provoked by Father McGlynn's support of Henry George's crusade against land monopoly revived the Church's traditional doctrine concerning the public regulation of property. McGlynn and his devoted following insisted that "private property in land" was an outrage against Christian ethics. But his religious superior, Archbishop Corrigan, denounced the proposal that the state confiscate economic rent as rank socialism, ordered McGlynn to cease propagating his views and on his refusal to do so excommunicated him for insubordination. In the end, however, Corrigan was overruled by the Pope's representative, Monsignor Francis Satolli, who in 1893 lifted the sentence against McGlynn on the ground that "there is nothing" in his opinions "contrary to the faith and teachings of the Church." McGlynn's views were of little moment in themselves; not many progressive Catholics accepted his entire program, regarding it as doctrinaire and unworkable. The significant thing is that the controversy convinced them that a moderate amount of state intervention was quite legitimate, the principle being the scholastic one that while private property is a natural right its exercise may be regulated by public authority in the common interest. Laws effectively controlling corporate monopolies, eliminating child labor, wiping out rotten tenements and curtailing the liquor traffic—these illustrated the approved type of state intervention.

This so-called liberalism seemed dangerous and sinful to Bishop McQuaid of Rochester and to many others of like disposition. But to men of more discerning mind effective measures in behalf of labor were necessary applications to the present day of the Church's age-old philosophy of justice and charity—an interpretation immensely strengthened by Leo XIII's labor encyclical of 1891. The American Church authorities did not, however, acquiesce in economic reform on grounds entirely or even mainly of justice and charity. They were motivated chiefly by practical consideration of a social and political character. They well knew that workingmen in vast numbers would leave the Church if it continued to ignore economic justice. But even more they feared a second Know-nothing persecution if they interfered with the liberty of Catholics to participate in social reform movements. Gibbons made much of this in his letter on the Knights of Labor, warning the Roman authorities that the "accusation of being un-American—that is to say, alien to our national spirit—is the most powerful weapon which the enemies of the Church can employ against her."

Considerations such as these defeated the efforts of Archbishop Corrigan to have Henry George's *Progress and Poverty* placed on the Index of Prohibited Books and secured Father McGlynn's restoration. The charges against Father McGlynn, "as they are understood by the American people," wrote a Brooklyn priest to Leo XIII in 1886, "raise the question of the right of the citizen to express his views on all questions that are non-essential." Cardinal Gibbons explained with his usual insight that the Church's teachings on socialism and private property were not directly involved in the controversy and that the fate of the single tax must rest with the whole people judging its expediency and justice as freely as any other proposed public policy. Or as the *Catholic Standard* of Philadelphia put it, to forbid Catholics to participate in the discussion and decision, as Archbishop Corrigan wished, would be to acknowledge "the truth of the accusation of our enemies that Catholics are not and cannot be truly loyal to the civil authorites of their country."

The economic crisis was not the only social issue disturbing the Church in the late nineteenth century. There were other issues whose power to arouse Catholic emotions was much greater than the labor question.[14]

For these further developments in Catholic social action, the student is referred to Professor Abell's books.[15]

Notes

1. Aaron I. Abell, *American Catholicism and Social Action: A Search for Social Justice, 1865–1950* (Notre Dame: University of Notre Dame Press, 1963).

2. Stephen Bell, *Rebel, Priest and Prophet: A Biography of Dr. Edward McGlynn* (New York: Devin-Adair, 1937), 23–24. By permission of the publisher.

3. Henry J. Browne, *The Catholic Church and The Knights of Labor* (Washington, D.C.: The Catholic University of America Press, 1949).

4. Aaron I. Abell, *American Catholic Thought on Social Questions* (Indianapolis–New York: Bobbs-Merrill, 1968), 162–76.

5. Bell, ix.

6. James M. Cleary, in J. H. Barrows, ed., *The World's Parliament of Religions*, 2 (Chicago: Parliament, 1893), 1066–67.

7. Such as Thomas McGrady and Thomas J. Hagerty. See Abell, *American Catholicism and Social Action*, 143–44.

8. Abell, *American Catholicism and Social Action,* 147–48; from William Stang, *Socialism and Christianity* (New York: Benziger, 1905).

9. Abell, *American Catholicism and Social Action,* 88.

10. John A. Ryan, *A Living Wage: Its Ethical and Economic Aspects* (New York: Macmillan, 1906), vii-viii.

11. Richard T. Ely, in Ryan, xi-xiii.

12. Ryan, 324–31.

13. Francis L. Broderick, *Right Reverend New Dealer: John A. Ryan* (New York: Macmillan, 1963); see also Abell, *American Catholic Thought,* 229–51.

14. Abell, "The Ideological Aspects of Catholic Social Reform in the Later Nineteenth Century," an unpublished typescript, given by its author to C. Howard Hopkins, of a paper read before a group of historians at Washington, D.C., in 1949. By the kind permission of Mrs. Abell.

15. See notes 1 and 4, above.

20 American Jews and the Kingdom

In spite of the fact that Judaism is a religion known, in the words of a Conservative rabbinical group, "for its worldliness and practical idealism," it did not produce a social gospel movement comparable to that in Protestantism, although numerous rabbis and laymen made great contributions to reform. This fact, which is a surprise to Nathan Glazer, author of *American Judaism,* a brief but thorough history, becomes "really surprising" when he turns to Reform Jews.[1] However, early Reform Judaism in America was seriously concerned with ethical and social issues, as was emphasized by the fifth and eighth points of the Pittsburgh Platform of 1885, the embodiment of Reform ideology:

> We recognize in the modern era of universal culture of heart and intellect the approach of the realization of Israel's great Messianic hope for the establishment of the Kingdom of truth, justice and peace among all men. . . .
>
> In full accordance with the spirit of Mosaic legislation which strives to regulate the relation between rich and poor, we deem it our duty to participate in the great task of modern times, to solve on the basis of justice and righteousness the problems presented by the contrasts and evils of the present organization of society.[2]

The biblical basis for the Reform leaders' concerns was vividly set forth by Rabbi Henry Berkowitz of Philadelphia, one of almost a dozen Jewish spokesmen to appear before the World's Parliament of Religions at Chicago in 1893. In an address called "The Voice of the Mother of Religions on the Social Question," Berkowitz declared that:

From the first Judaism proclaimed the dignity and duty of labor by postulating God, the Creator, at work, and setting forth the divine example unto all men for imitation, in the command, "Six days shalt thou labor and do all thy work." Industry is thus hallowed by religion, and religion in turn is made to receive the homage of industry in the fulfillment of the ordinance of Sabbath rest.

Against the iniquity of self-seeking, Judaism has ever protested most loudly, and none the less so against the errors and evils of an unjust self-sacrifice. "Love thyself," she says. This is axiomatic. Egoism as an exclusive motive is entirely false, but altruism is not therefore exclusively and always right. In the reciprocal relation between the responsibility of the individual for society and of society for the individual lies one of Judaism's prime characteristics. She has pointed the ideal in the conflict of social principles by her golden precept "Thou shalt love they neighbor as thyself; I am God." According to this precept she has so arranged the inner affairs of the family that the purity, the sweetness and the tenderness of the homes of her children have become proverbial.

With her sublime maxim, "Love thy neighbor as thyself; I am God," Judaism set up the highest ideal of society, as a human brotherhood under the care of a Divine Fatherhood. According to this ideal Judaism has sought, passing beyond the environments of the family, to regulate the affairs of human society at large. "This is the book of the generations of men," was the caption of Genesis (v. I), indicating, as the Rabbins taught, that all men are entitled to equal rights, as being equally the children of one Creator. The freedom of the individual was the prime necessary consequence of this precept. Slavery stood forever condemned when Israel went forth from the bondage of Egypt.

Judaism has calmly met the wild outbursts of extremists of the Antipoverty and Nihilistic types with the simple confession of the fact: "The needy will not be wanting in the land." The brotherly care of the needy is the common solicitude of the Jewish legislators in every age.

The freedom of the individual was recognized as involving the development of unlike capacities. From this freedom all progress springs. But all progress must be made, not for the selfish advantage of the individual alone, but for the common welfare "that thy brother with thee may live." Therefore, private property in land or other possessions was regarded as only a trust, because everything is God's, the Father's, to be acquired by industry and perseverance by the individual, but to be held by him only to the advantage of all. To this end were established all the laws and institutions of trade, of industry and of the system of inheritance; the code of rentals; the Jubilee year that every fiftieth year brought back the land which had been sold, into the original patrimony; the seventh or Sabbatical year in which the lands were fallow, all produce free to the consumer; the tithings of field and flock; the loans to the brother in need without usury, and the magnificent system of obligatory charities which still holds the germ of the wisdom of all modern scientific charity: "Let the poor glean in the fields," and gather through his own efforts what he needs; *i.e.,* give to each one, not support, but the opportunity to secure his own support.

A careful study of these Mosaic-Talmudic institutions and laws is of untold worth to the present in the solution of the social question. True, these codes were adapted to the needs of a peculiar people, living under conditions which do not now exist in exactly the same order anywhere. We can not use the statutes, but their aim and spirit, their motive and method we must adopt in the solution of the social problem even to-day.

The cry of woe which is ringing in our ears now was never heard in Judea. In all the annals of Jewish history there are no records of the revolts of slaves such as those which afflicted the world's greatest empire; no uprising like those of the Plebeians of Rome, the Demoi of Athens, or the Helots of Sparta; no wild scenes like those of the Paris Commune; no processions of hungry men, women and children crying for bread, like those of London, Chicago and Denver. Pauperism never haunted the ancient land of Judea. Tramps were not known there. We have here the pattern of what was the most successful social system that the world has ever known.

The hotly contested social questions of our civilization are to be settled according to the ideas neither of the capitalist, the communist, the anarchist, nor the nihilist, but simply and only according to the eternal laws of morality, of which Sinai is the loftiest symbol.[3]

No American Jew surpassed Rabbi Stephen S. Wise in battling "for American liberalism and for justice to all peoples." Imbued with the message of prophetic Judaism, Wise was also deeply influenced by the social gospel movement. He read the works of Josiah Strong and Lyman Abbott and especially admired Washington Gladden. At Gladden's death, Wise wrote to the editor of the *Ohio State Journal* in Columbus and praised "a nobly prophetic figure." Included in his tribute was an assessment which indicated Gladden's personal influence on Wise. "Gladden was the bishop of men of all creeds and churches."[4] As his biographer has observed, "The language and thought used by Wise in the pulpit and on the platform were as much that of 'Social Gospel' Protestants as that of the Hebrew prophets."[5]

Another devotee of Henry George in his youth, and founder and for thirty years rabbi of the Free Synagogue of New York, Wise was one of a group that called a mass meeting in the Metropolitan Opera House shortly after the catastrophic Triangle Fire of 1911 in which 146 persons, most of them young women workers in a clothing factory, lost their lives. In a powerful speech that recalls the ancient Hebrew prophets, Wise called the City of New York to penitence and action:

This ought to be a fast day of the citizens of New York, our day of guilt and humiliation. Let it not become a day of unavailing regret, but let it be a day of availing contriteness and redeeming penitence.

It is not the action of God, but the inaction of man that is responsible. I see in this disaster not the deed of God, but the greed of man. For law is divine, and this disaster was brought about by lawlessness and inhumanity. Certain calamities man can do no more than vainly deplore,—such calamities as the San Francisco earthquake and the destruction by volcano of Martinique. But this was not an inevitable disaster which man could neither foresee nor control. We might have foreseen it, and some of us did; we might have controlled it, but we chose not to do so. The things that are inevitable we can do no more than vainly regret, but the things that are avoidable we can effectively forestall and prevent.

It is not a question of enforcement of law nor of inadequacy of law. We have the wrong kind of laws and the wrong kind of enforcement. Before insisting upon inspection and enforcement, let us lift up the industrial standards so as to make conditions worth inspecting, and, if inspected, certain to afford security to the workers. Instead of unanimity in the shirking of responsibility, we demand that departments shall cooperate in planning ahead and working for the future, with some measure of prevision and wisdom. And when we go before the Legislature of the State, and demand increased appropriations in order to ensure the possibility of a sufficient number of inspectors, we will not forever be put off with the answer: We have no money.

This meeting is not summoned in order to appeal for charity on behalf of the families of the slain. What is needed is the redress of justice and the remedy of prevention. The families of the victims ought to be beyond the reach of the need of charity. Having denied them the justice of physical security, we ought at least be willing to give their survivors the justice of economic redress. They need justice, not charity. It is we who need charity, for dare we face inexorable justice? . . .

We know that we cannot and should not take away property without due process of law. Neither may we take away life with or without due process of law. Alas, for another one of a multitude of proofs that we regard property as sacred, and are ready to suffer a violation of the rights of life as if these were not sacred but violable, and violable with impunity.

This consuming fire will have been nothing more than a flash in the pan if other evils are suffered to go unchecked and uncorrected,—evils not less terrible because less swift and less sudden. It is just as necessary to protect women workers from the industrial and occupational diseases as it is to protect them from industrial accidents. We need to provide not only for security from accidents but security from the incidents of the industrial regime. I would have women workers safeguarded in every way,—safeguarded from the economically, physically, morally and spiritually disastrous consequences of over-work and under-pay and under-nourishment and insanitary housing, which seem to be the inevitable accompaniments of things as they are today. . . .

If the church and the synagogue were forces of righteousness in the world instead of being the farces of respectability and convention, this thing need not have been. If it be the shame and humiliation of the whole community, it is doubly the humiliation of the synagogue and of the church which have suffered it to come to pass. We may not be ready to prescribe a legislative program nor devise an industrial panacea, but we must demand and demand increasingly an ever-increasing measure of social equity and social justice.

The hour has come for industrial peace. It must be peace with honor,—say some. But it must be more than peace with honor. It must be peace with security as well. We would have no peace with honor for some, and, at the same time, deny security to all. The issue at stake is not the open shop but the closed door, which shuts out the toilers from safety and justice.

The lesson of the hour is that while property is good, life is better, that while possessions are valuable, life is priceless. The meaning of the hour is that the life of the lowliest worker in the nation is sacred and inviolable, and, if that sacred human right be violated, we shall stand adjudged and condemned before the tribunal of God and of history.[6]

That same year, Wise was invited to speak at the annual banquet of the

Chamber of Commerce of New York, as he says in his autobiography, "for the first and last time." Facing Andrew Carnegie, James J. Hill, J. P. Morgan, and Charles Schwab among the businessmen who made up his audience, Wise set forth unequivocally his attitude toward the relations between labor and capital, knowing that he could please this august assembly and lose his soul, or "displease them and keep it":

When I have read from time to time of religious noonday meetings held in shops and factories for the wage-earners, I have ventured to observe that the important thing is not so much to bring religious ministration to the daily toilers,—the soldiers of the common good,—as to bring it to the captains of industry and commerce, which you are. For the conscience of the nation, after all, will be that which you make it,—yours is the high and solemn duty not only of registering, but in large part of determining the character of the conscience of the nation. . . .

Not only ought the barter or trade side of business be completely moralized, but we need to ethicize what might be called the processes of creating and production, of distribution and consumption. No business order is just nor can it long endure if it be bound up with the evil of unemployment on the one hand and over-employment on the other, the evil of a man's under-wage and a child's toil, and all those social maladjustments incidental to our order which we lump together under the name of poverty. Let us not imagine that we can shift to the shoulders of over-worked charity the burdens that can be borne only by the strength of underworked justice. Yes, the stricken ask not the occasional tonic of charity, but the daily meat and substance of justice. We are never to forget that ours is a democracy, that a democracy, in the words of a high servant of the commonwealth means "the use of all the resources of nature by all the faculties of man for the good of all the people. . . . "

The conscience of the nation is not real unless the nation safeguard the workingman, safeguard him from the peril of over-work, as well as from the occasional accidents of industry. The conscience of the nation is not vital unless we protect women and children in industry, and protect them with half the thoroughness and generosity with which, for many decades, we have protected infant industries. We have not the right to speak of the importance of conserving the opportunity for initiative on the part of the individual as long as masses of individuals are suffered to perish without the opportunity of real life. The aim of democracy is not to be the production of efficient, machine-like men in industry. The first business of democracy is to be the industry of turning out completely effective, because completely free and self-determining, citizens.[7]

When he sat down, Wise wrote afterward, "the only comfortable man in the room was Admiral Peary (the polar explorer)—seasoned to subarctic temperatures!"

Scholarly research into the subject of this chapter has been minimal, but the authors are pleased to include an excerpt from an illuminating paper that was read before a group of historians by Professor Egal Feldman in 1968—"The Social Gospel and the Jews":

Liberal American Jews, it would appear at first glance, could hardly have felt themselves estranged during the era of the social gospel. Together with Christians they shared during the few decades before World War I many of the cheerful, optimistic, theological presumptions current at that time. Higher criticism, studies of comparative religion, the application of the theories of Darwinian evolution to biblical history, excited the intellect of many a progressive minded Jew and Gentile alike. The new Protestant view of God, as an immanent Deity, directly involved in the affairs of man, was not incongruent with the thoughts of many a Jew. Neither was the heavy emphasis placed by numerous American Christians upon the ethical and moral aspects of theology. Thinking Jews would have hardly disputed the prevailing belief in Christian circles that "the concrete problems of our day are social problems . . . the overshadowing question of our day is the social question . . . the dominating passion of our age is the social passion"; or that men must be judged by their works, rather than by their faith. "It is not enough that we believe: we must do." "Our relations with God cannot be right, if our relations with our fellow men are wrong," were propositions which Jews universally accepted. To Walter Rauschenbusch, the acknowledged theologian of the social gospel, the sins of mortals could be understood only in relation to the doings of present and past generations. "Sin is lodged in social customs and institutions and is absorbed by the individual from his social group. . . . The evils of one generation are caused by the wrongs of the generations that preceded, and will in turn condition the sufferings and temptations of those who come after," he wrote in 1918. Such a repudiation of the fatalism of original sinfulness would have undoubtedly elicited a nod of assent from many a Jew. And when such thoughts were officially endorsed by thirty-three Protestant denominations, with the establishment of the Federal Council of Churches of Christ, in 1908, it must have appeared to Jews that a new day had indeed dawned upon American Christianity.

Perhaps most encouraging was the revival of interest in Judaism evident in Protestant circles. To be sure, such an attentiveness to the life of an ancient people was motivated in part by the sudden influx of an unusual number of Jewish immigrants. But more important, however, was that the new interest in biblical history and comparative religion drove many a Christian to re-examine the sources of his faith. It was a kind of back-to-the-Bible movement that America witnessed during these years, wherein even the solution of modern social problems, problems of poverty and affluence, capital and labor, freedom and exploitation, was sought in the Old Testament. A Yale Divinity School lecturer went so far as to rename Exodus in 1905, calling it "The Story of an Ancient Labor Movement," a title which he believed would more appropriately "serve to indicate what is really the main theme of the narrative."

Since it was convenient for Christians to link the social message of Jesus to the thoughts of the Hebrew prophets there was a tendency to lean towards their moral and ethical writings. It was in the prophetic books that Walter Rauschenbusch sought a clue to a better present. "They are an integral part of the thought life of Christianity," he observed in 1907. "What other nation," but that of the Jews, he remarked with surprise, "has a library of classics in which the spokesmen of the common people have the dominant voice. It would be hard to find a parallel to it anywhere."

Ministers spoke frequently about the debt Christianity owed to Judaism. "Nearly everything we have that dignifies us and sweetens us and refines us and makes us significant . . . has come to us from them." "The world is at last awakening to a sense of its obligation to Israel." "Wherever men and women are toiling to prove that humanity is a great brotherhood, there we find . . . the influence of . . . leaders of Hebrew thought," were typical utterances. Edward C. Baldwin, author of *Our Modern Debt to Israel,* was convinced that the entire social gospel movement was but the rediscovery of Judaism by the Christian world. Unlike the historians of his day who sought the germ of constitutional government in the midst of Germanic forests, Lyman Abbott, whose popular magazine, the *Outlook,* was at the forefront of the revival of Judaism, attributed even the origin of modern democratic behavior to Jewish Biblical thought. "Every legislative hall, every courthouse . . . to say nothing of less visible and tangible manifestations of our national life and temper are monuments of our indebtedness to this ancient people," he wrote early in the century.

There is little need to delve deeply into Jewish thought to conclude that many of the humanitarian principles of the social gospel lay at the heart of Judaism. "Judaism is a God-centered faith whose chief concern is man." "The temptation to sin is real, and the desire on man's part to follow it stronger than his desire to choose the good," is a thought that would have fitted neatly into the conceptual framework of the social gospel. The belief in the immanence of God who joins with man in a striving towards the future Kingdom is an ancient belief in Jewish life. "The [first] benediction [in the daily prayers] underscores the relation of God to the world as that of Creator to creation with the added insight that His activity is not of the past but is ongoing and continuous." Faith and action, creed and deed, theory and practice, study and activity, were coupled throughout most of the history of Jewish theological thinking. "In Judaism," writes Abba Hillel Silver, "the life of contemplation or of study was of significance only insofar as it led to action." Judaism "did not accept a worship of God which does not involve the service of humanity."

Solomon Schechter, who early in the century assumed the presidency of the Jewish Theological Seminary of America, reflected substantial agreement with the aspirations of the social gospel. However, unlike his more liberal colleagues, he viewed the search for modern altruists among biblical and post-biblical figures to be somewhat unhistorical. Yet, like the social gospelers of his day, he stressed the idea of God's immanence and believed that for man "to work towards establishing the visible Kingdom of God in the present world" was "the highest goal religion can strive to reach." The Kingdom, explained Schechter, is inconsistent with "bad government," or a "state of social misery engendered through poverty and want. . . . All-wise social legislation in this respect must help towards its speedy advent."

Spokesmen for Reform Jewry frequently mentioned the social gospel, and as we have seen, it was included in their Declaration of Principles of 1885. Professor Feldman continues:

In almost perfect accord with the progressive wing of American Protestantism, American Reform Rabbis meditated over theories of evolution, glorified the ethical suggestions of the Hebrew Prophets and questioned the religious significance of ancient ecclesiastical rituals. "The task is to rescue from the morass of Rabbinism the prophetic ethical spirit underlying its minute regulations," wrote Kaufmann Kohler, a leading spokesman for Reform. Kohler understood the essential ingredient of Judaism to be man's consciousness of his social responsibilities, his obligations to those who surrounded him. Judaism "looks to the *deed* . . . not to the empty creed and the blind belief," he wrote. "The life of the recluse is of little use to the world at large and hence of no moral value. . . . Only in devotion to his fellows is man made to realize his own godlike nature."

The age of the social gospel, it would seem, therefore, had narrowed the theological gap between Jew and Gentile. Because of common agreements it became possible for the first time in many years for Jew and Christian to talk about matters which for centuries had been held to be sacred and mutually exclusive.[8]

Unfortunately, the ecumenical atmosphere generated by the Parliament of Religions, in which, as we have seen, Jews participated, lasted only until about the time of World War I. Liberal Jews and liberal Christians exchanged pulpits, interfaith worship services were held, a *Book of Common Worship* was compiled, and an occasional interfaith church appeared.[9] Glazer believes that at the turn of the century a historian of ideas might have forecast a merger of these groups. For numerous reasons, most of them beyond the scope of this book, no such amalgamation took place.[10] However, in the 1920's, the Central Conference of American Rabbis, the National Catholic Welfare Conference, and the Federal Council of Churches joined in challenging the twelve-hour-day–seven-day-week in the steel industry and later investigated several strikes jointly. Yet these forays into social action did not result in a Jewish social gospel, an understandable situation in the light of the overwhelming nature of Jewish problems since the early 1930's. Glazer believes, however, that Jewish social attitudes "derive more from nineteenth-century liberalism and socialism than from the Hebrew prophets."[11]

Notes

1. Nathan Glazer, *American Judaism* (2d ed.; Chicago: University of Chicago Press, 1972), 138–39.

2. Glazer, *American Judaism* (1st ed.; Chicago: University of Chicago Press, 1957), 152; from the *Yearbook of the Central Conference of American Rabbis,* 45 (1935), 198–200.

3. J. H. Barrows, *The World's Parliament of Religions,* 2 (Chicago: Parliament, 1893), 1150–51.

4. Stephen Wise to Editor, *Ohio State Journal,* July 3, 1918, First Congregational Church Archives, Columbus, Ohio; cited in Ronald C. White, Jr., "Social Christianity and the Negro in the Progressive Era, 1890–1920" (unpub.; Ph.D. diss., Princeton University, 1972), 178.

5. Carl H. Voss, *Rabbi and Minister: The Friendship of Stephen S. Wise and John Haynes Holmes* (Cleveland: World, 1964), 38–39.

6. Stephen Wise, *Challenging Years: The Autobiography of Stephen Wise* (New York: Putnam's, 1949), 62–64. By permission of G. P. Putnam's Sons, holder of the copyright.

7. Wise, 60–61. By permission.

8. Egal Feldman, "The Social Gospel and the Jews," *American Jewish Historical Quarterly,* 58, no. 3 (March, 1969), 308–12. We are deeply grateful to Professor Feldman for providing this essay and permission to reprint part of it.

9. Feldman, 312–16.

10. Glazer, 1st ed., 53; cited by Feldman, 316. Feldman believes that there was an element of anti-Semitism embedded in the social gospel, which prevented further rapprochement.

11. Glazer, 2d ed., 141. The broad field covered in this chapter offers many opportunities for further research.

VI

Looking Backward

Introduction

By 1920 the momentum of both the progressive movement and the social gospel was on the wane. From without, the climate of the country was changing. The political triumph of the progressive movement under Roosevelt and Wilson now seemed in disarray only to be replaced by the politics of normalcy of Harding and Coolidge. The tide of nationalism which boiled up in World War I spewed out to engulf the country in negative crusades—the Red Scare, the Ku Klux Klan, and anti-immigration legislation—all of which meant a widespread attack on civil liberties. After the post-war civil turbulence the twenties seemed to many observers to be marked by a rejection of progressive idealism and an upsurge of crass materialism.

From within, the voices of the foremost leaders of the social gospel —Walter Rauschenbusch, Washington Gladden, Lyman Abbott, and Josiah Strong—were all stilled between 1916 and 1922. Used to being partners with other progressives, the remaining social gospelers now found themselves and their causes out of sorts with the new ethos of normalcy. As action diminished, the liberal theology that was the ideological basis for many of the social gospelers came under attack. There had always been a pecking away on the right flank by the fundamentalists, but now a more subtle and devastating attack was articulated by the brothers Niebuhr, by John Bennett, and by others.

At this watershed of the social gospel as an historical movement, a whole cluster of issues and questions demand attention and critical evaluation. First, it is important to look again at the theological and social orientation of the movement. How can it best be defined? How did it exhibit continuity or discontinuity with its evangelical origins? The mature thought of Walter Rauschenbusch will be used as a basic resource.

A second question is raised by the whole confluence of events and ideas arising after World War I: Did the social gospel decline, become defunct, or revive in altered form? In answering this question we will consider the biblical realism of the new theology of Reinhold Niebuhr.

Niebuhr's type of neo-orthodoxy, self-consciously different from the Barthianism emanating from Europe, offered a devastating critique of liberal theology in general and the strategy of the social gospel in particular. The complaints against the social gospel reached a climax in the mid-thirties. H. Richard Niebuhr's sometimes forgotten essay, "The Attack upon the Social Gospel," sums up the arguments of the opponents, but in Niebuhr's typical manner presents a balanced accounting of the movement's weaknesses and strengths.

Finally, we must discover whether it is possible to speak of the social gospel in our own times. The question may be put this way: Was the social gospel an historical movement, however we may wish to date its terminus, or has it become also a continuing tradition in American religious life, albeit in ever renewed and changing forms? We make the case that the social gospel emerged with renewed vigor in the turbulent sixties as one of the not always recognized roots of the variegated social justice movement. The leading figure of that period, Martin Luther King, Jr., was quite conscious of his own debt to Walter Rauschenbusch and the social gospel. In the seventies one of the most remarkable religious phenomena is the extension of the social gospel among groups that for over a century have been associated hitherto with different histories and orientations. The book concludes with a new essay by John C. Bennett, one of the most important religious leaders of the last half-century. Author of one of the last social gospel statements, critic of liberalism, friend of the Niebuhrs, Bennett offers a fresh perspective on the heritage and present meaning of the social gospel.

21   Conservative or Liberal?

As we have seen throughout this volume, the social gospel is difficult to characterize by any single theological label. A movement that stressed action more than creed, the social gospel was capable of uniting diverse persons and groups rallying to various reform causes. This is not to downplay the movement's theological integrity, for certainly biblical and theological studies—for example, the understanding of the kingdom of God—undergirded much of its action. It is to say that ideas have consequences, and in the midst of what the social gospelers believed to be a "crisis" in America, there was no time for the luxury of intramural theological debate.

Even as we use such words as "liberal" and "conservative," it is important to determine whether these representations refer to theological belief or social strategy. The two were not synonymous, for liberal theology was sometimes linked with conservative social thought and more conservative theological persuasion could be combined with progressive or even radical social strategy. For example, Charles Stelzle, Presbyterian founder of New York's Labor Temple, espoused liberal positions on most social issues but was a conservative, Princeton-trained Calvinist in his theology.

In recent years "liberal" and "evangelical" (rather than "conservative") have been terms used in opposition, but Kenneth Cauthen insists that they must be used jointly to describe Walter Rauschenbusch and others for whom theology was a serious undertaking. These "evangelical liberals" made the person and work of Jesus Christ central, but at the same time sought a faith that could be mediated to intelligent modern people. They are to be contrasted with the "modernistic liberals" who come to the fore after World War I.

The liberalism which emerged in this country at the beginning of the twentieth century is one phase in this continuing struggle of the church to relate the enduring Christian message to a constantly changing cultural situation. One of the central concerns of theology since the eighteenth century has been the compatibility of Christianity with the modern mind. Thoughtful persons became increasingly conscious as the decades passed of the gulf between the ancient faith and the newly developing view of the world. Liberalism arose in an attempt to bridge this chasm. The central aim of liberal theology was to make it possible for a man, to use Fosdick's phrase, "to be both an intelligent modern and a serious Christian."

Liberalism, then, can best be understood in terms of its effort to harmonize Christ and culture under the conditions set by the late nineteenth and early twentieth centuries. However, not all liberals went about this task in the same way. Diverse forms of liberalism appeared. A fundamental difference between two groups of liberals can be specified in terms of the way each related the Biblical faith to modern culture. Thus, there are two basic types of liberalism. One will be called evangelical liberalism, and the other will be referred to as modernistic liberalism.

A. Evangelical Liberalism

The evangelical liberals can appropriately be thought of as "serious Christians" who were searching for a theology which could be believed by "intelligent moderns." They stood squarely within the Christian tradition and accepted as normative for their thinking what they understood to be the essence of historical Christianity. These men had a deep consciousness of their continuity with the main line of Christian orthodoxy and felt that they were preserving its essential features in terms which were suitable to the modern world. One of the evidences of the loyalty of the evangelical liberals to the historic faith is the place which they gave to Jesus. Through his person and work there is mediated to men both knowledge of God and saving power. He is the source and norm of the Christian's experience of God. In short, evangelical liberalism is Christocentric. In the words of William Adams Brown, "the new theology raises the old cry, 'Back to Christ.' Let no theology call itself Christian which has not its center and source in him."

This estimate of the centrality of Christ is closely related in the thought of the evangelical liberals to their way of dealing with the problem of revelation and reason. These men believed in special revelation in the sense that through the history and experience of Israel recorded in the Bible there has been given to mankind a unique and normative disclosure of the nature and will of God. The high point of this revelation is to be found in the life, work, and personality of the historical Jesus. His teachings were thought to be of universal and permanent relevance to the moral and religious quest of mankind, and it is to him that even modern men must look for the highest insights into the meaning of human existence. The revelation of God in Christ, then, is the norm of religious truth.

However, this revelation stands in direct continuity with reason and experience. The affirmations which Christianity makes about the existence and nature of God were seen to be fundamentally reasonable and in harmony with the available evidence. The high claims concerning Christ were thought to be validated by the moral and religious fruits which resulted from the impact of the personality of Jesus upon the believer. The Bible could be seen as the record both of God's progressive revelation of himself and of man's growing discovery of God in experience. It is not to be appealed to arbitrarily as a source of authoritative doctrine. Rather, the teachings of the Scriptures are to be accepted because of their intrinsic worth as measured by the mind and conscience of man. Thus, while the norm of religious truth was found in the act of God in Christ witnessed to by the Bible, this revelation was thought to validate itself in experience by virtue of its own inherent reasonableness and practical value.

The wide gulf between the thought patterns of the Bible and those employed in the modern world made it necessary to reinterpret many of the doctrines of orthodoxy in order to avoid intellectual embarrassment. One widely employed method of overcoming this hiatus was to set up a distinction between the religious experiences of men and the categories which gave expression to them. The experiences may remain the same from age to age while the categories change. Fosdick's phrase—"abiding experiences and changing categories"—attained wide currency among liberals as the means by which the permanent truth of the historic faith could be reinterpreted to fit the idiom of the contemporary world.

In short, evangelical liberalism represents the attempt of men who were convinced of the truth of historic Christianity to adjust this ancient faith to the demands of the modern era. . . .

B. Modernistic Liberalism

The modernistic liberals can best be thought of as "intelligent moderns" who nevertheless wished to be thought of as "serious Christians" in some real sense. They are called "modernistic" because they were basically determined in their thinking by a twentieth-century outlook. They had no real sense of continuing in the line of the historic faith. Rather, they were conscious that they were introducing something new. Nevertheless, they believed that there were elements of permanent significance in the Christian tradition which ought to be retained. However, the standard by which the abiding values of the Christianity of the past were to be measured was derived from the presuppositions of modern science, philosophy, psychology, and social thought. Nothing was to be believed simply because it was to be found in the Bible or Christian tradition.

The loose connection of the modernistic liberals with the traditional faith can be seen clearly in their estimate of Jesus. The thinking of these men was not Christocentric. Jesus was important—and even unique—because he illustrated truths and values which are universally relevant. However, these truths and values can be validated and even discovered apart from Jesus. He is not so much the *source* as he is the *exemplar* of the religious norm. Jesus might be psychologically helpful, but he was not usually thought to be logically necessary for the highest experience of God in human life.

One characteristic feature of modernistic liberalism was its intense concern with methodology. Having abandoned belief in revelation, these men, unlike the evangelical liberals, had no norm in the Bible, Christ, or tradition to which they could appeal. This made it necessary for them to discover a source and standard of religious truth independent of the historic faith. Hence, the search for a new methodology became a prime consideration and often overshadowed the efforts to define the content of religious truth. The most promising source of help along these lines was found by the modernists in empirical science. Here was a distinctly modern method of attaining and testing truth, the practical worth of which had already been demonstrated in the natural sciences. If the methods of observation and experimentation which had been so effective in unlocking the secrets of nature could be adapted for use in the realm of religion, the way seemed open to restore theology to a respectable place in the modern world. It would no longer be necessary to appeal arbitrarily to some external authority which had to be accepted on faith. Rather, it seemed possible to build up a body of religious truth which could take its place on an equal basis alongside the knowledge attained in physics, chemistry, biology, and the other empirical disciplines. All of the modernistic liberals to be considered in this undertaking found in the empirical method of science the surest way of attaining for theology a hearing in the modern scene.

In short, modernistic liberalism represents the attempt of men who were thoroughly immersed in contemporary culture to reinterpret what they felt to be of permanent truth and value in the Christian tradition in terms of the methods and categories of early twentieth-century science and philosophy. Modernism developed slightly later than evangelical liberalism and was strongest in the last fifteen years of the period under consideration.[1]

Walter Rauschenbusch is remembered as the foremost theologian of the social gospel. It is not always remembered that his theology was grounded in an evangelical piety that he never abandoned. Six generations of Rauschenbusches had served as Lutheran pastors in Germany. His father had become a Baptist, and Walter grew up in this evangelical church, where conversion was the entrance into the kingdom. Undergoing a profound Christian experience as a youth, Rauschenbusch believed he was called to be a minister. More than this he aspired to be an evangelist, which he esteemed as perhaps the highest calling for a minister.

One year before his death Rauschenbusch published *A Theology for the Social Gospel,* the culmination of his theological journey. He began this volume with what would become well-known words: "We have a social gospel. We need a systematic theology large enough to match it and vital enough to back it."[2] As critics would point out, this volume, prepared for a lectureship in doctrinal theology, lacked some of the fire and style of *Christianity and the Social Crisis,* but it is a more systematic attempt to deal with major theological ideas. There is much that could be quoted and analyzed, but what is of interest for our purposes is to note the continuing import of evangelical religion for the thought of the mature Rauschenbusch. Donald Meyer goes so far as to say, "Rauschenbusch, in other words, wished to 'add on' the social gospel to the evangelical personal gospel."[3] To be sure, the burden of Rauschenbusch's pastoral and teaching ministry had been to "add on" the social dimension, but this burden was picked up because of the overwhelming evangelical tendency in Rauschenbusch's day toward individualism and privatism. Nevertheless, in *A Theology for the Social Gospel,* Rauschenbusch takes great pains to reaffirm his solidarity with the evangelical faith. In the foreword, for example, he says:

I wish to assure the reader who hesitates in the vestibule, that the purpose of this book is wholly positive and constructive. It is just as orthodox as the Gospel would allow. I have dedicated it to an eminent representative of the older theology [Augustus Hopkins Strong] in order to express my deep gratitude for what I have received from it, and to clasp hands through him with all whose thought has been formed by Jesus Christ.[4]

Rauschenbusch affirms a more traditional theological position at several points. Early on, he insists on maintaining that the social gospel is neither alien nor novel.

In these introductory chapters my aim is to win the benevolent and serious attention of conservative readers for the discussions that are to follow. I have thus far tried to show that the spread of the social gospel will inevitably react on theology, and that this influence is likely to be constructive and salutary. Let us add the important fact that the social gospel imports into theology nothing that is new or alien.

Frequent attempts have been made in the history of our religion to blend alien elements with it. The early Gnostics and the mediaeval Albigenses, for instance, tried to combine historical Christianity with dualistic conceptions of the universe and strict asceticism. Modern Mormonism, Theosophy, and Christian Science represent syncretistic formations, minglings of genuine Christianity with new and alien elements.

The belief in the universal reign of law, the doctrine of evolution, the control of nature by man, and the value of education and liberty as independent goods,—these are among the most influential convictions of modern life and have deeply modified our religious thought. But they are novel elements of theology. They are not alien, but certainly they held no such controlling position in the theology of the past as they do with us. We may discover prophetic forecasts of them in the Bible, but we have to look for them.

On the other hand the idea of the redemption of the social organism is nothing alien. It is simply a proper part of the Christian faith in redemption from sin and evil. As soon as the desire for salvation becomes strong and intelligent enough to look beyond the personal sins of the individual, and to discern how our personality in its intake and output is connected with the social groups to which we belong, the problem of social redemption is before us and we can never again forget it. It lies like a larger concentric circle around a smaller one. It is related to our intimate personal salvation like astronomy to physics. Only spiritual and intellectual immaturity have kept us from seeing it clearly before. The social gospel is not an alien element in theology.

Neither is it novel. The social gospel is, in fact, the oldest gospel of all. It is "built on the foundation of the apostles and prophets." Its substance is the Hebrew faith which Jesus himself held. If the prophets ever talked about the "plan of redemption," they meant the social redemption of the nation. So long as John the Baptist and Jesus were proclaiming the gospel, the Kingdom of God was its central word, and the ethical teaching of both, which was their practical commentary and definition of the Kindom idea, looked toward a higher social order in which new ethical standards would become practicable. To the first generation of disciples the hope of the Lord's return meant the hope of a Christian social order on earth under the personal rule of Jesus Christ, and they would have been amazed if they had learned that this hope was to be motioned out of theology and other ideas substituted.

The social gospel is nothing alien or novel. When it comes to a question of pedigree and birth-right, it may well turn on the dogmas on which the Catholic and Protestant theologies are based and inquire for their birth certificate. They are neither dominant in the New Testament nor clearly defined in it. The more our historical investigations are laying bare the roots of Catholic dogma, the more do we see them running back into alien Greek thought, and not into the substance of Christ's message nor into the Hebrew faith. We shall not get away again from the central proposition of Harnack's History of Dogma, that the development of Catholic dogma was the process of the Hellenization of Christianity; in other words, that alien influences streamed into the religion of Jesus Christ and created a theology which he never taught nor intended. What would Jesus have said to the symbol of Chalcedon or the Athanasian Creed if they had been read to him?

The doctrine of the Kingdom of God was left undeveloped by individualistic theology and finally mislaid by it almost completely, because it did not support nor fit in with that scheme of doctrine. In the older handbooks of theology it is scarcely mentioned, except in the chapters on eschatology; in none of them does it dominate the table of contents. What a spectacle, that the original teaching of our Lord has become an incongruous element in so-called evangelical theology, like a stranger with whom the other doctrines would not associate, and who was finally ejected because he had no wedding garment! In the same way the distinctive ethics of Jesus, which is part and parcel of his Kingdom doctrine, was long the hidden treasure of suppressed democratic sects. Now, as soon as the social gospel began once more to be preached in our own time, the doctrine of the Kingdom was immediately loved and proclaimed afresh, and the ethical principles of Jesus are once more taught without reservation as the only alternative for the greedy ethics of capitalism and militarism. These antipathies and affinities are a strong proof that the social gospel is neither alien nor novel, but is a revival of the earliest doctrines of Christianity, of its radical ethical spirit, and of its revolutionary consciousness.[5]

Of fundamental importance for Rauschenbusch was the reality and implications of sin. He devoted six of nineteen chapters to a discussion of sin and evil. For Rauschenbusch the centrality of sin was vitiated both by the new theology's attempt to explain away sin in terms of the environment and the old theology's inability to recognize sin when confronted with it in society.

Any religious tendency or school of theology must be tested by the question whether it does justice to the religious consciousness of sin. Now, one cause of distrust against the social gospel is that its exponents often fail to show an adequate appreciation of the power and guilt of sin. Its teachings seem to put the blame for wong-doing on the environment, and instead of stiffening and awakening the sense of responsibility in the individual, it teaches him to unload it on society.

There is doubtless truth in this accusation. The emphasis on environment and on the contributory guilt of the community, does offer a chance to unload responsibility, and human nature is quick to seize the chance. But the old theology has had its equivalents for environment. Men unloaded on original sin, on the devil, and on the decrees of God. Adam began soon after the fall to shift the blame. This shiftiness seems to be one of the clearest and most universal effects of original sin.

Moreover, there is an unavoidable element of moral unsettlement whenever the religious valuation of sin is being reconsidered. Paul frequently and anxiously defended his gospel against the charge that his principle of liberty invited lawlessness, and that under it a man might even sin the more in order to give grace the greater chance. We know what the Hebrew prophets thought of the sacrificial cult and moral righteousness, but we are not informed about the unsettling effect which their teaching may have had. If we could raise up some devout priest of the age of Amos or Isaiah to give us his judgment on the theology of the prophets, he would probably assure us that these men doubtless meant well, but that they had no adequate sense of sin; they belittled the sacrifices instituted by Moses; but sacrificing, as all men knew, was the true expression and gauge of repentance.

In the early years of the Reformation, Catholic observers noted a distressing looseness in the treatment of sin. Men no longer searched their consciences in the confessional: they performed no works of penance to render satisfaction to God and to prove their contrition; they no longer used the ascetic means of holiness to subdue their flesh and to gain victory over the powers of darkness. Luther had taught them that God required nothing but faith, and that all accounts could be squared by agreeing to call them square. By any standard of measurement known to Catholics, the profounder consciousness of sin was with the old theology and its practical applications. In point of fact, the Reformation did upset the old means of moral control and did create widespread demoralization. But in time, Geneva, Holland, or Scotland showed a deeper consciousness of sin than Rome or Paris. The sense of sin found new outlets.

The delinquencies of a new movement are keenly observed because they are new; the shortcomings of an old system are part of the accepted scheme of life. If the exponents of the old theology have taught humanity an adequate consciousness of sin, how is it that they themselves have been blind and dumb on the master iniquities of human history? During all the ages while they were the theological keepers of the conscience of Christendom, the peasants in the country and the working class in the cities were being sucked dry by the parasitic classes of society, and war was damning poor humanity. Yet what traces are there in traditional theology that the minds of old-line theologians were awake to these magnificent manifestations of the wickedness of the human heart? How is it that only in the modern era, since the moral insight of mankind has to some extent escaped from the tuition of the old theology, has a world-wide social movement arisen to put a stop to the exploitation of the poor, and that only in the last three years has war been realized as the supreme moral evil? One of the culminating accusations of Jesus against the theological teachers of his time was that they strained out gnats and swallowed camels, judiciously laying the emphasis on the minor sins and keeping silence on the profitable major wrongs. It is possible to hold the orthodox doctrine on the devil and not recognize him when we meet him in a real estate office or at the stock exchange.

A health officer of Toronto told me a story which illustrates the consciousness of sin created by the old religious teaching. If milk is found too dirty, the cans are emptied and marked with large red labels. This hits the farmer where he lives. He may not care about the health of Toronto, but he does care for the good opinion of his own neighborhood, and when he drives to the station and finds his friends chuckling over the red labels on his cans, it acts as a moral irritant. One day a Mennonite farmer found his cans labeled and he swore a worldly oath. The Mennonites are a devout people who take the teachings of Christ seriously and refuse to swear, even in law-courts. This man was brought before his church and excluded. But, mark well, not for introducing cow-dung into the intestines of babies, but for expressing his belief in the damnation of the wicked in a non-theological way. When his church will hereafter have fully digested the social gospel, it may treat the case this way: "Our brother was angry and used the name of God profanely in his anger; we urge him to settle this alone with God. But he has also defiled the milk supply by unclean methods. Having the life and health of young children in his keeping, he has failed in his trust. Voted, that he be excluded until he has proved his lasting repentance." The result would be the same, but the sense of sin would do its work more intelligently.[6]

No doctrine received more prominence, nor was subject to more criticism in the following decades, than the doctrine of the kingdom of God. As Rauschenbusch emphasized, "This doctrine is itself the social gospel." In the excerpts from the section that follows, Rauschenbusch, the church historian, enumerates the consequences for theology when the kingdom of God was forgotten or downplayed.

If theology is to offer an adequate doctrinal basis for the social gospel, it must not only make room for the doctrine of the Kingdom of God, but give it a central place and revise all other doctrines so that they will articulate organically with it.

This doctrine is itself the social gospel. Without it, the idea of redeeming the social order will be but an annex to the orthodox conception of the scheme of salvation. It will live like a negro servant family in a detached cabin back of the white man's house in the South. If this doctrine gets the place which has always been its legitimate right, the practical proclamation and application of social morality will have a firm footing.

To those whose minds live in the social gospel, the Kingdom of God is a dear truth, the marrow of the gospel, just as the incarnation was to Athanasius, justification by faith alone to Luther, and the sovereignty of God to Jonathan Edwards. It was just as dear to Jesus. He too lived in it, and from it looked out on the world and the work he had to do.

Jesus always spoke of the Kingdom of God. Only two of his reported sayings contain the word "Church," and both passages are of questionable authenticity. It is safe to say that he never thought of founding the kind of institution which afterward claimed to be acting for him.

Yet immediately after his death, groups of disciples joined and consolidated by inward necessity. Each local group knew that it was part of a divinely founded fellowship mysteriously spreading through humanity, and awaiting the return of the Lord and the establishing of his Kingdom. This universal Church was loved with the same religious faith and reverence with which Jesus had loved the Kingdom of God. It was the partial and earthly realization of the divine Society, and at the Parousia the Church and the Kingdom would merge.

But the Kingdom was merely a hope, the Church a present reality. The chief interest and affection flowed toward the Church. Soon, through a combination of causes, the name and idea of "the Kingdom" began to be displaced by the name and idea of "the Church" in the preaching, literature, and theological thought of the Church. Augustine completed this process in his *De Civitate Dei*. The Kingdom of God which has, throughout human history, opposed the Kingdom of Sin, is today embodied in the Church. The millennium began when the Church was founded. This practically substituted the actual, not the ideal Church for the Kingdom of God. The beloved ideal of Jesus became a vague phrase which kept intruding from the New Testament. Like Cinderella in the kitchen, it saw the other great dogmas furbished up for the ball, but no prince of theology restored it to its rightful place. The Reformation, too, brought no renascence of the doctrine of the Kingdom; it had only eschatological value, or was defined in blurred phrases borrowed from the Church. The present revival of the Kingdom idea is due to the combined influence of the historical study of the Bible and of the social gospel.

When the doctrine of the Kingdom of God shriveled to an undeveloped and pathetic remnant in Christian thought, this loss was bound to have far-reaching consequences. We are told that the loss of a single tooth from the arch of the mouth in childhood may spoil the symmetrical development of the skull and produce malformations affecting the mind and character. The atrophy of that idea which had occupied the chief place in the mind of Jesus, necessarily affected the conception of Christianity, the life of the Church, the progress of humanity, and the structure of theology. I shall briefly enumerate some of the consequences affecting theology. This list, however, is by no means complete.

1. Theology lost its contact with the synoptic thought of Jesus. Its problems were not at all the same which had occupied his mind. It lost his point of view and became to some extent incapable of understanding him. His ideas had to be rediscovered in our time. . . .

2. The distinctive ethical principles of Jesus were the direct outgrowth of his conception of the Kingdom of God. When the latter disappeared from theology, the former disappeared from ethics. Only persons having the substance of the Kingdom ideal in their minds, seem to be able to get relish out of the ethics of Jesus. Only those church bodies which have been in opposition to organized society and have looked for a better city with its foundation in heaven, have taken the Sermon on the Mount seriously.

3. The Church is primarily a fellowship for worship; the Kingdom is a fellowship of righteousness. When the latter was neglected in theology, the ethical force of Christianity was weakened; when the former was emphasized in theology, the importance of worship was exaggerated. The prophets and Jesus had cried down sacrifices and ceremonial performances, and cried up righteousness, mercy, solidarity. . . .

4. When the Kingdom ceased to be the dominating religious reality, the Church moved up into the position of the supreme good. To promote the power of the Church and its control over all rival political forces was equivalent to promoting the supreme ends of Christianity. This increased the arrogance of churchmen and took the moral check

off their policies. For the Kingdom of God can never be promoted by lies, craft, crime or war, but the wealth and power of the Church have often been promoted by these means. The medieval ideal of the supremacy of the Church over the State was the logical consequence of making the Church the highest good with no superior ethical standard by which to test it. . . .

5. The Kingdom ideal is the test and corrective of the influence of the Church. When the Kingdom ideal disappeared, the conscience of the Church was muffled. It became possible for the missionary expansion of Christianity to halt for centuries without creating any sense of shortcoming. It became possible for the most unjust social conditions to fasten themselves on Christian nations without awakening any consciousness that the purpose of Christ was being defied and beaten back. . . .

6. The Kingdom ideal contains the revolutionary force of Christianity. When this ideal faded out of the systematic thought of the Church, it became a conservative social influence and increased the weight of the other stationary forces in society. If the Kingdom of God had remained part of the theological and Christian consciousness, the Church could not, down to our times, have been salaried by autocratic class governments to keep the democratic and economic impulses of the people under check.

7. Reversely, the movements for democracy and social justice were left without a religious backing for lack of the Kingdom idea. The Kingdom of God as the fellowship of righteousness, would be advanced by the abolition of industrial slavery and the disappearance of the slums of civilization; the Church would only indirectly gain through such social changes. Even today many Christians can not see any religious importance in social justice and fraternity because it does not increase the number of conversions nor fill the churches. . . .

8. Secular life is belittled as compared with church life. Services rendered to the Church get a higher religious rating than services rendered to the community. Thus the religious value is taken out of the activities of the common man and the prophetic services to society. Wherever the Kingdom of God is a living reality in Christian thought, any advance of social righteousness is seen as a part of redemption and arouses inward joy and the triumphant sense of salvation. When the Church absorbs interest, a subtle asceticism creeps back into our theology and the world looks different.

9. When the doctrine of the Kingdom of God is lacking in theology, the salvation of the individual is seen in its relation to the

Church and to the future life, but not in its relation to the task of saving the social order. Theology has left this important point in a condition so hazy and muddled that it has taken us almost a generation to see that the salvation of the individual and the redemption of the social order are closely related, and how.

10. Finally, theology has been deprived of the inspiration of great ideas contained in the idea of the Kingdom and in labor for it. The Kingdom of God breeds prophets; the Church breeds priests and theologians. The Church runs to tradition and dogma; the Kingdom of God rejoices in forecasts and boundless horizons. The men who have contributed the most fruitful impulses to Christian thought have been men of prophetic vision, and their theology has proved most effective for future times where it has been most concerned with past history, with present social problems, and with the future of human society.[7]

Notes

1. Kenneth Cauthen, *The Impact of American Religious Liberalism* (New York: Harper & Row, 1962), 27–30.

2. Walter Rauschenbusch, *A Theology for the Social Gospel* (New York: Macmillan, 1917), 1.

3. Donald B. Meyer, *The Protestant Search for Political Realism, 1919–1941* (Berkeley: University of California Press, 1960), 133.

4. Rauschenbusch, Foreword.

5. Rauschenbusch, 23–26.

6. Rauschenbusch, 32–36.

7. Rauschenbusch, 131–37.

22   Decline or Revival?

Most historians now believe that a portrait of the twenties as a decade of degeneracy has been overdrawn. As Arthur S. Link has reminded us, the progressive movement declined but did not become defunct after 1918. Several important groups within the movement—farmers, elements of labor, Democratic organizations in larger cities, and "a remnant of independent radicals, social workers, and social gospel writers and preachers"—"remained either in full vigor or in only slightly diminished strength."[1]

What interests us is how the remnant fared. Paul A. Carter, in *The Decline and Revival of the Social Gospel,* makes the case that the social gospel declined in the twenties. In the opening paragraph of Part II, "The Social Gospel under Fire, 1920–1929," he states:

> The Social Gospel . . . continued to live and flourish in America after the First World War. But between the generation of the muckrakers and the generation of the Red-baiters a great gulf lies in American history, and no movement which linked two such disparate generations could have carried over that gulf unchanged. For while the older Social Gospel had been in harmony with its secular milieu, Progressivism, the newer Social Gospel was in the deepest disharmony with its setting, "normalcy." And it is a stubborn fact that even the most wholehearted opposition to a social environment necessitates some adaptation to it.[2]

For Carter the social gospel declined both because of the relativizing of its ethic due to the World War and prohibition and because of the theological critique of the American version of neo-orthodoxy.

The decline was set in theological granite with the publication in 1932 of Reinhold Niebuhr's *Moral Man and Immoral Society.* A product of the social gospel, like Rauschenbusch he began his career as pastor of an inner-city parish (thirteen years in Detroit). He now became the social gospel's most trenchant critic. "The thesis to be elaborated in these pages," he wrote, "is that a sharp distinction must be drawn between the moral and social behavior of individuals and of social groups, national, racial, and economic; and that this distinction justifies and necessitates political policies which a purely individualistic ethic must always find embarrassing."[3] The social gospel had been anything but individualistic, but it had been "sentimental," according to Niebuhr, in assessing the possibilities and strategies for the reform of society.

It cannot be within the purposes of this volume to quote extensively from Reinhold Niebuhr, for his books and books about him are readily available, but it is important to hear briefly his critique of liberal religion and the social gospel. A basic complaint, sounded again and again, was a lack of realism about sin and society. It surfaced when men and women spoke about the Great War.

Thousands of Christians, who keenly felt the World War as an apostasy from the Christian spirit, consoled themselves with the thought that Christianity had not failed, because it had not been tried. The implication of this observation is that it will some day be tried. Not a few Christian historians have intimated that, but for the unhappy conversion of Constantine, which gave Christianity a premature popularity, the love spirit of the early Christian community might have been preserved for future history. All this leaves definite limitations of the human heart and imagination out of account. These limitations make it inevitable that the religious spirit of love should lose some of its force in proportion to the size of the communities which profess it, the impersonal and indirect character of social relations in which it operates, and the complexity of the situation which it faces. The Christian sects, such as the Quakers and other small religious communities, have preserved it more purely than the churches with their inclusive membership. It has characterised the lives of individual saints more than that of any religious communities, even small and intimate ones. All of which means that religion may increase the power and enlarge the breadth of the generous social attitudes, which nature prompts in the intimate circle; but that there are definite limits to its power and extension. All men cannot be expected to become spiritual any more than they can be expected to become rational. Those who achieve either excellence will always be a leavening influence in social life; but the political structure of society cannot be built upon their achievement.[4]

The social gospel also went astray in being too optimistic in its strategy for transferring the "spirit of love" or the "law of Christ" from the individual to the social sphere.

The weaknesses of the spirit of love in solving larger and more complex problems become increasingly apparent as one proceeds from ordinary relations between individuals to the life of social groups. If nations and other social groups find it difficult to approximate the principles of justice, as we have previously noted, they are naturally even less capable of achieving the principle of love, which demands more than justice. The demand of religious moralists that nations subject themselves to "the law of Christ" is an unrealistic demand, and the hope that they will do so is a sentimental one. Even a nation composed of individuals who possessed the highest degree of religious goodwill would be less than loving in its relation to other nations. It would fail, if for no other reason, because the individuals could not possibly think themselves into the position of the individuals of another nation in a degree sufficient to insure pure benevolence. Furthermore such goodwill as they did possess would be sluiced into loyalty to their own nation and tend to increase that nation's selfishness. . . . No nation in history has ever been known to be purely unselfish in its actions. The same may be said of class groups with equal certainty. Religious idealism may qualify national policies, as much as rational idealism, but this qualification can never completely eliminate the selfish, brutal and antisocial elements, which express themselves in all inter-group life.

The religious idealist, confronted with these stubborn obstacles to the realisation of his ideals, is tempted either to leave the world of political and economic relations to take the course which natural impulse prompts, or to assume that his principles are influencing political life more profoundly than they really are. He is tempted, in other words, either to defeatism or to sentimentality.[5]

In the spring of 1934, upon the occasion of the Rauschenbusch Memorial Lectures at Colgate-Rochester Divinity School, Niebuhr continued his attack upon "Christian Liberalism." Published in 1935 as *An Interpretation of Christian Ethics,* Niebuhr paid tribute in the preface to Rauschenbusch, "one who was not only the real founder of social

Christianity in this country but also its most brilliant and generally satisfying exponent to the present day."[6] Once into motion, however, Niebuhr launched a strong analysis and attack upon the illusions of liberalism.

The effort of the modern Church to correct the limitations of the orthodox Church toward the political order has resulted, on the whole, in the substitution of sentimental illusions for the enervating pessimism of orthodoxy. The orthodox Church dismissed the immediate relevancy of the law of love for politics. The modern Church declared it to be relevant without qualification and insisted upon the direct application of the principles of the Sermon on the Mount to the problems of politics and economics as the only way of salvation for a sick society. The orthodox Church saw the economic order as a realm of demonic forces in which only the most tenuous and tentative order was possible; the modern Church approached the injustices and conflicts of this world with a gay and easy confidence. Men had been ignorantly selfish. They would now be taught the law of love. The Church had failed to teach the law of love adequately because it had allowed the simplicities of the gospel to be overlaid with a layer of meaningless theological jargon. Once this increment of obscurantist theology had been brushed aside, the Church would be free to preach salvation to the world. Its word of salvation would be that all men ought to love one another. It was as simple as that. . . .

Yet it was wrong in the optimism which assumed that the law of love needed only to be stated persuasively to overcome the selfishness of the human heart. The unhappy consequence of that optimism was to discourage interest in the necessary mechanisms of social justice at the precise moment in history when the development of a technical civilization required more than ever that social ideals be implemented with economic and political techniques, designed to correct the injustices and brutalities which flow inevitably from an unrestrained and undisciplined exercise of economic power.[7]

Niebuhr does differentiate between the social gospel and other aspects of liberalism.

In justice to the wing of the liberal Church which has sought to interpret the "social gospel," it must be admitted that it was usually realistic enough to know that justice in the social order could only be achieved by political means, including the coercion of groups which refuse to accept a common social standard. Nevertheless, some of the less rigorous thinkers of the social gospel school tried to interpret the law of love in terms which would rule out the most obvious forms of pressure for the attainment of justice.[8]

In the following year, 1936, H. Richard Niebuhr presented a balanced essay weighing the merits of the social gospel against the arguments of its detractors. An excellent article, "The Attack upon the Social Gospel" summarizes the discussion of the day and offers a perspective on the relation of the social gospel to the newer theology.

The question of the Social Gospel is explicitly or implicitly involved in a great deal of the contemporary theological and religious discussion. To exponents of the "application of Christianity" to social problems the new movements—neo-Protestant or Barthian, neo-Evangelical or Buchmanite and neo-Catholic or Anglo-Catholic—appear to be retreats from the battlefield of social life back to the line of individualistic and other-worldly Christianity. They believe that those who are influenced by these movements intend to give up the endeavor to influence group behavior as impossible in a world lost in sin or to devote themselves to the cultivation of a spiritual life in quietist isolation from a confusing civilization. Representatives of the post-liberal movements, on the other hand, are inclined to speak of the Social Gospel as though it were the epitome of all those humanistic, melioristic and anti-revolutionary tendencies in modernist religion against which they protest. They think of the Social Gospel as a message of self-help, as an optimistic faith that men can enter the kingdom of God without profound revolution, as the expression of cultural Protestantism which is more interested in civilization and its improvement than in God's judgment and love. Very important issues are at stake and it will not do to attempt a superficial synthesis of ideas

which are antithetical, yet it seems to the present writer that the issues
are still confused and that the debate may become more fruitful if
certain distinctions are made. Above all else it seems that the issue of
the objective should be distinguished from the issue of the means. The
first question is whether the individual or society is the proper object of
Christianity's mission; the second, whether the Church is to employ
direct or indirect means.

The Social Gospel is characterized by the conviction that social
units of every sort are the primary human realities to which the Church
ought to address itself, or that, in dealing with individuals, not the
isolated soul but the social individual—the citizen, class-member, race-
member—should be regarded as the being who is in need of redemption.
In this respect it is the heir of sociological science rather than of liberal
philosophy. It rejects the doctrine of eighteenth- and nineteenth-
century liberalism which proclaimed with Bentham that "the community is a fictitious body" and which regarded all societies as based
upon contracts into which independent individuals entered for the sake
of promoting common interests. However true this liberalism may have
been of a period in which new societies were being established, the
Social Gospel has noted that it is not true of our time. Now, at least,
society appears to precede the individual, to mold his character, to
determine his interests, to bestow rights upon him. The individual is
what he is by virtue of the place in society which he occupies; or, if this
is too extreme a statement, the interaction between society and individual is such that an interpretation which always makes the individual the
first term is manifestly wrong. The Social Gospel has seen sin and
righteousness as characteristics of group life; it has noted that vicarious
suffering is laid upon group for group rather than upon individual for
individual; it has seen the problem of salvation as a social problem and
it has worked for the conversion or "change" of societies rather than of
individuals who, no matter how much they may be changed, yet remain
bound by common social evils and participants in common social sin.

This social interest of the Social Gospel is as pertinent to our time
as the individualist gospel was to the eighteenth and early nineteenth
centuries. In that earlier period Christianity confronted individuals who
had been emancipated from political, ecclesiastical and economic
bonds, who had sometimes also—as in the case of the American
frontiers—been freed from the restraint which popular mores had imposed upon them. These emancipated individuals not only became
perilous to one another but were in danger of losing significance from
lives which had become ends-in-themselves. The bases of a new com-

mon life needed to be laid; the individual needed to be related to a source of meaning which transcended his particular desires and his self-hood; he needed to be given an inner discipline which would direct his new freedom; those who had become victims of the free egotism of others needed to be rescued from despair and its consequences. How well Evangelicalism (Methodism, Pietism, the American revival movement) met these problems, how splendidly it succeeded in supplying inner discipline in place of vanished external restraints, how effectively it related lives to a transcendent God, how genuinely it gave new faith, courage and zest to suppressed individuals—these facts are frequently overlooked by men who regard the whole individualistic movement as an error which might have been avoided, or who note that the Evangelical answer no longer suffices in an age which poses a different problem. But it is possible to give all due credit to the effectiveness of the individualistic gospel without maintaining that it is adequate for our day.

It is true that every person has interests, problems and responsibilities as a self which is directly related to God; no full presentation of the gospel can ever leave these out of account. Yet it seems evident that in our time the doom and the salvation, the creation, sin and redemption with which men are concerned are social rather than individual in character. The emancipated individuals of our day are the societies, the races and classes which have made themselves laws to themselves; which commit crimes against other classes, races and nations and believe they will go unpunished; which suffer injustice and suppression as groups; which are faced with the problem of their own futility and emptiness. It is in this area that the reality of sin and hell, and the necessity of salvation have become most apparent. In that sense the modern situation is more like that of the Hebrew nation in the time of the prophets than like that of eighteenth-century individuals. The question of personal salvation is important but, as in the whole of Hebrew history, it is secondary to the question of social salvation. It is true that in this situation much can be done for men as independent individuals, and the Oxford Group movement has demonstrated something of the possibilities. But insofar as this movement deals with persons as the primary factors and tends to overlook the fact that the amount of honesty, purity and love which persons can exercise while they participate in the dishonesties, impurities and hatefulness of capitalism, nationalism and racialism is very limited, it will continue to be regarded with many reservations not only by exponents of the Social Gospel but by all who see the problem of society as the problem of the day. But it may be that this movement will not remain as individualistic as it now appears to be, while there is nothing in either neo-Protestantism or in neo-Catholicism which is inimical to the social approach. On the contrary the exponents of these movements may claim with considerable right that their return to sixteenth- and thirteenth-century modes of thought is due precisely to the necessity of overcoming the individualism of the more recent past. After all, both Catholics and Protestants were interested in the conversion of societies, in the ordering of social life, in the fate not only of men but of humanity. It is certainly true that both neo-Protestants and neo-Catholics have a far more social conception of the Church than many even of those who represent the Social Gospel in its liberal form, for whom the Church remains too often a contract society. And both of these groups with their orthodox conceptions of original sin, of historic revelation, of general judgment and of the salvation of mankind are operating with ideas which have direct relevance to men's existence as members of mankind and its societies. Doubtless these ideas will need to be rethought, but there is nothing individualistic about them, and those who believe that in them the solution to the human problem is to be found not only can but must participate in the social direction of the Social Gospel.

It is at the point of the second issue that the real divergence of the day is to be sought. The Social Gospel has been directed not only toward the changing of social entities but it has largely sought to accomplish this end by indirect means, and by way of self-help. The means which it has employed are indirect from the religious point of view. It has used political and economic means to gain the end. Its exponents have sought to influence legislatures to enact laws, schools to teach attitudes, political parties to adopt programs. Or it has sought to work through the labor movement, using economic means for the purpose of changing society. It has worked for international peace by trying to influence governments to adopt treaties or by writing to congressmen with requests to vote for this or that law. Such measures are doubtless good in their place but as used by the church they represent the strategy of indirect action. They are not only efforts to get some other organization to do something about the intolerable situation but also presuppose the convictions that religion as such has no direct bearing on social life, that prophetic and Christian analysis of the situation with corresponding direct religious action are unimportant and that the analysis of society in terms of its political and economic arrangements is fundamental.

In the second place the strategy of the Social Gospel has largely been a strategy of self-salvation, or of salvation by works. It has tended to speak of social salvation as something which men could accomplish for themselves if only they adopted the right social ideal, found adequate motivation for achieving it and accepted the correct technical means. The social ideal has been regarded as the product of men's independent ethical insight, the knowledge of correct means as the product of social science, and religion has been looked to for the motivation. God, in this theory, becomes a means to an end; he is there for the sake of achieving a human ideal and he does not do even this directly but only through the inspiration which he offers to those who worship him. The failure of this whole scheme of social salvation had driven many Social Gospel advocates to look for nonreligious motivation in the self-interest of classes or races, in which case even the last vestige of a religious strategy has been given up.

It is against this indirect, self-help strategy, rather than against the social objective of the Social Gospel, that the major protest of the day is being made. There are significant differences, of course, between neo-Protestant and neo-Catholic movements, but they seem to agree in this: that whatever place be given to the indirect strategy the primary attack of Christianity upon the social situation or the social individual must be direct, not via governments and economic units, but via the Church or the word of God. They agree in the second place in regarding salvation, whether social or individual, as a divine process, not as something man can achieve by moralistic means.

From the neo-Protestant point of view the strategy of the Social Gospel rests upon a false analysis of the social situation, and the false strategy results from this false analysis. A true analysis will see that our social injustice and misery cannot be dealt with unless their sources in a false faith are dealt with. So long as the faith of man remains "capitalistic," that is, a faith in the security which can be given economically, so long the profit-system and the system of private property cannot be budged. So long as any sort of this-worldly security remains the object of confidence our nationalisms and mammonisms will flourish. Both just and unjust live by faith, though by different kinds of faith, and our social no less than our individual lives are an expression of these faiths. From the neo-Protestant point of view repentance for the *sins* of social life is not enough; there needs to be repentance for the *sin,* for the false faith, for the idolatry which issues in all these sins. Men will be ready for no radically new life until they have really become aware of the falsity of the faith upon which their old life is based. But an attack upon faith requires the direct action of the Church rather than indirect action.

In the second place neo-Protestantism's analysis of the situation in which social groups live runs counter to the analysis upon which the doctrine of self-salvation is based. The Social Gospel is related to the neo-Protestant movement somewhat as Utopian Socialism is related to Marxism. Utopianism also believed in the saving power of the ideal, motivated by sympathy and love of the good. Whatever the quarrels may be between "deterministic" and "synergistic" Marxians they all recognize the priority of the historic process to which the party must adjust itself; Marxian salvation at least is not self-salvation. In another sphere, with a far more profound analysis of the total situation than Marxism offers, neo-Protestantism would base its strategy on the priority of God—not as a human ideal, or the object of worship, but as the moving force in history—who alone brings in His kingdom and to whose ways the party of the Kingdom of God on earth must adjust itself. But strangely enough the Social Gospel, when it recognizes the inadequacy of Utopianism, tends to accept Marxist rather than Christian determinism as offering the correct analysis.

The strategy toward which neo-Protestantism is feeling its way is not only the direct strategy which attacks false faith and proclaims true faith, or the strategy of action corresponding to the way of God in history as revealed in the event Jesus Christ, but for both of these reasons it is also a revolutionary strategy, which regards the death of the old life as inevitable and as necessary before a new beginning can be made.

Our interest here, however, is not that of trying to set forth the strategy of an orthodox Christianity which is thoroughly alive to the problem of the day. The development of this strategy still lies in the future. The question is rather whether such a strategy does not need to be developed. The issue between the Social Gospel and the new movements lies here, not at the point of social versus individual salvation.

The present situation may be compared to that which existed at the beginning of the eighteenth century. The rationalist effort to deal with the problem of emancipated individual life in terms of moral self-salvation and by means of indirect and melioristic action through education and reason failed. Then came the direct, revolutionary Evangelical approach based upon a theory of salvation in which—whatever the differences between Calvinists and Arminians—the adjustment of human ways to the way of God as revealed in Jesus Christ was demanded. The new movements in Christianity, it seems to the present writer, must not be interpreted as reactions to Evangelical individualism, but as efforts to discover in our own day the social equivalent of the Evangelical strategy.[9]

Perhaps it is only fair that Rauschenbusch be given the last word in this section. Rauschenbusch and the social gospel were accused again and again of an optimism that missed the tragic sense of life, especially in the social arena. The critics missed the note of realism present in *Moral Man and Immoral Society.* Donald B. Meyer quarrels with this interpretation, at least as it concerns Rauschenbusch, and perhaps Gladden. The social gospel was not all of one piece, and Rauschenbusch spoke of corporate evil in ways not that dissimilar to Niebuhr. Speaking of the breadth of Rauschenbusch's understanding of sin, Meyer comments: "So far as the nature of human nature was concerned, Rauschenbusch again had exhibited a realism that liberals were later to be accused universally of having lacked."[10] This realism was set forth, among other places, in the chapter "The Super-Personal Forces of Evil," in *A Theology for the Social Gospel.*

Individualistic theology has not trained the spiritual intelligence of Christian men and women to recognize and observe spiritual entities beyond the individual. Our religious interest has been so focused on the soul of the individual and its struggles that we have remained uneducated as to the more complex units of spiritual life.

The chief exception to this statement is our religious insight into the history of Israel and Judah, into the nature of the family, and the qualities of the Church. The first of these we owe to the solidaristic vision of the Old Testament prophets who saw their nation as a gigantic personality which sinned, suffered, and repented. The second we owe to the deep interest which the Church from the beginning has taken in the purity of family life and the Christian nurture of the young. The third we owe to the high valuation the Church has always put on itself. It has claimed a continuous and enduring life of its own which enfolds all its members and distinguishes it from every other organization and from the totality of the worldly life outside of it. It is hard to deny this. Not only the Church as a whole, but distinctive groups and organizations within the Church, such as the Friends or the Jesuit Order, have maintained their own character and principles tenaciously against all influences. This is the noblest view that we can take of the Church, that the spirit of her Lord has always been an informing principle of life within her, and that, though faltering, sinning, and defiled, she has kept her own collective personality intact. Paul's discussion of the Church as the body of Christ (I Cor. xii) is the first and classical discussion in Christian thought of the nature and functioning of a composite spiritual organism.

The Church is not the only organism of that kind, though pre-eminent among them all. Others are less permanent, less distinctive, less attractive, and less self-assertive, but the spiritual self-consciousness of the Church is built up on the social self-consciousness which it shares with other social organisms. . . .

This conception is of great importance for the doctrine of sin. I have spoken in the last chapter about the authority of the group over the individual within it, and its power to impose its own moral standard on its members, by virtue of which it educates them upward, if its standard is high, and debases them, if it is low. We need only mention some of the groups in our own national social life to realize how they vary in moral quality and how potent they are by virtue of their collective life: high school fraternities; any college community; a trade union; the I.W.W.; the Socialist party; Tammany Hall; any military organization; an officers' corps; the police force; the inside group of a local political party; the Free Masons; the Grange; the legal profession; a conspiracy like the Black Hand.

These super-personal forces count in the moral world not only through their authority over their members, but through their influence in the general social life. They front the world outside of them. Their real object usually lies outside. The assimilative power they exert over their members is only their form of discipline by which they bring their collective body into smooth and efficient working order. They are the most powerful ethical forces in our communities.

Evil collective forces have usually fallen from a better estate. Organizations are rarely formed for avowedly evil ends. They drift into evil under sinister leadership, or under the pressure of need or tempta-tion. For instance, a small corrupt group in a city council, in order to secure control, tempts the weak, conciliates and serves good men, and turns the council itself into a force of evil in the city; an inside ring in the police force grafts on the vice trade, and draws a part of the force into protecting crime and brow-beating decent citizens; a trade union fights for the right to organize a shop, but resorts to violence and terrorizing; a trust, desiring to steady prices and to get away from antiquated competition, undersells the independents and evades or purchases legislation. This tendency to deterioration shows the soundness of the social instincts, but also the ease with which they go astray, and the need of righteous social institutions to prevent temptation.[11]

Faced with the corporate terror of Nazi Germany, a later generation would recover the biblical doctrine of "the principalities and powers." One of the few who understood the horror of World War I, the tenacity of the social dimension of sin, seen in institutions and ideologies, pushed Rauschenbusch to posit a kingdom of evil. Not a systematic theologian, Rauschenbusch does not so much explain as describe its reality and power.

The solidaristic spiritual conceptions which have been discussed must all be kept in mind and seen together, in order to realize the power and scope of the doctrine to which they converge: the Kingdom of Evil.

In some of our swampy forests the growth of ages has produced impenetrable thickets of trees and undergrowth, woven together by creepers, and inhabited by things that creep or fly. Every season sends forth new growth under the urge of life, but always developing from the old growth and its seeds, and still perpetuating the same rank mass of life.

The life of humanity is infinitely interwoven, always renewing itself, yet always perpetuating what has been. The evils of one generation are caused by the wrongs of the generations that preceded, and will in turn condition the sufferings and temptations of those who come after. Our Italian immigrants are what they are because the Church and the land system of Italy have made them so. The Mexican peon is ridden by the Spanish past. Capitalistic Europe has fastened its yoke on the neck of Africa. When negroes are hunted from a Northern city like beasts, or when a Southern city degrades the whole nation by turning the savage inhumanity of a mob into a public festivity, we are continuing to sin because our fathers created the conditions of sin by the African slave trade and by the unearned wealth they gathered from slave labour for generations. . . .

This is what the modern social gospel would call the Kingdom of Evil. Our theological conception of sin is but fragmentary unless we see all men in their natural groups bound together in a solidarity of all times and all places, bearing the yoke of evil and suffering. This is the explanation of the amazing regularity of social statistics. A nation registers so and so many suicides, criminal assaults, bankruptcies, and divorces per 100,000 of the population. If the proportion changes seriously, we search for the disturbing social causes, just as we search for the physical causes if the rhythm of our pulse-beat runs away from the normal. The statistics of social morality are the pulse-beat of the social organism. The apparently free and unrelated acts of individuals are also the acts of the social group. When the social group is evil, evil is over all.[12]

Notes

1. Arthur S. Link, "What Happened to the Progressive Movement in the 1920's?" *American Historical Review,* 64 (July, 1959), 845.

2. Paul A. Carter, *The Decline and Revival of the Social Gospel* (rev. ed.; Hamden, Conn.: Archon Books, 1971), 31.

3. Reinhold Niebuhr, *Moral Man and Immoral Society* (New York: Charles Scribner's Sons, 1932), xi.

4. Niebuhr, 72–73.

5. Niebuhr, 74–76.

6. Reinhold Niebuhr, *An Interpretation of Christian Ethics* (New York: Harper & Brothers, 1935), 1.

7. Niebuhr, *Interpretation of Christian Ethics,* 169–70; 171.

8. Neibuhr, *Interpretation of Christian Ethics,* 172. Included among "the less rigorous thinkers" were Shailer Mathews, Gerald Birney Smith, Francis McConnell, and E. Stanley Jones.

9. H. Richard Niebuhr, "The Attack upon the Social Gospel," *Religion in Life,* 5 (Spring, 1936), 176–81. Copyright renewal 1964 by Abingdon Press.

10. Donald B. Meyer, *The Protestant Search for Political Realism* (Berkeley: University of California Press, 1960), 130.

11. Walter Rauschenbusch, *A Theology for the Social Gospel* (New York: Macmillan, 1917), 69–70, 71–72.

12. Rauschenbusch, 78–79, 81.

23   The Past Is Prologue

It can be affirmed now that the concerns of the social gospel did not
become extinct in the twenties. Buffetted by a different political and
social climate, toughened and made more sophisticated by the infusions
of the Niebuhrs, this heritage stood behind the social strategies of
Martin Luther King and others in the new activism of the late fifties
and sixties. As one example, one of the early dissenters from the
tragedy that was Viet Nam, the junior Senator from South Dakota,
spoke of his own vision for social justice as rooted in the social gospel.
As a graduate student at Northwestern, George McGovern had written
a dissertation on the Ludlow, Colorado, strike and massacre. Earlier,
as a seminary student at Garrett Biblical Institute, he had been inspired
by the writings of Walter Rauschenbusch, which he said still informed
his political, social, and religious thinking.

A decade earlier it was Martin Luther King who stirred the nation
to face its greatest moral iniquity and most unfinished task. Where
did King get his vision and his strategy? Since his death much emphasis
has been placed on the teachings on nonviolence of Mahatma Gandhi,
and to be sure much credit must go to this source. However, as King's
lieutenant and later Congressman Andrew Young has pointed out,
King was first and always a Baptist preacher. Unlike many other black
preachers in the South, however, King had the advantage of excellent
theological training at Philadelphia's Crozier Theological Seminary and
at Boston University. The graduate school at Boston University was
noted for a type of liberalism that was in part a product of the social
gospel, but it was at Crozier that King found the theological basis for
his social concern. As he tells the story,

Not until I entered Crozier Theological Seminary in 1948, however, did
I begin a serious intellectual quest for a method to eliminate social evil.
Although my major interest was in the fields of theology and philoso-

phy, I spent a great deal of time reading the works of the great social philosophers. I came early to Walter Rauschenbusch's *Christianity and the Social Crisis,* which left an indelible imprint on my thinking by giving me a theological basis for the social concern which had already grown up in me as a result of my early experiences.[1]

King was concerned that Rauschenbusch, in this volume, seemed unduly optimistic, and that he came close to identifying the kingdom of God with a particular political and social system.

But in spite of these shortcomings Rauschenbusch had done a great service for the Christian Church by insisting that the gospel deals with the whole man, not only his soul but his body; not only his spiritual well-being but his material well-being. It has been my conviction ever since reading Rauschenbusch that any religion which professes to be concerned about the souls of men and is not concerned about the social and economic conditions that scar the soul is a spiritually moribund religion only waiting for the day to be buried. It well has been said: "A religion that ends with the individual, ends."[2]

King gave eloquent expression to his social theology on many occasions. In speeches, sermons, and articles he exhibited not only a gift for a rhetoric filled with pictures and power, but an underlying theological sensitivity that must be pondered apart from the drama of the moment to be fully appreciated. This social theology was evident in 1963, when, confined in a Birmingham jail, he responded to eight clergymen who criticized his tactics. In his *Letter from Birmingham Jail,* King answers the charge of "outsiders coming in." He stresses that he was invited in by the Alabama Christian Movement for Human Rights, an affiliate of his own organization, the Southern Christian Leadership Conference.

But more basically, I am in Birmingham because injustice is here. Just as the prophets of the eighth century B.C. left their villages and carried their "thus saith the Lord" far beyond the boundaries of their home towns and just as the Apostle Paul left his village of Tarsus and carried the gospel of Jesus Christ to the far corners of the Greco-Roman world, so am I compelled to carry the gospel of freedom beyond my own home town. Like Paul, I must constantly respond to the Macedonian call for aid.

Moreover, I am cognizant of the interrelatedness of all communities and states. I cannot sit idly by in Atlanta and not be concerned about what happens in Birmingham. Injustice anywhere is a threat to justice everywhere. We are caught in an inescapable network of mutuality, tied in a single garment of destiny. Whatever affects one directly affects all indirectly. Never again can we afford to live with the narrow, provincial "outside agitator" idea. Anyone who lives inside the United States can never be considered an outsider anywhere within its bounds.

You deplore the demonstrations taking place in Birmingham. But your statement, I am sorry to say, fails to express a similar concern for the conditions that brought about the demonstrations. I am sure that none of you would want to rest content with the superficial kind of social analysis that deals merely with effects and does not grapple with underlying causes. It is unfortunate that demonstrations are taking place in Birmingham, but it is even more unfortunate that the city's white power structure left the Negro community with no alternative. . . .

One of the basic points in your statement is that the action that I and my associates have taken in Birmingham is untimely. Some have asked, "Why didn't you give the new city administration time to act?" The only answer that I can give to this query is that the new Birmingham administration must be prodded about as much as the outgoing one before it will act. We are sadly mistaken if we feel that the election of Albert Boutwell as mayor will bring the millennium to Birmingham. While Mr. Boutwell is a much more gentle person than Mr. Connor, they are both segregationists, dedicated to maintenance of the status quo. I have hope that Mr. Boutwell will be reasonable enough to see the futility of massive resistance to desegregation. But he will not see this without pressure from devotees of civil rights. My friends, I must say to you that we have not made a single gain in civil rights without determined legal and nonviolent pressure. Lamentably, it is a historical fact that privileged groups seldom give up their privileges voluntarily. Individuals may see the moral light and voluntarily give up their unjust posture; but, as Reinhold Niebuhr has reminded us, groups tend to be more immoral than individuals.

We know through painful experience that freedom is never voluntarily given by the oppressor; it must be demanded by the oppressed. Frankly, I have yet to engage in a direct action campaign that was "well timed" in the view of those who have not suffered unduly from the disease of segregation. For years now I have heard the word "Wait!" It rings in the ear of every Negro with piercing familiarity. This "Wait" has almost always meant "Never." We must come to see, with one of our distinguished jurists, that "Justice too long delayed is justice denied."[3]

In the body of the letter, King expresses his disappointment in both the white moderate and the leadership of the white church. In holding up to the light the outmoded sentiments of whites who might call themselves "liberals," King articulates his own tough-minded strategy.

I must make two honest confessions to you, my Christian and Jewish brothers. First, I must confess that over the past few years I have been gravely disappointed with the white moderate. I have almost reached the regrettable conclusion that the Negro's great stumbling block in his stride toward freedom is not the White Citizen's Counciler or the Klu Klux Klanner but the white moderate who is more devoted to "order" than to justice; who prefers a negative peace which is the absence of tension to a positive peace which is the presence of justice; who constantly says "I agree with you in the goal you seek, but I cannot agree with your methods of direct action"; who paternalistically believes he can set the timetable for another man's freedom; who lives by a mythical concept of time and who constantly advises the Negro to wait for a "more convenient season." Shallow understanding from people of good will is more frustrating than absolute misunderstanding from people of ill will. Lukewarm acceptance is much more bewildering than outright rejection.

I had hoped that the white moderate would understand that law and order exist for the purpose of establishing justice and that when they fail in their purpose they become the dangerously structured dams that block the flow of social progress. I had hoped that the white moderate would understand that the present tension in the south is a necessary phase of the transition from an obnoxious negative peace, in which the Negro passively accepted his unjust plight, to a substantive and positive peace, in which all men will respect the dignity and worth of human personality. Actually, we who engage in nonviolent direct action are not the creators of tension. We merely bring to the surface the hidden tension that is already alive. We bring it out in the open where it can be seen and dealt with. Like a boil that can never be cured so long as it is covered up but must be opened with all its ugliness to the natural medicines of air and light, injustice must be exposed, with all the tension its exposure creates, to the light of human conscience and the air of national opinion before it can be cured.

In your statement you assert that our actions, even though peaceful, must be condemned because they precipitate violence. But is this a logical assertion? Isn't this like condemning a robbed man because his possession of money precipitated the evil act of robbery? Isn't this like condemning Socrates because his unswerving commitment to truth and his philosophical inquiries precipitated the act by the misguided populace in which they made him drink hemlock? Isn't this like condemning Jesus because his unique God-consciousness and never-ceasing devotion to God's will precipitated the evil act of crucifixion? We must come to see that, as the federal courts have consistently affirmed, it is wrong to urge an individual to cease his efforts to gain his basic constitutional rights because the quest may precipitate violence. Society must protect the robbed and punish the robber.

I had also hoped that the white moderate would reject the myth concerning time in relation to the struggle for freedom. I have just received a letter from a white brother in Texas. He writes: "All Christians know that the colored people will receive equal rights eventually, but it is possible that you are in too great a religious hurry. It has taken Christianity almost 2,000 years to accomplish what it has. The teachings of Christ take time to come to earth." Such an attitude stems from a tragic misconception of time, from the strangely irrational notion that there is something in the very flow of time that will inevitably cure all ills. Actually, time itself is neutral; it can be used either destructively or constructively. More and more I feel that the people of ill will have used time much more effectively than have the people of good will. We will have to repent in this generation not merely for the hateful words and actions of the bad people but for the appalling silence of the good people. Human progress never rolls in on wheels of inevitability; it comes through the tireless efforts of men willing to be coworkers with God, and without this hard work time itself becomes an ally of the forces of social stagnation. We must use time creatively, in the knowledge that the time is always ripe to do right. Now is the time to make real the promise of democracy and transform our pending national elegy into a creative psalm of brotherhood. Now is the time to lift our national policy from the quicksand of racial injustice to the solid rock of human dignity. . . .

Let me take note of my other major disappointment. I have been so greatly disappointed with the white church and its leadership. Of course there are some notable exceptions. I am not unmindful of the fact that each of you has taken some significant stands on this issue. I commend you, Reverend Stallings, for your Christian stand on this past Sunday, in welcoming Negroes to your worship service on a non-segregated basis. I commend the Catholic leaders of this state for integrating Spring Hill College several years ago.

But despite these notable exceptions, I must honestly reiterate that I have been disappointed with the church. I do not say this as one of those negative critics who can always find something wrong with the church. I say this as a minister of the gospel, who loves the church; who was nurtured in its bosom; who has been sustained by its spiritual blessings and who will remain true to it as long as the cord of life shall lengthen.

When I was suddenly catapulted into the leadership of the bus protest in Montgomery, Alabama, a few years ago I felt we would be supported by the white church. I felt that the white ministers, priests and rabbis of the south would be among our strongest allies. Instead, some have been outright opponents, refusing to understand the freedom movement and misrepresenting its leaders; all too many others have been more cautious than courageous and have remained silent behind the anesthetizing security of stained-glass windows.

In spite of my shattered dreams I came to Birmingham with the hope that the white religious leadership of this community would see the justice of our cause and with deep moral concern would serve as the channel through which our just grievances could reach the power structure. I had hoped that each of you would understand. But again I have been disappointed.

I have heard numerous southern religious leaders admonish their worshipers to comply with a desegregation decision because it is the *law,* but I have longed to hear white ministers declare, "Follow this decree because integration is morally *right* and because the Negro is your brother." In the midst of blatant injustices inflicted upon the

Negro I have watched white churchmen stand on the sideline and
mouth pious irrelevancies and sanctimonious trivialities. In the midst of
a mighty struggle to rid our nation of racial and economic injustice I
have heard many ministers say, "Those are social issues with which the
gospel has no real concern." And I have watched many churches commit themselves to a completely otherworldly religion which makes a
strange, unbiblical distinction between body and soul, between the
sacred and the secular.[4]

The extension of the social gospel continues in the seventies. It is possible to discuss several examples but the most dramatic may be among
religious bodies that two generations ago would have been at logger-
heads with the original social gospel. On Thanksgiving weekend, 1973,
some fifty "evangelicals," mostly young, female and male, black and
white, gathered in the dingy environs of the Y.M.C.A. Hotel on South
Wabash Avenue in Chicago for a workshop entitled "Evangelicals and
Social Concern." Emanating from that conference has come a loosely
knit but energetic movement calling itself Evangelicals for Social
Action.

The result of their combined efforts was *The Chicago Declaration*.
Commented upon widely in both the religious and secular press, it
needs to be read in full to accurately catch the thrust and flavor of
the movement.

As evangelical Christians committed to the Lord Jesus Christ and the
full authority of the Word of God, we affirm that God lays total claim
upon the lives of his people. We cannot, therefore, separate our lives in
Christ from the situation in which God has placed us in the United
States and the world.

WE CONFESS that we have not acknowledged the complete claims
of God on our lives.

WE ACKNOWLEDGE that God requires love. But we have not
demonstrated the love of God to those suffering social abuses.

WE ACKNOWLEDGE that God requires justice. But we have not
proclaimed or demonstrated his justice to an unjust American society.
Although the Lord calls us to defend the social and economic rights of
the poor and the oppressed, we have mostly remained silent. We

deplore the historic involvement of the church in America with racism and the conspicuous responsibility of the evangelical community that have divided the body of Christ along color lines. Further, we have failed to condemn the exploitation of racism at home and abroad by our economic system.

WE AFFIRM that God abounds in mercy and that he forgives all who repent and turn from their sins. So we call our fellow evangelical Christians to demonstrate repentance in a Christian discipleship that confronts the social and political injustice of our nation.

WE MUST ATTACK the materialism of our culture and the maldistribution of the nation's wealth and services. We recognize that as a nation we play a crucial role in the imbalance and injustice of international trade and development. Before God and a billion hungry neighbors, we must rethink our values regarding our present standard of living and promote more just acquisitions and distribution of the world's resources.

WE ACKNOWLEDGE our Christian responsibilities of citizenship. Therefore, we must challenge the misplaced trust of the nation in economic and military might—a proud trust that promotes a national pathology of war and violence which victimizes our neighbors at home and abroad. We must resist the temptation to make the nation and its institutions objects of near-religious loyalty.

WE ACKNOWLEDGE that we have encouraged men to prideful domination and women to irresponsible passivity. So we call both men and women to mutual submission and active discipleship.

WE PROCLAIM no new gospel, but the gospel of our Lord Jesus Christ, who, through the power of the Holy Spirit, frees people from sin so that they might praise God through works of righteousness.

By this declaration, we endorse no political ideology or party, but call our nation's leaders and people to that righteousness which exalts a nation.

WE MAKE THIS DECLARATION in the biblical hope that Christ is coming to consummate the Kingdom and we accept his claim on our total discipleship till he comes.[5]

Some observations can be made about the Evangelicals for Social Action in light of both the social gospel and the Chicago declaration. It should be clearly noted that the correlation with the social gospel is our interpretation, not theirs. For most evangelicals the social gospel is still today a phrase to be placed on the enemies list. Not understood or defined, the term implies to many a departure from the simple gospel in favor of moonlighting with sociology, politics, and all other things secular. Stung by the various events and crises of the sixties, many evangelicals searched for a way to become meaningfully involved in society's problems and challenges. They had heard it said that the way to change society was to change individuals, but the change-the-heart theory did not seem to be working. Belief in the Bible and in racism seemed too often to be synonymous and belief in Jesus and in peace seemed not to have anything to do with each other. That evangelicals could arrive at such a merger of Christ and culture was certainly to miss part of the legacy of their own origins.

But most evangelicals did not know the story of their own past. Now these younger evangelicals are trying to make the story known. They have read and digested Timothy L. Smith's *Revivalism and Social Reform* and thus they know that nineteenth-century revivalism did connect personal salvation and piety with social reform. David O. Moberg, in *The Great Reversal,* a study in Christian ethics, treats the question of what happened to this reform impulse. "The Great Reversal" is a Timothy L. Smith phrase referring to the setback for the reform impulse as revivalism moved from Dwight L. Moody to Billy Sunday to Billy Graham.

In many ways this newer generation is "evangelical liberal," although they prefer the word "radical," this conveying their desire to get "back to the roots." Much of the impetus for their transformation has been their perception of "conservative evangelicals," a designation meant to "conserve" a fidelity to scripture and the gospel. These younger leaders have perceived that "conservative" has meant in reality a fidelity to the cultural status quo. Thus the declaration contains the indictment: "We must resist the temptation to make the nation and its institutions objects of near-religious loyalty."

In attacking human misery one deals head on with the doctrine of the nature of human nature. The old social gospelers were accused of not taking sin seriously, but we have seen how this critique was sometimes turned around quite effectively on their opponents. The Evangelicals for Social Action are repentant for the selectivity of their past attacks on sin. Actually taking pride in their awareness of sin, older evangelicals restricted their vision to individual sins or certain sins of social consequence. Thus Ronald J. Sider, chairperson of the movement and Dean of Messiah College (Mennonite), comments: "Conservative Christians have always condemned pot, pubs, and pornography, but they have expressed less holy horror in the face of institutional racism and oppressive economic systems."[6]

Finally there is a move from love toward justice. In fact, the largest paragraph in the declaration concerns justice. The evangelicals are saying in effect that they have known something of love but not enough of justice and both are biblical mandates. For the 1970's justice is linked to the advocacy of the rights of the oppressed. The problem with benevolence is that it is up to the giver to decide who receives the gift. The message of the prophets is that the oppressed have a claim on us, whether we like it or not. Racism and peace are not high on the list of designated mission projects. The declaration targets both "personal attitudes" and "institutional structures," but there is a clear message that if we follow justice we need be aware that our own systems and the comforts they bring to some will be under more direct scrutiny.

What is the future of the Evangelicals for Social Action? Workshops on more specific agendas are happening and are being planned. Quite significant is the dialogue developing between the National Council of Churches, the sucessor of the Federal Council, and these particular evangelicals. If the newer labels of division are "evangelical" versus "ecumenical" Christians, these conversations are a step across the bridge. The National Council has listened, and the Unit Committee of the Division of Church and Society has responded (October, 1974) positively to the Chicago Declaration. Taking its cue from the confession-affirmation pattern of the declaration, the Church and Society unit confesses its own shortcomings largely in terms of its diffidence to make certain that its actions spring from a central commitment to the gospel and biblical mandates.

Notes

1. Martin Luther King, Jr., *Stride toward Freedom* (New York: Harper & Row, 1958), 91.

2. King, 91.

3. Abridged from pp. 78–79, 82–83, of Martin Luther King, Jr., "Letter from Birmingham Jail," April 16, 1963, *Why We Can't Wait* (New York: Harper & Row, 1963).

4. King, "Letter," 87–90, 93–95.

5. Ronald J. Sider, ed., *The Chicago Declaration* (Carol Stream, Ill.: Creation House, 1974), 1–2. Courtesy of Dr. Sider.

6. *Chicago Declaration*, 30.

VII

Conclusion

"Christians are called to engage in both evangelism and social action. We are commissioned to proclaim the Gospel of Christ to the ends of the earth. Simultaneously, we are commanded to struggle to realize God's will for peace, justice and freedom throughout society."

Fifth Assembly,
World Council of Churches

Note: Teacher, clergyman, administrator, and prolific writer, John Coleman Bennett has been an influential participant in, and a discerning critic of, the religious life of the half-century since he first wrote about it in 1926. He attended Phillips Exeter Academy, Williams College, Union Theological Seminary, New York, and Mansfield College, Oxford. His long and stimulating career as teacher began at Union in 1930, when America was slipping into the Great Depression. After a seven-year term at Auburn Seminary and five years at Pacific School of Religion, he returned to Union as professor of social ethics in 1943. From 1955 to 1964 he was Dean of the Faculty and from 1964 to 1970 President of the Seminary. He was Vice-president of the New York State Liberal Party during ten of those years.

Starting in his graduate days at Oxford, Professor Bennett has written at least one editorial, review, commentary, or article a month and edited, contributed to, or himself written two dozen books or brochures, all dealing with the religious-ethical aspects of contemporary issues. The student who is unfamiliar with Dr. Bennett's writing may well begin with the volume of essays in his honor, *Theology and Church in Times of Change,* ed. Edward L. Long, Jr., and Robert T. Handy (Philadelphia: Westminster, 1970), and follow it with Bennett's *Social Salvation* (New York: Scribner's, 1935; new ed., 1946) and *Christian Realism* (New York: Scribner's, 1941). The reader will find the following essay, written for the present book in August, 1975, not only a succinct summary of much that has been said in the preceding pages, but an "unpolemical," "cool and balanced" critique of the social gospel—as Bennett's lifelong friend and colleague, Reinhold Niebuhr, once characterized not only his writing but his teaching, administration, and ecumenical statesmanship.

The Social Gospel Today

The words "social gospel" might well be used to refer to a continuing movement or emphasis in the life of the Church, but they are most often used to designate a particular movement in North American Protestantism that had its greatest influence in the half-century before 1930. In this chapter I shall summarize the most important criticisms that have been made of the social gospel, but my main interest is in calling attention to the lasting effects of the movement and to current tendencies which express, often in a more radical way, fresh responses to the imperatives to which the social gospel was a response. Very often the critics of the social gospel owe to it a great debt.

I have identified the social gospel as North American and Protestant, but it had parallels in Roman Catholicism since the reign of Pope Leo XIII at the end of the nineteenth century. It also had parallels among Anglicans and in the Free Churches of Great Britain and among Protestants on the continent. Also, the social gospel strongly influenced the missionary movement and through it many churches in Asia especially. I have referred to North America because it had great influence in Canada[1] as well as in the United States.

The criticisms of the social gospel which have been prevalent in recent decades have concerned chiefly its theological assumptions and, closely related to them, the sense of historical reality which characterized its representatives. They were not all alike and some representatives were more vulnerable than others to these criticisms. To criticize them is chiefly to say they were products of their own time and place. The social gospel did express an optimistic view of history that has been refuted by events more effectively than by theological criticism. There was little sense of the tragic dimension of history or of the depth and stubbornness of sin and evil. Walter Rauschenbusch in his idea of corporate sin, of superpersonal forces of evil, of the kingdom of evil, of the cultural transmission of sin was able to grasp conceptually many of the problems which it is easier for us to perceive than it was for his generation.

For a short time the First World War, which for Rauschenbusch was a bitter and disillusioning experience, was for many of his contemporaries the final crusade for peace and democracy, but it proved to be the beginning of the end of the climate that was favorable to the facile Progressivism that prevailed during the period of the social gospel. In Europe the war was an important factor in the emergence of neo-reformation or neo-orthodox theology for which Karl Barth was the primary inspiration and which had a delayed response on this side of the Atlantic in the 1930's. Perhaps the theological event that marks the beginning of a change in the theological climate here was the publication of Reinhold Niebuhr's *Moral Man and Immoral Society* in 1932. Niebuhr was himself a product of the social gospel, but he was also, as Donald B. Meyer says, "its climactic critic."[2] The social gospel did not prepare Christians to face the experiences of the 1930's and 1940's: the Great Depression, the malignant realities of Hitlerism in Germany and of Stalinism in the Soviet Union, above all, the horror of Auschwitz, the appalling destruction of the Second World War and the anxieties of the nuclear age. The threatening nature and the baffling complexity of today's global problems were outside its ken, but they were outside everyone else's ken until recently; and a theology that takes for granted a deeper understanding of sin and tragedy and human finiteness in history is better able to prepare people to live with them.

Closely related to this criticism of the social gospel was the criticism of its tendency to identify the mission of the church, the Christian ideal, even the kingdom of God, with particular social objectives, movements, systems, programs. Sometimes it was democracy. Sometimes it was socialism. Sometimes it was the labor movement. Sometimes, for a more limited but very influential group, it was pacifism. There was a tendency to speak of "Christianizing the Social Order," which was the title of one of Rauschenbusch's books, of Christian solutions to problems. There was a tendency to speak of love as the immediate clue to policy and to neglect the distinctive role of justice, which, when it is embodied in social movements and structures, is fraught with ambiguities and compromises. Yet in a society in which there are so many partly valid claims and counterclaims, and in which both the maintenance of order and struggles to overcome oppression involve forms of coercion, the idea of justice is less misleading than the idea of love when we describe our goals and our methods. The relation between love and justice needs to be carefully thought through, but the social gospel was weak at this point. Gustavo Gutierrez, whose "liberation theology" is sometimes criticized as a replay of the social gospel, so far as its expectations are concerned, in one sentence provides warnings against the very errors for which the social gospel is criticized. He says that the Christian hope that is a gift of God "keeps us from any confusion of the Kingdom with any one historical stage, from any idolatry toward unavoidably ambiguous human achievement, from any absolutizing of revolution."[3] The social gospel was not revolutionary in the current Latin American sense of revolution, but there was much talk about a Christian revolution, about transformations of society which were radical but which could be expected to come by evolution.

A third criticism has to do with the use of the teachings of Jesus by the representatives of the social gospel. I think that in the main their use of the Old Testament prophets has been sustained. The most serious criticism has been their use of the kingdom of God in the teaching of Jesus to refer to a future Christianized social order. I think that the full weight of New Testament scholarship is against this. There are great differences between scholars but not on this point. Many have stressed a chiefly futuristic eschatology with the kingdom thought of as beyond history. Others have stressed a realized eschatology which is important for our present experience, but for them this is seen to be either a matter of personal even private experience or it is seen to be a redemptive reality that is corporate but belonging to the experience of the Christian community. In neither case does this involve the kingdom as the fulfillment of human ideals for social or political progress. Others find in the achievements of social justice or of better political structures or of more humane social relationships signs of the kingdom or ways of serving the kingdom or partial embodiments of the kingdom, but they are always careful to preserve the transcendence of the kingdom both as an ultimate fulfillment of God's purposes beyond history and as a source of judgment upon all human achievements. While this criticism of what now seem to be naive views of the kingdom is, I believe, valid, there is today a revival of interest in the social and political implications of the teaching and example of Jesus and especially of his identification with the poor and oppressed. There is even today considerable discussion of whether or not he was influenced by the Zealots, of whether or not he was a political revolutionary. The answer to that second question is usually "no," but there is much being written today about the social implications of the teaching of Jesus which remind one of the social gospel.

Two criticisms of the social gospel have been greatly emphasized recently. One that is often put quite polemically is based on the neglect of the issue of racial justice. The other has to do not only with the neglect of women's liberation but also with rather conservative views of the role of women which were reflections of the long-standing patriarchal culture. Most of the social gospel writers failed to emphasize the American white-black problem. This was partly because they were located in the North and it seemed at the time to be a southern problem. It may have been partly because their confident views of progress had no room for an awareness of the depth of stubbornness of the roots of racial discrimination. White people generally failed to perceive these until some of them were pushed by a new generation of blacks in the 1950's. Also, there was preoccupation with the economic issues which were seen by Rauschenbusch to belong to the completely unredeemed aspect of American life. I wrote a book in 1935 entitled *Social Salvation* which was a transitional work between the social gospel and Christian Realism, which followed it in some circles, and I am surprised to find that I had neglected race in my own preoccupation with the economic problems of the Depression and with the threat of war. Even the special economic discrimination against black people did not get attention.

I think that the lack of concern for the discriminations against women was so much a part of the culture that it is understandable. It is not surprising that Rauschenbusch, who believed in women's suffrage, saw the role of women as largely limited to the family, preferably large families, but it is to me somewhat surprising that as progressive a figure as Lyman Abbott did not even believe in women's suffrage. Here again a change of outlook has come because of changed external conditions including the fact of smaller families and especially from pressure by women, who have come to see their role as that of second-class citizens in both the church and community and who are seeking change.

These criticisms may explain why the social gospel is generally considered to be a dated movement. I am much concerned to show what the social gospel achieved that may be permanent and how far the Christian social imperatives to which it responded are widely seen to have today as strong a claim as ever. Many elements of the social gospel are now receiving fresh expression though in a context that is very different situationally and theologically. These differences alter the content of the new expression of much that was in the social gospel in important respects.

1. The struggles in the name of the social gospel to achieve particular social goals in American life had considerable success. One cannot isolate the contribution of the social gospel as such to this success for it flourished in an age of many forces that were making for social reforms;

the larger achievements of the period of the New Deal which were made possible by the pressure of events were prepared for by Roman Catholic and Jewish and many secular influences as well as by the social gospel. In 1932 the Federal Council of Churches, after several years of study, sponsored a statement concerning the social ideals for which the churches should stand. This statement was surely a product of the social gospel. Seventeen goals are projected. Ten of them called for specific economic changes such as social insurance, the right of labor to organize, a minimum wage, and the abolition of child labor. Of these ten objectives there have been very solid gains in regard to at least eight. It is significant that the only mention of race is in a general call for "equal justice for all; mutual good will and cooperation among racial, economic and religious groups." Since the chief emphasis of the social gospel had been on economic justice, I think that it is fair to speak of its considerable success in terms of its objectives even though the deeper causes of economic injustice remained little changed. We see how true this is in the 1970's, when we are aware of the continuing poverty of thirty million people and the dominance of an economic individualism in the federal government as well as in the business community which inhibits direct action by government to provide employment for the unemployed victims of a recession even when there is such a socially catastrophic situation as the unemployment of 40 percent of young people, especially of minorities, in major American cities.

2. The social gospel within the churches went far to counteract the Protestant support for this economic individualism. Today, in new movements of theology, there are strong attacks on privatistic interpretations of sin and salvation, but the social gospel had already done much to discredit these in theology and in the teachings of churches. The very common ideas in earlier periods concerning poverty and wealth, concerning wealth as a reward for virtue, and concerning the sinful responsibility of the poor for their poverty, have not so much been refuted as they have been allowed to die. The depression of the 1930's cured many people of this whole complex of ideas. The rationalizations of the capitalistic status quo which dominated Protestant thought in 1880 have lost their credibility in the Protestant circles to which I am referring. They never had the same acceptance in Catholic thought. Again, events have had a great deal to do with this, but the social gospel was the religious and theological preparation that helped Protestants to see the meaning of these events. The support of the labor movement by Protestant leadership, inspired by the social gospel, was a victory over what today seem incredible teachings in high Protestant

theological circles which regarded the organization of labor as an interference with the laws of individualistic economics that were believed to
be the pattern of divine providence. I do not believe we can exaggerate
our debt to the social gospel for helping to clear away a mountain of
individualistic inhibitions to social change that is now seen very widely
in the churches to be as necessary.

3. The third contribution of the social gospel is that it decisively
emphasized the faith and conviction that God was identified with the
poor, the deprived, the neglected, the oppressed groups in society and
that Christian love required a concern to transform social and political
structures in the interest of social justice. There were variations in regard to methods and there was a spectrum among representatives of the
social gospel in regard to the extent to which this transformation could
take place within the capitalistic system. Probably the main tendency
was to think in terms of reformed capitalism, but some of the most influential persons involved, including Rauschenbusch, were Christian socialists. The concern for social justice was always central, though, as I
have pointed out, there was little clarity about the relation between justice and love. This concern has grown in strength and in the radical
nature of its economic and political implications since the period of the
social gospel.

4. The fourth contribution of the social gospel was that its concerns became institutionalized in the denominational and ecumenical
structures of the Church. The reading of the history of denominations,
of the Federal Council of Churches, and of international ecumenical institutions that prepared the way for the World Council of Churches impresses me very much in this regard. I am amazed at the sheer energy
released by the social gospel in the establishment of innumerable official and unofficial agencies of Christian social action. The Federal
Council of Churches, which was one of the predecessors of the National
Council of Churches, was from the beginning inspired by the social
gospel.

Also, the social gospel had considerable influence on the development of the international ecumenical institutions which expressed the
same commitment to social justice and peace. The first major ecumenical conference which represented these concerns met in Stockholm in
1925. The influence of the social gospel on the planning of that conference and on the American delegates was enormous. Out of the Stockholm Conference came the "Universal Christian Council for Life and
Work," which was the continuing ecumenical agency representing these
same concerns. It was finally absorbed by the World Council of

Churches. The social gospel also had great influence on "the World Alliance for Promoting International Friendship through the Churches," which though unofficial was an important factor in the early ecumenical movement. The theology that dominated this ecumenical activity changed in the 1930's as a result of the influence of the broad revival of Reformation theology especially on the European continent. The Oxford Conference on Church, Community and State in 1937 was a landmark in this change in theological emphasis. It was by no means narrowly Barthian, or even neo-orthodox, but the first three criticisms of the social gospel that I have mentioned were characteristic of the thinking of this conference. Yet probably most of the influential Americans present were themselves products of the social gospel. There was institutional continuity between Stockholm and Oxford, and there was also continuity in the commitment to social justice. The criticisms by the Oxford Conference of what it called "the economic order of the industrialized world" were devastating, and its discussion of the ethics of property had more radical implications than most social gospel teaching, though Oxford refused to identify Christian ethics with any economic system. The Oxford Conference, and all ecumenical thinking that followed it, necessarily dealt with a wide range of new problems such as those created for the Christian mind and conscience by the totalitarian state in Hitler's Germany and in Stalinist Russia (a source of disillusionment among many Christians who saw hope in Communism) and by the prospect of the Second World War. In all of this history there were many continuities as well as differences from the outlook of the social gospel, but here I have in mind especially the institutional continuities.

I have already said a good deal about the later movements which reflect the same imperatives to which the social gospel was a response. I shall conclude this chapter by giving some examples of these.

One of the movements in this country which followed the social gospel and which regarded itself as opposed to the social gospel went by the name of Christian Realism. This was in large measure the creation of Reinhold Niebuhr. His criticism of the social gospel's view of progress in history is known to everyone familiar with his thought at all. But for many years his commitments in regard to social justice were more radical than the social gospel. Indeed, in the 1930's he used Marxism as an interpretation of history to counter the social gospel though he soon rejected what he regarded as the post-revolutionary utopianism of Marxism. He stressed the class struggle and the role of the proletariat as the agent of revolutionary change in this country when he wrote *Moral*

Man and Immoral Society. Christian Realism became embodied in the
"Fellowship of Socialist Christians" of which Niebuhr was the chief
leader, and the Fellowship was considerably influenced by Paul Tillich,
who found in it the nearest approach in the United States to the movement of Religious Socialism, of which he was one of the founders during the 1920's in Germany. This Christian Socialism as such eroded as
interests were diverted by the threat of Hitlerism and by the Second
World War and also by the social changes brought about by the New
Deal, which seemed to many in this Socialist Christian movement to be
the most viable approach to social transformation in this country.

Ecumenical social thinking internationally, as it has been expressed
by the Assemblies and by various conferences and programs of the
World Council of Churches, became more intense and radical on issues
of social justice. The Geneva Conference on Church and Society in
1966 and the Uppsala Assembly in 1968 stimulated many initiatives
under the umbrella of the World Council which made the Council a
sounding board for the aspirations of countries in the third world that
need radical change. This trend has been parallelled by social teaching
and social initiatives in the Roman Catholic Church as illustrated by the
encyclicals *Mater et Magistra, Pacem in Terris,* and *Populorum Progres-
sio* and by aspects of the teaching of Vatican II. During the period since
the Vatican Council there have been many initiatives and movements in
the Catholic Church which, while they were in part stimulated by papal
teaching, have gone far beyond that teaching in their commitment to
revolution. The Theology of Liberation, which I shall discuss later, is
one example of these in Latin America.

Today socially oriented movements and theologies which presuppose radical criticisms of the status quo have become widespread on
several continents. In Europe both the Theology of Hope of Juergen
Moltmann and the Political Theology of Johannes Metz and Dorothee
Soelle do for our time much that the social gospel did for its time.
There has been a very pervasive discussion of "the theology of revolution," though this as a separate theological movement has not gone far.
While there is no agreement on strategies for revolution or on the issue
of violence, there has been an enormous amount of ferment in the
churches concerning the responsibilities of Christians and churches in
situations that call for revolutionary change. In this country the civil
rights movement in the days of Martin Luther King, Jr., inspired a spirit
and attitudes in the churches that had many similarities with those inspired by the social gospel. King himself was strongly influenced by persons who had themselves been products of the social gospel. Today

James Cone's Black Theology, which is a revolutionary theology and a theology of liberation, expresses a more militant spirit, suited to the stage of greater frustration of the black struggle for justice and full dignity which has followed the springtime of the early civil rights movement. Black Theology is as powerful a challenge to the social conscience of white American Christians as they have ever received. It is an indigenous American parallel to the Theology of Liberation, which has had its greatest influence in the third world, especially in Latin America. One of the most surprising developments has been the emergence among theologically conservative "evangelicals" of a radical social movement that has considerable strength among a new generation of evangelicals, and in comparison with some of its manifestations, especially a new journal named *Post American,* the liberal social gospel seems tame. Whatever may be true of the social gospel as a movement, there is no general return to a pre–social gospel individualism and privatism.

Of these contemporary movements I shall say more about the Theology of Liberation, which has been stimulated by the desperate social conditions in many Latin American countries and which has become best known in North America through a book by a Roman Catholic theologian in Peru, Gustavo Gutierrez, entitled *A Theology of Liberation.* This theology has some points in common with the social gospel. There is the same emphasis on social justice though in an entirely different situation. There is in both much use of the Old Testament prophets and of the teachings of Jesus, especially his idea of the kingdom of God. There is a similar emphasis on hope for the future, though I have already quoted Gutierrez to show that he takes pains to guard against too close identification of the Kingdom of God with any new social order. He does use the word "utopic" to denote both the rejection of the old and the announcement of the new which is the object of Christian hope. The theology of liberation did generate a degree of optimism within the struggle for social change which has often been criticized as the social gospel has been criticized. (This optimism may have faded a good deal since the overthrow of Allende in Chile and the closing off of that country as a center of revolutionary influences.) There is one great difference between the outlook of the social gospel and that of this theology. The new is in this case expected to come after a social and political revolution, a revolution expected to be violent. The social gospel assumed that the new would come as the fulfillment of the intentions of existing American institutions. There was no thought among its most influential representatives that there would be need for illegal or violent

revolution. I cite this theology only to show that today the social objectives of the social gospel are as much sought as ever but now in a more
radical form.

No one did more to create the theological climate that caused the
social gospel as a particular movement to erode than Karl Barth, for
Barth was the great Protestant theologian who was the major stimulus
behind the revival of theology that came to be known as neo-orthodoxy. Barthianism as such has never been a great theological force in
North America, but Barth's influence was an important factor in a
much wider theological trend. Yet Barth himself was a socialist, and he
never abandoned his radical criticism of capitalism, of the philosophy
and institutions of economic individualism. The social gospel was mild
in comparison with Barth, but both represented a strong commitment
to social justice. I shall quote one passage that Barth wrote in 1946:

> The Church is witness of the fact that the Son of Man came to
> seek and to save the lost. And this implies that—casting all false
> impartiality aside—the Church must concentrate first on the
> lower levels of human society. The poor, the socially and eco-
> nomically weak and threatened, will always be the object of its
> primary and particular concern, and it will always insist on the
> State's special responsibility for these weaker members of society.
> That it will bestow its love on them, within the framework of its
> own task (as part of its service), is one thing and the most impor-
> tant; but it must not concentrate on this and neglect the other
> thing to which it is committed by its political responsibility: the
> effort to achieve a fashioning of the law such as will make it im-
> possible for "equality before the law" to become a cloak under
> which strong and weak, independent and dependent, rich and
> poor, employers and employees, in fact receive different treat-
> ment at its hands; the weak being unduly restricted, the strong
> unduly protected. The Church must stand for social justice in the
> political sphere.[4]

One would not be surprised to find that passage in the literature of the
social gospel, for these words are close to the heart of its teaching.

Notes

1. For an authoritative account of an important period of the social gospel
in Canada, see Richard Allen, *The Social Passion - Religion and Social Reform in
Canada, 1914–1928* (Toronto: University of Toronto Press, 1973).

2. Donald B. Meyer, *The Protestant Search for Political Realism* (Berkeley: University of California Press, 1960), 2.

3. Gustavo Gutierrez, *A Theology of Liberation* (New York: Orbis, 1973), 238.

4. From an essay entitled "The Christian Community and the Civil Community," which is available in several publications. One is Karl Barth, *Against the Stream* (London: S.C.M., 1954).

Index

Index

Figures in italics indicate important references or summaries